BRADFORD

Walking the Americas

Also by Levison Wood

Walking the Nile
Walking the Himalayas

Walking the Americas

*1,800 Miles, Eight Countries, and
One Incredible Journey from
Mexico to Colombia*

Levison Wood

Atlantic Monthly Press
New York

First published in Great Britain in 2017 by Hodder & Stoughton
A Hachette UK company

Typeset in Bembo by Hewer Text UK Ltd, Edinburgh

Printed in the United States of America

First Grove Atlantic hardcover edition: March 2018

Library of Congress Cataloging-in-Publication data available for this title.

ISBN 978-0-8021-2749-5
eISBN 978-0-8021-6564-0

Atlantic Monthly Press
an imprint of Grove Atlantic
154 West 14th Street
New York, NY 10011

Distributed by Publishers Group West

groveatlantic.com

18 19 20 21   10 9 8 7 6 5 4 3 2 1

For Alberto

Contents

Introduction   1

1. Hampton Court   6
2. Mornings in Mexico   14
3. The Americas   26
4. Meeting an Explorer   36
5. Departure   46
6. Yucatán   55
7. Ruins   66
8. Trouble in Paradise   81
9. Boot Camp   94
10. Borderlands   108
11. El Petén   120
12. Barrios   133
13. The Ascent   148
14. Escape to Nicaragua   161
15. Land of Fire   171
16. Chirripó   187
17. Paradise Found   199
18. Panama   209
19. Crossing the Panama Canal   223
20. The End of the Road   235
21. The Last Jungle   247

Contents

22. The Darién Gap   259
23. New Scotland   271
24. Colombia   280

Acknowledgements   289

Introduction

Much have I travell'd in the realms of gold,
And many goodly states and kingdoms seen;
Round many western islands have I been
Which bards in fealty to Apollo hold.
Oft of one wide expanse had I been told
That deep-browed Homer ruled as his demesne;
Yet did I never breathe its pure serene
Till I heard Chapman speak out loud and bold:
Then felt I like some watcher of the skies
When a new planet swims into his ken;
Or like stout Cortez when with eagle eyes
He star'd at the Pacific – and all his men
Look'd at each other with a wild surmise –
Silent, upon a peak in Darien.

                                                            Keats

The young poet clearly did not know his history, or maybe he just didn't care all that much. Of course, it wasn't Cortés that discovered the Pacific for Europe, but Balboa, another Spanish knight in shining armour.

My journey attempts to link the two. Mexico to the Darién, bringing out a little bit of the past along the way. This book doesn't intend to present a comprehensive geo-political narrative, nor does it pretend to cover the vast history of this complex and often misunderstood region. It is, instead, a tale of adventure in the modern age.

Perhaps the title is misleading. Those readers who picked up this book expecting a jaunt across the United States will be sorely disappointed. I don't even set foot in that great country. Nor do I so much as peek a glimpse at anything in South America. Except literally dipping my toes into Colombia, this book is solely a journey through Central America. But, like Keats, in his bid to avoid an extra syllable, I decided that anything more than 'Americas' would be a mouthful, so I've left it at that. Moreover, for almost a hundred years after Columbus first laid eyes upon this verdant region, the Americas *was* Central America. For its formative decades, Central America and the Caribbean coastline was the hub of the 'New World'.

When a young Italian clerk embarked on a career in the merchant navy to go and explore the oceans of the West, he had little idea that his name would go down in history and become the basis of two entire continents and the most powerful country on earth.

Amerigo Vespucci was born into wealth, but sought adventure. He worked for the House of Medici in late fifteenth-century Florence, and under their backing managed to accompany four expeditions to chart the recently discovered coastline of the New World.

After Christopher Columbus had sighted land and discovered Central America for Europe in 1492, it seemed as if the Earth had changed forever. Suddenly an entirely new hemisphere had come into existence and it needed to be conquered.

I can imagine that it must have sent young men all over Europe into a frenzy. There it was, a new horizon, hitherto unknown, ready and waiting. There were stories of wealth beyond dreams, pyramids made of gold, and all sorts of monsters and tyrants to vanquish. Until 1507, it didn't even have a name. A German map-maker called Martin Waldseemüller decided that had to change and he called the new landmass after the Italian explorer. America was born.

More ships set sail and it soon became apparent that the age of discovery had only just begun. Inevitably, with discovery came colonisation. After the maps were updated, the conquistadors followed. Hundreds of Spanish warriors sailed across the waves to set up new trading outposts in an empire that eventually stretched from Texas to Argentina. These early pioneers acted as agents of the Spanish Crown – instructed to find gold and riches, convert the native Indians to Catholicism, and destroy those who would not be subjugated.

One of the first Spaniards to set out on the conquest was Hernando Cortés. Wildly ambitious, this was a man who, on landing on the muggy, mosquito-ridden coast of Mexico in search of gold in 1519, sensed that his sailors might be at risk of bottling. To prevent any such desertion, he bored holes in the hulls of all the ships so that they couldn't sail, and instructed his men to march onwards.

Like other Spanish colonisers who would follow, they advanced inland, razing forests, annihilating settlements, smashing ancient Mayan buildings to the ground and plundering gold. They demolished temples and put Christian altars in their place. They forced the people they came across to convert from their native faiths to Catholicism. While Mayan culture prized the capture of living prisoners above all, the Spanish had no qualms about killing the enemy – whether warrior or civilian – both on and off the battlefield. Cortés only let those men live who could be his interpreters, or those women who could act as his spies.

As the Spanish came cantering into American villages on horseback, the Mayans could be forgiven for thinking that the Gods had descended. In some settlements, as many as thousands of people would come out of their homes, lining their watery causeways in canoes to admire these mysterious creatures from heaven. Cortés was the first to bring horses to the American mainland and though he had only sixteen of them, the snorting and rearing of these vast beasts was a sufficient scare tactic to terrorise the unwitting native people.

The Spanish also had the benefit of far more sophisticated weaponry – armed with iron and steel swords, lances and pikes, they were a tough match for the Mayan warriors, who had little more than flint-tipped spears, stones and padded-cotton armour. Everything about their technology was alien to the Central Americans: gunpowder, helmets, even the wheel. Once, when invited to meet a tribal king, Cortés ordered his men to disassemble the warships, smuggle them in piece by piece along a canal bored through the mountain, then reconstruct them and – like the Trojan horse – lay siege from within.

As the conquistadors moved across Mesoamerica during the sixteenth century, they were often outnumbered – sometimes as much as ten to one – but here another factor started to come into play. Unknowingly, the Spanish had a secret weapon – disease. The inhabitants of the New World had no immunity to foreign and fatal illnesses such as smallpox and typhoid. As the interlopers ploughed through the jungle, resupplying repeatedly with infected soldiers and settlers, they brought an infinite number of viruses and bacteria from the Old World. Perhaps as many as ninety per cent of the indigenous peoples were wiped out in the first century of Spanish invasion, as the colonisers swept across the region.

The Maya and other native populations had little choice between succumbing to a biological apocalypse and the violence of the invading Europeans. The Spanish inevitably won out, and for over 350 years dominated every aspect of life throughout Central and South America. The indigenous culture was virtually decimated. America became the playground of the Spanish Crown, in which there was little respect for the previous way of life. Traditions, languages, entire cities disappeared, and within the space of a couple of generations, five thousand years of history were forgotten.

What became of those people, the ancient Maya, and tribes like them? What do the present-day Central Americans feel about their colonial roots and their indigenous ancestry? What impact do their northern neighbours have on the region, and how do they see the rest of the world? For centuries, Central America was the hub of the gold trade, facilitated by slaves and the trafficking of people; nowadays, how do cocaine and the other drugs define an entire sub-continent? And as for the people – are they still slaves, and who traffics them?

These were but some of the questions I wanted answering, and which are the basis of this book. And even if no answers were forthcoming, I could still at least be silent upon a peak in Darién.

I

Hampton Court

'Eight hundred pounds for a piece of glass?'

'Yes, but you'll need two,' said Nigel the builder, his hands as big as spades, leaning against the crumbling remains of the bathroom wall, chewing on something inedible.

'Do you want chrome or brass?' shouted Danny from somewhere downstairs. Or at least, it would have been downstairs if there were any. Instead, I peered into a dusty hole where the stepladders melted into a grey, throat-filling cloud of evil muck. My head was spinning now.

'Look, the carpet man will be here in two days, so that floor needs to be finished. Slate grey or natural oak?' It was Nigel again.

'Bollocks,' squealed the electrician, as he cut through the wrong wire.

Only Kevin seemed to maintain his sense of humour. He chuckled at Jeff's misfortune, 'You're as shite as these southern fairies.'

'Chuck us a screwdriver,' barked Jeff, 'and shut up.'

'Tea, anyone?' My poor mother levitated between the piles of bricks and plasterboard with a tray full of cups of tea and sandwiches. Somewhere in the garden, a radio pumped out 1980s power ballads.

'Five days left!' My dad bellowed above the noise of a drill. 'Five days. What's not done then, isn't getting done.' My heart sank and I jumped through the hole in a bid to escape the pandemonium.

I had gone over my budget by half and there was no chance on earth that the house would be finished on time. I still hadn't bought any furniture and I was living on a diet of cuppa soup and bacon sarnies that were covered in a fine layer of sandy grime. The property looked like a bomb had gone off, but it didn't stop the builders living in camp cots among the debris.

'It'll be fine,' said Tracey, calm as ever.

'Shouldn't you be fluffing some pillows or something?' Kevin winked at the interior designer. He looked like he was about to pat her on the head.

'Piss off,' she said, ever so politely. Then she smiled at me with the patience of a Buddhist monk, 'Go outside, get some fresh air and plan a holiday.'

'But there's no bloody stairs yet,' I whimpered pathetically.

'It'll be fine, I promise, these things all come together at the last minute.'

I went outside into the garden, which I tried to imagine as a little haven of peace. It would be soon, I promised myself, when the massive pile of rubble and wood had been shifted. I wondered to myself who had lived in this place before me. The wallpaper belonged in a 1970s disco. 'Who puts wallpaper like that in a seventeenth-century house anyway?' I shuddered.

'Don't you worry, I have just the paint. It's called Elephant's Breath,' said Tracey, without even a glimmer of irony.

'Elephant's Breath?' my dad regurgitated, half-hanging out of the bathroom window. He'd been eavesdropping. 'I've got one you'd prefer. It's called Grasshopper's Fart. It's by Harrow and Balls.'

'Farrow and Ball,' Tracey repeated with a smile. 'I'll take care of them. Now you go for a walk in the park and I'll sort all this out.'

I left the troubled premises in a sullen mood and went for a walk around Hampton Court Palace Gardens. In through the massive gate topped by limestone lions, I entered the magical estate: rose bushes, apple trees; a wilderness filled with daffodils, criss-crossed with ancient paths and a hidden maze. The boughs of the willow trees in their spring bloom hid the red-brick chimney stacks and gargoyle-encrusted rooftops of the magnificent house. Deer, once the favourite sport of old Henry – when he wasn't philandering – ran wild in the parkland beyond, and the Thames, that glorious river, was just a few hundred metres on the far side of the royal courtyard.

I cheered up pretty quickly. I often had to pinch myself that I lived so close to Henry VIII's old gaff – reminding me that I was very fortunate indeed. It really was quite astonishing to think of the history of the place; what scandals and love stories must have occurred within these hedgerows and ivy-clad walls. But despite the nostalgia, I couldn't help but think of my bank balance, which was ebbing away with increasing alacrity. I winced as I totted up the daily expenditure and realised how woefully unprepared I was to take on the full refurbishment of a crumbling 300-year-old house that seemed to be falling apart.

I took a deep breath. 'It'll be worth it,' I told myself.

In fact, the house was well over 300 years old, if the date on the deeds was to be believed. It said 1670, as a rough estimate. The land had been acquired during the reign of William of Orange by a certain Mr Abraham Fish, tree-planter-in-chief to the Royal Palace. It was all fields and hunting grounds then – the favourite palace of the lot, since it was far enough away from London to avoid the smell of the open sewers. It was my dream home. After six years of homeless vagabonding, sleeping on mates' floors, short-term rents and the occasional squat, I had saved up enough to cover the extortionate cost of a deposit for a house and finally put down roots on the leafy fringes of my capital.

In spite of the grandeur, when William of Orange, the Dutch prince, moved into the palace in 1689, he was not best pleased with his new lot. Obliged to become King of England after wedding Mary II – surely one of the oddest royal relationships in British history – he was envious of the neighbouring French monarch.

King Louis XIV, who was well known for being rather flash, had created such delights as the Palace of Versailles, and this inspired a competitive spirit in William, who wanted to please his wife by doing some refurbishments of his own. He employed the services of the esteemed architect Sir Christopher Wren to knock down the majority of the original Tudor structure and rebuild it in a far more elegant and contemporary style. No dodgy wallpaper for this royal family. As I ambled past the ornate baroque fountains, I wondered if the Dutch King had to choose his own paint.

'Gold or silver doorknobs, your Royal Highness?' bowed Sir Chris, nine years later. At the grand old age of sixty-six, he was no doubt wishing he'd left on a high with St Paul's Cathedral and the fifty-one other churches he had reconstructed after the Great Fire of London. It was 1698 and works had been going on much longer than anyone had expected. King William was beginning to tire of the refurb project (his queen had died four years earlier and it had been her idea in the first place) and he preferred the cosmopolitan living of Kensington anyway. The palace was finally completed in 1700, but only after poor Wren underestimated the budget (I could certainly sympathise) and got the sack, his deputy taking on the commission instead. For King William, the glory was short-lived. He fell off his horse in the gardens of his new palace only two years later and died.

It was in 1700 that the world's first piano was made in Italy. It was the year that Edinburgh burnt down, and the year that the poet John Dryden passed away. It was also the year that Spain handed over its crown to King Louis XIV, much to William's annoyance, his blood pressure presumably reaching astronomical levels by now. But apart from that, it was a fairly uneventful year. And that is exactly how William wanted to keep things. There was a precarious peace with Spain and a small war with France – as ever. But, by and large, England was doing rather well, trading cotton, iron and spices in far-flung places around the world with the East India Company.

Meanwhile, 5,200 miles away, on a boiling hot beach in Central America, Scotland was having a far less pleasant time. For many years, the Scottish economy had been in turmoil, burdened by a series of disastrous civil wars and a declining ship-building industry. There had been crop failures, famine, and restrictions on fishing in the North Sea. The Scots were jealous of England's growing fortunes and all around, European countries like France, Spain and Holland were developing as world trading nations. The Scots had decided they'd had enough; it was time to build their own empire.

In the summer of 1698, soon after Sir Christopher stomped out of Hampton Court after being told he was too expensive by King William, a fleet of five ships led by the *Caledonia* set sail from the port of Leith on the east coast of Scotland. Stood on the wooden decks, waving the lochs goodbye for the last time were 1,200 bold adventurers bound for the New World. They had their sights set on a remote patch of jungle called the Darién – 60 by 100 miles wide – in Panama, of all places. The expedition leaders, who had spent years collecting donations from wealthy Scots and the general public alike, determined that if Scotland could create a 'New Caledonia' on the little isthmus, away from the main pirate route, then they could potentially have a stake in transatlantic trade, and maybe, just maybe, find a way to become the gatekeepers of the Pacific. It was a visionary, ambitious project that anticipated the building of the Panama Canal some two hundred years later.

Many of the 1,200 volunteers were former soldiers and sailors, with plenty of fighting experience; others were peasants seeking a better life in a foreign country. When the gang of colonists arrived on the shores of the Caribbean in November that year, they immediately set about building a wooden fort called St Andrews. It was accompanied by a village called New Edinburgh, to accommodate families, and the surrounding land was planted with fields of maize and corn. The expedition went well for a while, but soon the newcomers realised that there was no reliable source of fresh water. Things went rapidly downhill from there. Disease set in and life was hampered by the unwillingness of the native Indians to trade with the Scots, because all they had to barter with were a few trinkets and nothing of value.

Things went from bad to worse when they discovered that the spot they had chosen for the New Scotland was a completely useless harbour; trading ships refused to come in for fear of being battered by the waves. Malaria, or the fever, as it was known, became rife and soon the settlers were dying at the rate of ten a day, until fewer than three hundred remained alive.

The whole expedition had been a massive disaster, but that

didn't stop Scotland sending a resupply ship a year later, and another ship called the *Rising Sun*, with another 1,000 hopeful colonists a year after that. What they discovered, though, must have horrified them. Deserted huts, a rotting fort, and hundreds of overgrown graves already being reclaimed by the jungle. Still, the stout-hearted Scotsmen did not give up. They tried to rebuild New Edinburgh, until the inevitable happened.

The Spanish empire had ruled over Central and South America for more than 150 years at this point, and the Spaniards had no desire to see an irritable little Scottish colony take over a potentially important trade route in Panama – even if their efforts did seem futile. They attacked in January 1700, besieging the Scots for over a month. Hundreds died – mainly of fever and starvation, rather than battle – until at last they surrendered. Out of the original 2,500 settlers, only a handful of survivors made it back to Scotland alive.

Of course, Scotland blamed the lack of English support for the scheme, and there is a fair probability that if England had financed and helped to defend the colony, then perhaps the story might have had another ending. But hindsight is, of course, a wonderful thing. Scotland was now virtually bankrupt; the aristocracy broke, the public angry. There seemed no alternative other than to throw in their lot with England, which by now had the awesome combined strength of an alliance with Holland and Austria. By the time King William fell off his horse in 1702 and was succeeded by the ruthless and clever Queen Anne, the moment had come to accept a joint future. On the first of May 1707, Scotland signed a treaty enabling an act of union. The United Kingdom was born.

I walked along the riverbank, enjoying a moment of peace and quiet away from the house. Tracey was probably right, it would all come good in the end. The sun was shining, and I heard the squawking of geese. A little ferry in the style of an old steamer navigated its way under Hampton Court bridge, and the tourists stood smiling at the picturesque scene of little England all around them.

2

Mornings in Mexico

The first time I visited Central America was as a young soldier on leave; I was green and reckless and the memories are hazy. I have visions of spit-and-sawdust bars, pristine beaches and endless tequila. I was only there for a week, but it was a week that changed my life. I met a Mexican girl called Ceci and promised her that I'd come back.

I did go back, a few times. Whenever I had leave, I would fly across the Atlantic like a hopeless romantic chasing a distant dream. Once, I even managed a free trip courtesy of Her Majesty. In 2007, my company of Paratroopers had been attached to a Scottish Regiment to do some jungle training in the rainforests of Belize. It was some way up the coast of the Caribbean from where the early settlers of the Darién scheme had landed, but I was sure that some of our own experiences must have matched theirs.

As a unit on exercise, we spent six weeks chopping our way through the thick vines, making shelters out of leaves, shooting pop-up targets and sneaking down sodden rivulets in search of an elusive enemy. We always won in our play-fights with the soldiers of the Belize Defence Force, mainly because they were usually asleep. All in all, it was excellent training, and jolly good fun. I'm still not sure how six weeks in Belize was considered the best training for the deserts of Afghanistan where we deployed to a few months later, but who was I to argue?

The best bit of that particular trip, though, was that because my Paras were only on attachment to the jocks, we were given free rein. When the exercise had finished, the whole Officers' Mess hired a mini bus and sped off for some R&R. And where else to go but Cancún, Mexico?

It was a messy affair. The soldiers quickly caught on to where we had disappeared and they were allowed to follow. Before we knew it, the entire Regiment followed suit, so that almost four hundred men, fresh from six weeks living in hammocks, descended like the Spartans onto the resort. Needless to say, not all who entered, returned in one piece.

I remember one chap, a young corporal, who went missing for three whole days. They ended up having to call out the Royal Military Police, who spent the time searching high and low throughout the brothels in the district. It was only when everyone had assumed he'd either been washed out to sea, or knifed in a back alley, that he was discovered somewhere near the border, alive, but minus his shirt and passport. He had lost all his money on a prostitute with whom he'd fallen in love. It turned out to be unrequited.

But I will save the tales of hedonism and debauchery for another time. After four days, I escaped. We were all pretty much done-for anyway, so I saw it as my chance to explore the region some more. I travelled to Mérida to meet up with Ceci, who showed me the wonders of the Yucatán, and it was her that convinced me, some years later, when I finally left the army, to go and live there and try my hand at photography. So I did. In the spring of 2010, I turned up in the Yucatecan city of Mérida with nothing but my notepad, a camera, and a newfound sense of freedom.

What struck me the most in those halcyon days was the rain. Much of the three months I lived in that ancient town was spent holed up in *Casa Zocalo*. It was a little townhouse near to the cathedral. The *casa* was basic and barely furnished. In my room, there was a simple bed, a dusty wardrobe and a full-length mirror. But the ceiling was high so that it was cool enough to breathe. The electricity came and went, and the fan, which belonged in a bygone era, clattered into life at will. There was a courtyard directly outside my room, beyond a small marble terrace, on which there was a hammock, where I could lie and watch the rain come down, pummelling the garden and the tropical plants that sprouted from every corner. It usually began with a tentative warning; a few fat globules and then, before you even had time to run indoors, the heavens would open and sheets of warm water fell from the blackness above. The noise of the water was an inescapable beating, like a primordial drum. Even the sound of the outside world was temporarily dumb, as the high walls of the house acted like an inverted speaker and kept out the car horns and market chatter beyond. That little courtyard seemed suddenly as if the world itself belonged only there.

A tiny bathing-pool was dug in its centre. Its inviting shallows were disturbed by the watery onslaught that appeared in the form of a million cannon balls. When it rained, the pool overflowed and the surrounding grass grew at a ferocious rate. Around the edges of the high walls were tropical plants and flowers. They were rejoicing after months of drought. Reds and greens and purples danced around with the pouring rain. Only when the rain stopped, would the animals come out. Steam would lift like a cloud from the garden and almost immediately it was filled with chattering parakeets and shifty little lizards.

Usually a fat iguana would make his way slowly out of the bushes, emerging to bask in the triumphant sunlight – once upon a time, the god of these lands. The lizard's eyes were partially closed, but he was ever alert. He'd wait for a juicy spider to scamper across the lawn, before darting to gobble it up. In the surrounding palm trees, the parrots would sing, thanking the heavens for a chance to bask in the rays and dry their sodden feathers. Cats would stretch off and stalk from the terrace, treading carefully over the grass, so as not to get too wet in search of their prey. Only the dog remained still. He was too idle to move in the searing heat, instead rolling lazily wherever there was shade.

I was the only guest in the *casa*. The owner of the house was an old woman called Gracialla. Her father had recently passed away and I was given his room. She sometimes joked that his ghost still lived there, but I didn't have any unpleasant encounters. The bed was a fairly new addition. Until recently, most Yucatecans slept exclusively in hammocks, but Gracialla had decided to move with the times, succumbing to modernity. Gracialla wanted a simple life, but needed her own money to survive, as she didn't have any children to support her. She usually woke early and wandered off to buy fresh tortillas from the market, dressed in an *huipil*, the characteristic white dress of the Yucatecan Mayans. When she returned, she would not stand for me to be still asleep and would sing at the top of her voice, '*Desayuno!*', the Spanish word for breakfast. It was served on a wooden trestle-table in the courtyard, and as the only guest, I would help myself to the delicious burritos and refried beans.

I thought it would have been a conducive atmosphere to photography, but, after two weeks I realised that I was simply getting lazy. The humid air, the ferocious sun, the diet of pure carbohydrates and the plentiful tequila meant that entire days would often disappear in a haze of food and sleep and rain. After five years in the army, I was quite happy to have a break and do nothing. Some evenings I'd explore the downtown area and marvel at the old square and its sixteenth-century Spanish architecture.

Other times I would visit Ceci at her parents' house and immerse myself in local culture, trying my hand at Spanish. '*Si, Dona Leonor, muy bien*,' I'd say to her mother, as she rattled off breathless prose in my general direction. I actually took up Spanish classes, but the two hours of classroom time were exhausting in the heat of the rains, and I don't think I took much on board.

'Why don't you get out and about more?' said Ceci one day. 'Go and explore, otherwise when you run out of money, you won't even have any pictures to sell.' It was a good point, I supposed.

'You've spent all that money on a new camera and you have barely used it.' It was true. I'd blown a good deal of my savings from the army on a brand-new, top-of-the-range Nikon, with the intention of making a little sideline business in travel photography. I dreamt of selling pictures to guide books and magazines, and maybe one day even having an exhibition of my own.

'You go to such wonderful places and take pictures, but you never take any here,' she nagged.

'That's not true,' I protested. 'I got a great shot of that iguana last week.'

'One iguana, that's it?'

'And the cathedral.'

'Ridiculous. How much did that thing cost you?'

I wasn't about to tell her that, but she had a point, I had not exactly got my money's worth yet.

'Such a shame,' she carried on. 'We have such a colourful country and Mérida has *mucho* charm. Why don't you take pictures of all the little *casas* and saloons? And the birds and the *tolocs*? Or you could go to *Chichen Itza* and see the ruins again? Or even go to Palenque and the jungle? There's a beautiful place in the mountains called San Cristóbal de las Casas, there's heaps of the indigenous culture remaining up there – all the women wear an *huipil*.'

'Why don't you wear an *huipil*?' I asked her. 'Then I could take pictures of you.'

She laughed. 'I'm not some Mayan curiosity. Go and explore, I have work to do.'

I took her advice and went on a photography spree.

Fortunately, I had chosen a good week for it. The rain seemed to come only for a couple of hours a day and almost perfectly on time, at two o'clock in the afternoon. As long as I looked at my watch, I could plan around it and make sure I'd found shelter in a canteen or a saloon by that time. I would wake early and take photographs of anything that caught my eye. I enjoyed the freedom and the creativity involved in photography. There is something rather liberating in capturing a moment, an event, or merely the look in someone's eye through a lens. People talk about photographers 'having an eye'. I wasn't sure about that, and I certainly don't know if I had an eye or not. I had never taken a lesson in my life, but understood the basics from an artistic point of view. The rule of thirds in composition, the use of light and framing, and making the most of colour. But I was not technically adept.

When I learned a new trick, like most novice photographers, I would play with it like a child and be very happy with myself. I loved experimenting with depth of field to create what is known in the industry as 'bokeh' – when the subject is in focus and the background is blurry. When you figure out how to get it right, then suddenly you feel as though you've just turned pro. Of course, nothing could be further from the truth.

I travelled around the Yucatán peninsula and as far afield as Campeche, San Cristóbal de las Casas and Palenque, in search of bokeh. I took pictures of the *Cascadas de Agua Azul*, the blue waterfall, one of the most remarkable things I'd seen, not to mention the Sumidero Canyon. I snapped away at the howler monkeys that swung between the pyramids of the ancient Mayan city at Palenque, high in the celestial cloud forest, and at the old men that sat on doorsteps in the old colonial plazas. In Chiapas there were the colourful Zapatistas, and all over the peninsula were grand *cenotes*, deep pools formed from sinkholes hidden away in the forests.

One of the highlights of the road trip was visiting *haciendas*, the old factories and ranches of the Spanish era. Some of them were still working farms making *henequen* rope or *mezcal*. Many had since been converted into tourist lodges, or cattle ranches, but they were all reminiscent of another time and era, and as far as taking pictures was concerned, you couldn't really go far wrong. *Rancheros*, cowboys, stallions, sombrero-wearing *muchachos* and beautiful farm girls in flowing white frocks.

Soon my memory cards were full and I was happy that I had taken my passion to another level and learned lots of new skills. In the process, I think I learned one particularly useful thing about the process of photography – that while it's important to understand the technical aspects, and to know your camera inside and out, it is far more important to be bold. You need to speak to people and get them to relax. You need to spend an hour or so chatting about their life, their passions, their wants and needs, before you even get your camera out. They must trust you, and that cannot be forced. They must like you, and you can't force that either. If they don't open up, then you have not done your job well enough, and you must leave them alone.

So, with new lessons learned and feeling pretty satisfied that the creative juices had been flowing – perhaps even a little too self-assured that I could even sell one or two of the images to a guidebook or a magazine – I boarded a long-distance bus. I hate long-distance bus rides, but since it was the only way to get back to Mérida, I treated myself to a VIP tourist coach, which involved fourteen hours in the relative luxury of a shiny bus that had only twenty-six seats instead of the usual fifty-six. They even gave you a packed lunch with sandwiches wrapped in cling film.

Normally I can never sleep on buses, although I generally try and get the window seat, so I can at least have the vain hope of a few minutes shut-eye. The bus was not full and most people had two seats to themselves, so it was rather annoying when, shortly before we pulled out of the station, a man got on and chose to sit next to me. He didn't look like the rest of the passengers. Since this was the VIP bus and it cost significantly more than the 'local bus', which stopped at all the local villages *en route*, most of the people were wealthy Mexicans – well-dressed and well-mannered. This man was swarthy, in a cheap tracksuit, and wore a baseball cap. He did not acknowledge me when he sat down, preferring to stare at a magazine instead.

Nevertheless, I thought nothing more of him as we pulled off and began the long journey. The road weaved through small villages and towns, where peeling red churches towered above the adobe walls. Soon it was dusk and I had dozed off fitfully, as my head banged relentlessly against the smeared glass window. I must have been so exhausted from my recent travels that I slept like a baby for almost the whole journey back. It wasn't until the coach jolted into the bus station that I woke up with a start and a terrible headache.

Wiping the sleep from my eyes and stretching, I realised that the man who had been next to me was gone. We must have stopped off somewhere in the night, although I had no recollection of it. It felt as if I had slept for only a few minutes, but it must really have been several hours. The passengers around me were shuffling about, collecting up their belongings as we waited for the doors to open so that we could get off and stretch our legs. I stood up, giving a vague nod to the lady sat in the chair in front, and reached for the overhead compartment.

Suddenly I felt sick. I stood on my tiptoes, looking left and right, but it was not to be seen anywhere. My bag was gone.

No, surely not, I thought, panicking. I looked under the seats, but it wasn't there either.

The bastard, I thought. It could only have been the man next to me. I had been travelling light, inside my bag was everything that I owned. It had my laptop, some travel money, some nice sunglasses. But most importantly, it contained my shiny new camera and lenses, and all the bloody photographs that I had gone to some incredible lengths to take.

Crestfallen, I sat down and noticed a couple of things. The bottle of water that I had been drinking was still in the seat pocket, and it looked odd. I couldn't put my finger on it, perhaps it was a little cloudy. I could not tell for sure, but it occurred to me that maybe I'd been drugged. That was why I had slept so well. But when? How? Then I remembered I'd got up to use the toilet just after the man had got on. Perhaps it was him? Surely it was him. The fucking bastard. And then I saw something else. Tucked in behind the bottle of water was my passport. Shit, my passport, what was it doing there? It had been in my bag.

And then it dawned on me that the thief, the man next to me, must at least have had the grace to leave behind my passport. Fucking bastard.

I stormed down the aisle, pushing past the other passengers, and shouting at the bus driver, 'Who was the man next to me? Show me the passenger list!' The driver just shrugged, looking bored.

Another passenger, a lady, then said in English, 'Sorry, amigo, it happens all the time. You won't get an answer from this man, it isn't his fault, you can blame the company, they let on undesirables who steal things from tourists.'

I wanted to punch the driver out cold, for surely he must have known what was going on. What bloody corruption.

'Hope you didn't have anything valuable?' said the lady in a conciliatory tone. I wanted to tell her that I'd just lost a three-thousand-pound camera, not to mention a month's worth of photographs. Instead, I said nothing and sulked off the bus.

In Mérida, I told Ceci about my loss. She let me feel sorry for myself, while I reported everything to the police. They simply laughed and shrugged their shoulders, as if it were my fault for not knowing about the scams that go on in these parts. I was suddenly very much out of love with Mexico.

'I have a plan,' said Ceci the day after. 'I know a guy, he's a photographer. I've made a call and he's said he'll lend you a new camera.'

'But I don't have any money now, half of what I had was in that bag.'

'He doesn't want any money. He'll just lend you the camera, and he said he'd love for you to visit his studio.'

I figured that she was doing her best to comfort me, and while I was in no mood to socialise, I thought it best to humour her and meet this chap who had made the generous offer. I arrived at his studio on a suburban street in Mérida. From the outside, it looked like a ramshackle little place, but inside it was all mod cons. The blast of air-conditioning came as a relief from the relentless heat outside, and as I wiped my brow of sweat in the reception, I noticed a beautiful and flirtatious girl behind the desk.

'*Hola*,' she said coyly, about to carry on, but was interrupted as a man burst into the room from the doorway.

Alberto, a trendy, good-looking man with wide-set eyes and a chunky nose greeted me with enthusiasm. ''Ello Levi,' he said, with such a characteristic Mexican accent that I couldn't help breaking into a smile, despite my foul mood. 'I heard all about you and your problem. So, you had your camera stolen, eh? Fucking assholes, no?' He grinned. 'Fucking Mexicans!'

At that, we both laughed out loud.

'Well, no problem, amigo, come this way.'

I followed Alberto through the glass door into the studio itself, where big lights shone against bright white walls, and sheets that were draped as backdrops. There was a white table in the middle of the room. On it there was a selection of fruits: bananas, grapefruit, kiwis and a solitary apple.

'Hang on, my friend, I just need to finish this.'

He picked up a plastic spray-bottle and squirted a haze of water over the fruit.

'Makes it look fresh and tasty,' he grinned, with a conspiratorial wink.

Picking up his camera, a large, full-frame professional SLR, battered from years of use, he began snapping away with a close-up macro lens.

'It's for a restaurant. They want bananas, not so glamorous as bikini girls,' he chuckled to himself.

When he'd finished, he put the camera down and led me to a cabinet that contained a collection of camera bodies and lenses.

'Which do you need?'

I was embarrassed. I was a complete novice in the presence of a true professional. My meagre snaps were the vain product of a restless desire to eke out a career in anything other than finance or security, which were what most of my army pals had gone into. I knew nothing of lenses or formats or apertures. I knew still less of f-stops and ISOs and colour balance.

I think Alberto sensed my hesitation. He smiled, 'Here you go, it's a good camera.' He handed me another Nikon similar to his own, and three lenses; a long telephoto zoom, a 50mm prime and a wide-angle, too.

'Now, let's go explore.'

3

The Americas

The history of Central America in the decades and centuries after Colombus's rediscovery is generally seen as a rather dismal time, particularly for the indigenous inhabitants. Disease, war, famine and genocide were the inevitable consequences of the Spanish invasion of the region. It was one of the darkest periods in any colonial expansion, resulting in millions of deaths. Moreover, the loss of human life was compounded with the loss of entire civilisations. Cities, cultures and languages succumbed to the new order and the old ways disappeared, it seemed, without a trace. Well, almost.

If it were not for the curiosity of a couple of amateur archaeologists, perhaps the ancient Mayan civilisation would never have been uncovered. The story of two friends who set off on one of the most remarkable expeditions of the early nineteenth century changed the way everybody in Europe and the United States thought about Central America for good.

John Lloyd Stephens was a thirty-three-year-old American writer and lawyer and Frederick Catherwood was a thirty-seven-year-old British artist and architect.

At a time when almost all of Central America was involved in violent rebellions and insurrections, the adventurers boarded a boat in New York bound for Belize, which was then known as British Honduras. They were on a mission to explore something that the Spanish, in their endless quest for gold and riches, had overlooked – the ancient cities of Mayan civilization, now engulfed by the rainforest.

Through his fame as a travel writer, Stephens had managed to land himself a job as US ambassador to what was then the United Federation of Central America – a loose jumble of countries and city states that had recently become independent from Spain. The only problem was that the loose jumble of countries and city states now wanted independence from their new federation. Countries and territories jostled for autonomy; the entire peninsula was alight with civil war.

That didn't deter Stephens, whose passion for antiquities had resulted in him meeting the equally fanatical Catherwood at an archaeological dig in Egypt. So, when Stephens landed the new job, he sent his English friend a letter asking if he would like to come along on a free trip to see what ruins they could find in the jungles of Mexico and Guatemala. There were rumours, he said, of entire lost cities awaiting discovery. But even so, Stephens – enthusiasm and wide-eyed curiosity aside – remained a little sceptical. He wrote that their journey was in the *hope*, rather than the expectation of finding wonders. Surely no one could have anticipated the wonders that the two men would actually find.

When they reached Belize, Stephens and Catherwood travelled inland without the vast entourage that was so common at the time. They based their movements on word of mouth, often arriving in an unmapped village and trusting the hearsay of the locals to locate the ruins of their ancestors in the next.

It took them weeks of hacking through jungles and avoiding the warring tribes until they finally rediscovered the city of

Copán. It must have been a joyful moment for the pair of explorers:

> Working our way through the thick woods, we came upon a square stone column ...The front was the figure of a man curiously and richly dressed, and the face, evidently a portrait, solemn, stern, and well fitted to excite terror. The back was of a different design, unlike anything we had ever seen before, and the sides were covered with hieroglyphics ...The sight of this unexpected monument put at rest at once and forever, in our minds, all uncertainty in regard to the character of American antiquities, and gave us the assurance that the objects we were in search of were interesting, not only as the remains of an unknown people, but as works of art, proving, like newly discovered historical records, that the people who once occupied the Continent of America were not savages.

Stephens would write and Catherwood would draw – impeccably documenting the ancient monuments in intricate detail. They would log the time it took to walk from one settlement to another, meticulously listing ornaments, pyramid shapes, sculptures and skulls. They soon identified hieroglyphics and complex systems of astronomy amongst the ruins. It seemed that the civilisation that created these monuments was far more complex than anyone could have imagined.

Where the conquistadors hadn't destroyed the Mayan edifices, they had paid no heed to them – preferring instead to paint the indigenous Americans as bloodthirsty savages who lived in huts and worshipped the devil. Clearly, nothing could have been further from the truth.

Over the course of the next decade, the explorers documented all the magnificent relics they found in a series of travel books and illustrations that became standard texts on indigenous Central American culture. Both of the men died tragically young. Catherwood drowned at fifty-five, when his boat sank crossing the Atlantic, but not before having cashed in on the boom in San Francisco in the wake of the gold rush. Stephens had moved south, taking on the running of the Panama Railroad Company. He died at his home in New York, aged just forty-six, plagued with the ailments of his jungle days.

But even though neither of the explorers lived to see their work celebrated, they left a legacy that changed world history forever. When the intrepid pair set out to uncover the Mayan story, Stephens wrote that the inhabitants of Mesoamerica were still viewed by many as a separate race – without art, architecture, culture or language. But Stephens and Catherwood demonstrated that long before Christopher Columbus set sail, an advanced, massively developed and intelligent civilisation had flourished in the Americas.

I had been fascinated by the Mayans since learning about 'American Indians' as a child from story books. I remember reading about the myth of El Dorado, and the legends of these strange tribes that lived in the jungle – but what really intrigued me was how far they'd come – not just in terms of civilisation, but *physically*, across the world. I couldn't work out how pyramids could exist in the jungles of America when they should really be in Egypt – that was where they were supposed to be in my seven-year-old mind.

And how did a people who didn't really exist come to know an alphabet, learn to read the stars, travel across oceans on canoes and build massive cities without any metal, or even the use of a wheel? None of it made any sense, and even as I grew up and properly studied the history of the world, there was something unnerving about the fact that these 'Indians' knew more than 'we' did, when the Europeans were still in the Stone Age.

The only conclusion I could reach was that these people were the ultimate explorers. They were the ones who had travelled the furthest away from the original home of Homo Sapiens in Africa, were they not? They'd walked all the way from the rift valley, across the Middle East and China, and somehow over the frozen Bering Strait into Alaska. Not content with that, they continued south. Forming clans and tribes along the way, and over the course of thousands of years, but these early explorers kept on going. The hardest, most curious of them, the ones who refused to settle, walked all the way through the jungles of Central and South America and formed three of the great civilisations – the Aztec, the Inca, and the earliest of them all, the Maya.

What led them on this insatiable quest, we will probably never know. Surely it wasn't just the need for new grazing, or chasing wildlife to eat – after all, in those days there were endless supplies of food and little competition for it. Whatever it was that drove these brown-skinned Asiatics to populate the Americas, they did it with a skill and fortitude that is often overlooked by the history books.

After I met Alberto in his studio, he took me under his wing as photography mentor for a while. We'd go out to abandoned railway stockyards and capture images of beautiful texture: rusty nails and deep-grained wooden sleepers. We'd go out to the Mayan ruins at Mayapan and Acanceh and photograph the rough-hewn limestone blocks. At Tekit we explored the ancient graveyards, where dusk brought a range of colours that I previously thought impossible to combine. 'Follow the light,' he insisted. I learned about white balance and slow shutter-speeds. Back in his studio, he taught me how to edit, sharpen and saturate, 'but not too much,' he'd say. 'The first thing to remember as a photographer is that it must be real.'

I liked Alberto. He was honest, genuine and generous. He was a lot of fun, too. At thirty-six, he was a few years older than me, but had an almost child-like enthusiasm for life. Nothing seemed to worry him, and adventure was at the very core of his soul.

'What are you doing when you get back home?' he asked me one day.

'I think I'll go to Africa,' I said, explaining that a friend of mine had asked me to procure an ambulance for a hospital in Malawi. I'd suggested that rather than importing one in a shipping container and wasting a whole lot of money, she allow me to fundraise, buy one in the UK, and drive it 10,000 miles overland to its destination. 'As long as it still works at the end,' said Ruthie. 'Of course,' I'd promised.

'You're driving to Malawi?' Alberto's eyes were wide open now. 'Shit, I don't even know where that is.' He shook his head. 'Can I come?' he continued.

'Sure,' I said, and gave it no more thought.

Five months later, after 4,000 miles of driving across Europe and the Middle East, I was sitting in a café in downtown Damascus with two makeshift ambulances parked outside. Guess who burst through the door.

'Eyy, Levi!' There he was, the mad devil. 'You never thought I'd show up, did you?'

Turns out that Alberto, the fashion-and-fruit photographer from Mérida, Mexico, who'd never really travelled very much, was now in Syria. He was about to drive through eight countries and the length of Africa with me.

'Actually, I had a hunch you might,' I told him. He grinned.

'Now, where can we get tacos in this town?' he said, only half-joking.

But that's a digression; a story I won't go into now. I mention it because it was on that particular adventure that Alberto first came up with the idea of a Central American journey.

'Imagine it, Lev, a road trip – we'd start in Mérida at my house and go all the way to South America. Jungles, beaches, parrots, pyramids and hot girls,' he winked. 'No Sharia law there,' he continued. 'No suicide bombs, no nasty deserts, good food and best of all – great beer and cocktails. It's my dream trip. Don't forget about it, Lev.'

I didn't forget about it. I'd told him that one day I would go back to Central America and we'd do the trip together.

Six years later, having spent six months trekking through the wild foothills of the Himalayas a year previously, not to mention nine months traipsing the length of the River Nile, I thought that a four-month walk following the spine of Central America would pose no particular problem. The house was almost finished and summer had arrived. I could do with a break from London, anyway, I thought.

So there I was, standing in the garden at Hampton Court, amid the dust, dodgy wallpaper and Grasshopper's Fart paint. I called Alberto. We hadn't spoken properly since saying goodbye over half a decade ago in Malawi – possibly something to do with the fact that by going on that journey he had pretty much bankrupted himself, plus I heard he'd got married. But I wanted to keep my promise, and it seemed as good a time as any.

The number rang through and a familiar voice answered.

'Eyy, Levi.' It was him alright, and he didn't sound too angry.

'Alberto, you remember that trip we talked about doing one day? The Central American trip.'

'Of course.'

'Well, how about this summer, in six weeks' time?'

The line went quiet for a few seconds. I remembered back to the aftermath of the Africa trip. He'd sent me an email a few weeks later explaining that the two-month expedition had cost him his entire business. The photography studio was gone and he'd had to sell half his cameras and, damn it, been forced to get a *real* job. I'd not heard from him since.

'*Chinga*,' was his response. I knew it meant something very rude in Spanish.

And then he launched into a story that I found very difficult to believe. But I suppose he had no reason to make it up.

'Three days ago, I was on the beach in Tulum with some English girls. They were clients actually. We were doing a photo shoot. Did I ever tell you what happened to my business after Africa?' he said.

'Yes, I seem to remember it didn't work out.'

'Yeah, exactly, I had to sell everything. It was a tough time, but you know what, it was worth it. Every moment in Africa was amazing and I saw things that nobody gets to see. Those experiences are worth more than a few cameras and lights, so even though I lost it all, I don't mind. But I had to get a proper job.'

'Sorry about that,' was all I could reply.

'There I was, in my late thirties, working for some bastard

making all the money. But I was the one doing all the work, seriously, everything. It was a production and he just sat on his ass in Miami watching the dollars come in, and there was me making coffee for the models.'

'It could have been worse,' I suggested.

'Models!' He almost sounded angry now. 'People think, being a fashion photographer, I sit under a coconut tree with a piña colada, getting drunk with super-hot girls in bikinis on either side of me.'

It had crossed my mind.

'No, I have to make coffee for them, and order their taxis and ask them what kind of skinny latte they want. You know, there was this one girl who only ate cabbage soup. Cabbage soup! She's like a rabbit, Lev. Well anyway, one day, I'd had enough. I was going to quit, but the universe had a different idea. The boss of the client's production company approached me and asked if I'd like to work directly with them. Of course, I felt a bit bad on my own boss – he might have thought I was stealing his customers, but it wasn't like that. They asked me, and of course, I said yes. Now I run these massive productions myself. I do all the same work, but earn ten times more.'

'So, you're doing well?'

'Very well, I'll show you my houses when you come to Mexico.'

'So, you're up for it then?' I asked him, eager to get to the point.

'Let me finish the story,' he said.

'Sure.'

'Anyway, as I was saying. There I was, three days ago, on the beach in Tulum with some English girls, clients. We were doing a photo shoot for some fashion magazine. And one of these

English girls started to complain about something. I asked her what was wrong, and she said that she'd lost her book. A book, she said. I mean, there's lots of things to complain about, but it was only a book and we were busy. We had models to film and bikinis to try on and rabbit food to arrange. But no, she wanted her book. She said she'd nearly finished it. We looked everywhere; in the hotel, in the minibus, by the swimming pool. It was lost, I told her, now back to work. She was sad, she said. She said I'd like the book, it was about a guy travelling and stuff and he'd been to Africa as well, travelling all the way to Malawi. Anyway, of course she found it. It was in her bag after all, the silly girl. She showed me the book. It was called *Walking the Nile* by Levison Wood.'

Alberto laughed down the phone.

'It's true. That was three days ago, and I had no idea what you've been doing the last few years, but now I can see. So now you ring me up, asking to come and drive the length of Central America, what choice do I have? It's, how do you say in English? Fate, destiny? Everything happens for a reason, and so, of course I'll come. But I've just sold my chopper motorbike, what will we drive?'

I broke the news to him.

'Erm, we're not driving. We're walking.'

The line went quiet again.

'*Chinga*,' he said.

'I'll see you in six weeks.'

4

Meeting an Explorer

Apart from the jaguar, there are no large predators in Central America to worry about; an absence of which would represent, I felt, a great improvement on life along the Nile. Having said that, there are much the same amoebic and bacillary dysenteries to deal with, yellow and blackwater and dengue fevers, malaria – of course – and cholera, typhoid, hepatitis, tuberculosis and rabies. Then there's some very special extras. Bot fly, for instance, whose larvae bore into your scalp, eat your flesh from the inside and then, forty days later emerge as inch-long maggots. Chagas disease, likewise, is rather gruesome. Here, the assassin bugs bite you on the face, and then, gorged, defecate next to the puncture. When you scratch the resulting itch, you rub the shit and their cargo of protozoa into your bloodstream and then between one and twenty years later, you die from incurable brain damage.

River blindness is no less pleasant. Blackfly transmit a particularly determined kind of worm that migrate into your eyeball. Then there's leishmaniosis – a flesh-rotting disease, a bit like leprosy, which eats away at your warm extremities. Let's not forget Zika virus either, which emerged as a freak exotic malady in 2015, causing an epidemic of shrunken-headed babies across Latin America.

I asked my friend and tropical-disease expert Dr Will Charlton what he thought my chances were. I was assured that if I didn't succumb to at least one or two of the above, then I should consider myself very lucky indeed. Of equal concern was, of course, all the stuff that I would likely encounter in or around my jungle campsites to come. Vampire bats have been known to bite humans and transmit rabies, giving rise to the zombie myth. The bushmaster viper can grow up to twelve feet long, but generally bites only if you stand on it. The fer-de-lance (seven and a half feet) can be more aggressive and chase you across the road. Anacondas are likely to be found in the rivers and will crush you to death.

In Belize, the tarantulas can grow to the size of saucers; black widow spiders inhabit every drainpipe and are fifteen times as poisonous as a rattlesnake, whereas bullet ants are a mere nuisance with only twenty-four hours of excruciating, debilitating agony on the cards. My personal horror was the prospect of yet more crocodiles lurking in the depths of the swamps I would inevitably have to wade through.

The political situation was no less horrifying. Decapitations in Mexico, stabbings in Belize, forestry wars in Guatemala, murders in Honduras, kidnappings in Nicaragua, hijackings in Panama, and a whole host of drug and gang violence in Colombia. And that's not to mention the hurricanes, volcanoes, earthquakes and floods that happen every year in virtually all of those countries. I'd been warned explicitly about the perils of walking through the favelas of Belize city, and the cartel neighbourhoods of San Pedro Sula and the remote lawless border regions of El Petan. But, of course, the most terrifying place of all was the Darién Gap – that squalid stretch of jungle that has been the demise of explorers for centuries, as the poor Scots found out three hundred years ago.

Nowadays, the Darién is barely less inhabitable that it was during those early ill-fated expeditions, in fact it's probably worse. For fifty years, it's been the refuge of the guerilla group FARC, who have launched a campaign of violence against the Colombian government from their jungle hideouts. Even now it's a sanctuary for criminals, gun runners, drug smugglers and human traffickers. Newspapers rarely cover the story of what's known in NGO circles as 'the other migrant crisis'. While Europe and the Middle East are in turmoil as the war in Syria rages on, and a steady flow of migrants from Africa try their luck at floating across the Mediterranean, there's another, equally desperate group of people trying to get into the United States.

While Mexicans have been digging tunnels and jumping fences for years, there were now reports of thousands of migrants, mainly from Cuba but also other parts of Latin America, and even from Bangladesh, Nepal and Afghanistan, making the arduous trek from Colombia into Panama. Of course, they didn't do it alone, it was part of the vast network of criminal gangs that rule the region with an iron fist – and a Kalashnikov. And they weren't exactly known for being friendly to outsiders wanting to nose about their business.

Over the last twenty years, the Darién Gap has swallowed up more people than perhaps anywhere else in the western hemisphere. Stories abound of journalists and backpackers getting kidnapped and released only after months of starvation and psychological torture at the hands of the notorious FARC rebels. Some though, sadly never escape. In 2013 one poor chap, a Swede called Jan Philip Braunisch, set off to attempt to become one of the handful of foreigners to have ever succeeded in crossing the infamous jungle. He'd been enchanted by the impossibility of the task; the fact that it is the only break in the 17,000-mile Pan-American Highway and has defeated armies and conquerors alike for centuries.

Unfortunately for him, he was kidnapped almost immediately upon entering rebel territory and not heard from in over two years. It was only when his family was handed a bag of bones that they discovered he had been executed in the jungle. The suspicious rebels had assumed he was a CIA operative working with the Colombian anti-narcotics units and didn't want their lucrative trade disrupted. Throughout the 1990s and 2000s, the FARC systematically targeted Westerners and anyone else they could blackmail to fund their campaign of terror. The journalist Robert Young Pelton spent ten days detained by the gang before they let him loose in Colombia. He was one of the lucky ones. In 2003, he described his experiences to *National Geographic* the day after he made it home:

The basic problem of the Darién Gap is that it's one of the toughest hikes there is. It's an absolute pristine jungle, but it's got some nasty sections with thorns, wasps, snakes, thieves, criminals, you name it. Everything that's bad for you is in there ... We had probably been travelling a week before it happened ... at about 11.44 in the morning, three Kuna Indians passed us on the trail, and all of a sudden we heard automatic gunfire for about three minutes, about a half a mile from us. Our guides ran away – they dropped our stuff and just took off ... I suggested we walk into the ambush, as opposed to try to hide or run away ... So we decided to talk very loudly in English and keep together as a group and let them know we were coming. It took about a half hour for them to calm down because they were so amped up ... they were wired and twitchy, shouting and yelling ... they killed four people from Paya, and they burned Púcuro to the ground ... The Darién Gap is an extremely dangerous place ... It's used as a conduit for drugs. There are no police there, there's no military, the trails aren't marked ...The jungle there is not viewed as a place that is pristine and beautiful – it's looked at as a place where you get killed.

Not exactly reassuring stuff, I thought to myself. It wasn't just the FARC either; there were dozens of other paramilitary groups and criminal gangs operating in the green vastness of the Darién Gap, making it without a doubt one of the most hostile regions that I was ever likely to encounter. What I needed was the advice of an expert; someone who knew the Darién, who knew the jungle, and could put me in touch with people that could try and help me not to get killed.

He was ramrod straight in a pinstripe Savile Row suit and a Regimental army tie. His polished, black Oxford shoes glinted in the half-light of the summer evening. His perfectly white hair was combed impeccably over a seventy-nine-year-old head.

'Evening, Colonel,' I said, being greeted with a vice-like handshake.

'Let's sit down,' he said. 'This'll do.'

I was expecting that we would go upstairs to the library, or at least into the tea room, but the Colonel was clearly in a rush and wanted to deal with me as quickly as possible. So, we plonked ourselves down on some ancient wooden chairs in the entrance hall of the Royal Geographical Society in South Kensington.

It is always magical entering the hallowed halls of the society and I have never grown tired of walking along the creaky corridors, looking at the old paintings and busts of the great explorers. All of my Victorian heroes look down from the walls: Baker,

Stanley, Burton and Speke. In a side room, where a four-hundred-year-old Chinese map of the world hangs proudly from the wall, is a model of Mount Everest – it is the same one that Edmund Hillary used to plan his famous ascent of the mountain in 1952. I imagine all the fabulous eccentrics to have trodden the same halls and it never ceases to amaze.

Outside, two statues peer down on the unsuspecting tourists from Beijing who are busy photographing the Albert Memorial, having spent the day marvelling at the dinosaurs inside the Natural History Museum. One is David Livingstone, the other Ernest Shackleton. But the RGS usually remains unnoticed; bypassed by the masses.

The Colonel looked every inch the London gentleman. He was the kind of explorer that looked just as comfortable sipping whisky in a Pall Mall club as he was in a pith helmet in the jungle. He reminded me of the explorers of old, a last bastion of a noble creed in these changing times. I'd read his book years ago. The front cover has a photograph of him in a safari suit, holding a pair of binoculars, while riding an elephant. He used to be 'the chap at Sandhurst in charge of adventure training': which, in the words of the Commandant of the time meant 'sending cadets overseas, to the benefit of their character, and at the least possible detriment to the Empire.'

'Blashers', as he was known to those allowed into his inner circle, was something of an enigma. He lived in Dorset with his wife and dogs, and had only just discovered the Internet in this, his seventh decade. This was the man who almost single-handedly invented white-water rafting, when, as a Captain in the Royal Engineers, he led the first team to descend the Blue Nile and realising he was going to be late for a tea party, floated down the river on an improvised inflatable tyre.

This was the very same chap, who, being fascinated by the musical sensibilities of the Wai Wai tribe of Guyana, had decided to hack a path through 350 miles of rainforest to deliver a grand piano to their jungle hideout. Not only that, but he had returned several times to make sure the thing was properly tuned.

Colonel John Blashford-Snell, OBE, veteran of thirty-seven years of service in the Army, founder of the Scientific Exploration Society and Operation Raleigh, and leader of over one hundred expeditions; he'd once even designed a pith helmet 'to meet the needs of all explorers'.

'So, you're having a go at the stopper, are you?' he said, with the clipped tones of an old public-school boy. 'El Tapon, in Spanish. It's what the locals call the Darién Gap.'

'I certainly hope so,' I replied, not wanting to sound too confident, given the fact that he was one of the few people to have completed this expedition and that was over forty years ago.

I needn't have been so coy.

'Well, you'll have a jolly good time, I'm sure.' He attempted a smile, but it only served to cause a creaked wince in his weathered face. He was here for a meeting with someone very important, so I knew I didn't have much time.

'Did you bring a map?'

I opened a 1975 atlas of Central America. He shook his head, tutting, and pulled a laptop close instead, where Google Earth displayed the digital route in bright red.

'I went this way, you see, to the east a bit and over the Atrato river, but of course I had a Land Rover with me, which made things complicated, so you should have it easier.' His ancient finger prodded the screen.

'How many men did you take?' I asked, wondering how on earth he managed to get a vehicle through an impenetrable swamp.

'Oh, rather a lot, sixty perhaps. A few whites and plenty of natives. Ended up having to get some prisoners from a hard-labour camp in the jungle, though, we needed all the help we could get. Got an excellent deal with the Commandant – he gave them to me for a fortnight for a crate of scotch.'

My God, I thought. He's mad.

'We only lost seven on the last trip,' he said, barely raising an eyebrow.

'Lost seven?' I asked. 'Who?'

'Our Colombian escort.'

'You mean they went missing?

'Oh, no,' he carried on, 'ambushed. Killed the lot of them, they did. Very inconvenient as they were bringing our weekly resupply. Poor buggers.'

'What? Who killed them?'

'Bandits, I imagine. Or FARC, perhaps, truth is we never did find out. Had to push on, you see.'

He opened his briefcase and pulled out a folder, handing it to me. It was a photocopy of the expedition diary. I flicked through with interest and he pointed out some black-and-white photographs from the expedition. Everyone in the pictures was in jungle fatigues. This had been very much a military-run expedition, in conjunction with the Panamanian and Colombian armies. All of the images looked like they had been plucked straight from a Vietnam war album.

'Well, there basically was the beginnings of a war at that time. It got much worse though,' he said.

One of the photographs showed the famous Land Rover in

the middle of a forest river valley, being driven up some ladders onto an inflatable raft.

'All bloody rivers and swamps, so we had to float the thing most of the way.'

I didn't dare ask why he had decided to take a Land Rover in the first place.

'Who's that?' I asked, pointing at another picture of a white man surrounded by boxes of equipment.

'That's the expedition cameraman. Bloody hard job carrying cameras in those days, all film, none of this digital nonsense back then. Game fellow, he was, walking backwards the whole time. Only problem was that he was a vegetarian. We were all eating monkeys and iguanas, and he lived on nothing but onion rings.'

'I don't plan on taking any vegetarians,' I said.

'Good. The Kuna won't tolerate it.'

'The Kuna?'

'The Kuna tribe. Troublesome people, they are. They have rings through their noses and believe in dragons, but nowadays all they're interested in is the money.'

'Did they give you any hassle?' I asked.

'Oh, just the usual aggro over food and supplies. Although in Colombia we did have a gunboat escort us upriver, so they generally gave us a wide berth.'

'A gunboat?'

Now I was in awe, and suddenly felt woefully unprepared. I didn't have a gunboat.

'Well, it wasn't much use to be honest. The thing sank with its crew. You're far better without,' he said in a comforting tone.

But the truth was that I was relatively ill-equipped. Not only did I lack a gunboat, I also didn't have an army of prisoners traded for scotch, or a sixty-man backup team, or a light aircraft capable of parachute resupply, or the full backing of the British Army, not to mention resupply teams from the Colombian and Panamanian military. I read in his report that he'd carried boxes of dynamite to blow holes in the jungle.

'Well, the dynamite was quite useful,' he conceded. 'See if you can get hold of some. In the Congo, we were up against some rather frightful tribals. Armed to the teeth with guns and spears and they were always shooting at us, so we had to scare them off. We didn't fire back. We put on little displays, like getting the plane to fly low over the jungle and we chucked bricks out of it. Then I'd hide my engineers in the bushes and set off sticks of dynamite, so they thought the aircraft could drop bombs. Bit of theatrical action, you see, never goes amiss. Yes, see if you can get some dynamite.'

I replied that I'd ask around.

'I'm sure you'll have a cracking time,' he said, genuinely.

I was flicking through the report as he spoke and noticed a picture of him in full military fatigues topped by a white pith helmet, and a contingent of chaps marching in three columns behind him. It occurred to me that his idea of a cracking time might be fairly unique.

'If nothing else, you'll have fun with the Embera,' he carried on. 'They're another tribe with rings through their noses, but less hostile than the Kuna. They're up for a laugh. I remember it was Burns Night in the jungle, so of course, we had to celebrate. We had some of the Indian guides and their women with us and gave them some haggis and whisky. They seemed to enjoy it. They didn't quite get the hang of reel dancing, though. There we were in the middle of the jungle with all of these topless girls, tits jiggling all over the place, as the Gay Gordons played on the radio.'

5

Departure

To the north lay almost one thousand miles of unbroken water. I pondered what I would encounter if I were to travel in that direction. Probably the swampy estuary of the Mississippi River, if my calculations were correct. But the rickety little fishing boat that scuttled me along the coast of the northern Yucatán would hardly make it ten miles into the Gulf of Mexico before it would break up in the waves, and it wouldn't take too long to get eaten by sharks in those tepid waters. And in any case, it was the wrong the direction entirely, I should have been thinking about what was to my left – to the south – instead.

The boat, powered by a little 45 hp motor, bounced across the frothy waves in a westerly direction, keeping the shore never more than a few hundred metres away, and my mind wandered. It became difficult to focus, difficult to comprehend and accept that I was on yet another life-altering journey, another walk into the unknown. Perhaps it was too much of the sea air, but I couldn't shake the feeling that maybe I'd bitten off more than I could chew this time.

It had started less than forty-eight hours before, in the sweltering heat of Cancún.

'*Señor*,' said the bell-boy. 'Press this button here, is very easy.' The short, dark, twenty-something man in a white frilled shirt smiled patiently as he handed me the plastic control to the air-conditioning. There were far too many buttons to press and try as I might, I couldn't get the thing to work. Nobody has air-conditioning in London. I'd already lain sweating on the bed for an hour, staring at the pathetic fan that creaked around the ceiling. It did nothing but agitate and swirl the hot air around the room. The sheets of the bed were soaked through and I was too idle to move, let alone exert any mental energy on the remote AC unit. It was only on the fifth attempt to ring reception that my call was answered, and the promise of a porter made things become bearable.

Even after the ambient temperature had reached a tolerable level, I carried on lying there, still, listening to the noises of a resort that bore no resemblance to the beginnings of what was to come.

On the bedside table lay stacks of glossy leaflets advertising jet-skis, banana boats, parasailing, and some sort of jetpack that propels you out of the water, whilst attached to what can only be described as a giant vacuum cleaner. It promised the full 'James Bond experience'. Other 'experiences' to be had included Coco Bongo's superhero show, with its comprehensive cast of lycra-clad champions, who, according to the literature, promised to entertain several thousand inebriated revellers, in addition to the lure of as much tequila as you could drink. Señor Frogs adopted a similar approach. Sixty-five-dollar entry got you free drinks as well as luminous face paint, and the option of a T-shirt included in the price. La Platino needed no such affectation and was far more direct: 'Two-for-one sexy babes'. Happy hour, every hour.

The Gideon Bible, which was, of course, for one of the most devoutly Catholic countries in the world an essential item in every hotel room, lay hidden beneath the pile, presumably unopened.

Afternoon wore into evening, but the heat remained. I'll treat myself to a day on the beach tomorrow, I told myself. For now, I only went as far as the balcony to look down on the scene of paradise below.

The sun was setting on the lagoon and it cast a deep-maroon glow over the Caribbean sky. The shadows of palm trees were stretched long over the hot tarmac of the famous strip. I could already hear the monotonous thud of music in the beach bars down the road. People would be getting ready to party, I thought. Make-up was undoubtedly being applied by the coachloads of American college girls, and the boys, barely out their teens, were no doubt preparing for the night ahead with buckets of tequila washed down with cheap beer. Part of me wanted to join them in a nostalgic last dash at youth. The other, greater part of me, was resigned to feeling old and I looked forward to an early night in on my own.

A gecko scuttled across the wall, and I observed as he darted after a limp spider. Below, the stragglers from the beach came wading in. A Mexican family washed their feet in turn at the poolside tap, getting rid of the sand acquired from an afternoon swimming in the glinting shallows. A child carried an inflatable crocodile. Not far away, in the lagoon on the other side of the road, the real things, I pondered, were just waking up for their evening hunt.

Like the crocodiles, I watched hordes of the young men, livened by their tequila buckets and emboldened with uniform T-shirts, each with his own profanity displayed across the back, as they stormed down the avenue in the direction of La Platino – no doubt contemplating the two-for-one sexy babes. The music got louder as dusk turned to night and the resort came to resemble an open-air flashing disco. As far as the eye could see to the north and south were twenty-storey hotels, enormous white megastructures designed for the sole pursuit of pleasure.

In between, high walls designated where one hotel stopped and another began, but truth be told, they all looked identical. Palm trees and artificially irrigated cacti poked from rock gardens. Three-tiered swimming pools, all spotlessly perfect, vied for synthetic attraction. A limousine cruised slowly down the strip passing by endless shopping malls, all selling the same nylon hammocks, ceramic geckos, oversized sombreros, tequila shot-glasses, pyramid-shaped keyrings and Lucha Libre wrestling masks. The cargo of this lewd motor car was a pack of pink-tiara-wearing bachelorettes and a bride-to-be on one final vodka-fuelled adventure.

I sighed. Hardly an auspicious place to begin what was potentially going to be my biggest expedition to date. 'No, I'm having a night in.' I looked around the room at the equipment strewn across the floor. Compass, check. Satellite phone, check. Memory cards, spare batteries, jungle boots, machete, first-aid kit, Spot Tracker, diary, daysack, sweat rag, socks, mosquito repellent, head torch, canvas hat, river shoes, tourniquet, field dressing, penknife, cameras, check, check, CHECK. I packed it all away into the bag, and then, just to be sure, emptied it all out again onto the floor.

And then I went out in search of a tequila. Just one wouldn't do any harm.

The boat sped up and every wave that we smashed through felt like a tsunami. I was soaked through and hungover. Anyone that's had a tropical hangover knows that they should never do it again. Especially when you have a three-hour boat ride ahead of you. We lurched and banked, if that's the right term? I'm not a nautical type of chap, and can't stand the sea at the best of times, never mind after half a bottle of Don Julio. Still, I kept it in and kept my eye on the horizon.

'*Cinco minutos*,' shouted Jose, over the noise of the engine. The stern, moustachioed fisherman, my trusty captain for the day, pointed to a small spit of land, and I had never been so glad to see the sight of a beach in my life. They were the first and only words I'd get out of the man the entire journey.

As the shore got closer, I noticed the knotted mass of mangrove swamps and gnarled scrubland beyond the perfect white sands. For as far as I could see, there was only that: white sands and tangled bushes, as flat as the earth before Columbus and the first Latin navigators proved the theory wrong.

I thought of those Italians, Portuguese and Spaniards as we came in to anchor. It was on this stretch of coastline that history was made. Columbus beached at Hispaniola, now Haiti and the Dominican Republic, in 1492 on his famous journey. His later voyages took him to the Bahamas, Cuba, and within sight of the Honduras coast. The Caribbean islands didn't take long to become a base for further explorations, and with them, conquest.

Twenty-five years later, in 1517 a Spaniard called Cordoba landed with a group of men a few miles to the east of where I was currently speeding along. His views were undoubtedly rather similar to mine. Little has changed in the barren landscape of the Yucatán. It was him that gave the place its name, and probably not for the first time, it was the result of a miscommunication.

When the smiling little Indians paddled out in their dugout canoes to gaze at the vast warship anchored just off their beach, there was, of course, no way of communicating. The Spanish assumed that they must be Muslims. Cordoba asked them what this place was called, and the Indians replied, as you would, 'I don't know what you are saying. I don't understand.' Which, in the Mayan language, sounded something like 'Yu-ka-tan'. Cordoba and his band of merry men reported back that they had discovered the land of Yucatán. When, in actual fact, they didn't have a clue where they were.

Of course, as word got back to the outposts in Cuba and in turn to Spain that the Indians had gold earrings and nose rings, then the invasion began in earnest. Two years later, the infamous Hernan Cortés and his conquistadors arrived at the same coastline. Where old Columbus came in peace, in his quest to prove a trade route, Cortés came in full shining armour, sword in hand, to conquer the new world for himself.

It took a mere three years for him to decimate the Aztec empire and install himself as Governor of Mexico. The rest of Central America was soon to follow.

Looking out at the mangroves, though, I wondered what on earth was going through the minds of those first conquistadors. What drove them to think anything other than fever and mosquitoes lay ahead? Perhaps it was the shame of going home empty-handed that led them to battle through the swamps in their steel suits and feather-adorned helmets? Whatever it was, I didn't envy them. I suppose at least I was relatively unencumbered, with nothing more than a rucksack and a camera.

This was not a palm-fringed paradise, the kind you'd expect from the Caribbean coast. There was something malign, sinister in the air. The beach was littered with the debris of centuries all around, the sickly sweet smell of rotting vegetation, and death perhaps.

The boat lurched forward into the shallows and Jose chucked in a small anchor to stop us drifting back out to sea. I thanked the weathered old fisherman for his trouble, giving him his pesos, and shook the brown hand that was as gnarled and knotted as the roots of the bushes beyond.

'*Hasta luego!*' I said. 'See you again.'

Jose forced a smile, but he looked doubtful.

With my rucksack slung on one shoulder I jumped into the warm sea, which splashed up to my knees, and waded ashore. Before I could trudge up to the dry sand, Jose had already pulled up the anchor and put the motor in reverse. I watched as he backed up, pointed east, and with nothing more than a tip of the finger to the heavens to acknowledge his departure, he sped off into the distance, bouncing over the waves. I felt like one of those hapless Spaniards with Cortés, my boat gone, and with no option but to set off on foot.

I had managed to avoid being seasick, but as I stood there with sodden feet and trousers, I suddenly felt very alone. To the east and west was nothing. To the north, a vast shark-filled sea. And to the south, the direction that I was to travel, a flat, featureless swamp. The only consolation came from my map. If it proved correct, then five miles away was the village of Sisal, and from there a road that led thirty miles south to Mérida, where I hoped that Alberto would be waiting.

I dumped my rucksack on the shore, which was strewn with driftwood, and opened it to take out my boots. The sun bore down and the sand was hot to touch. Sitting on a smooth rock, I noticed that all around were millions of beautiful shells. There were tiny clams and gigantic conch and the remains of some sort of horseshoe crab, a living fossil which has swum in these waters since before even the dinosaurs roamed the plains.

Sixty-five million years ago, a meteor shot through the solar system at forty times the speed of sound and entered the earth's atmosphere. It was so big that even the powerful forces that burn up most space rocks did little to shrink the enormous asteroid as it ploughed through the sky. There were no people then to look up and shriek with terror, but I have no doubt that some sort of fear passed through the minds of whichever dinosaur happened to be grazing on the spot where I was doing up my shoe laces.

Exactly forty miles from here, the meteor hit the earth with an ear-shattering bang; it was the equivalent of a billion times more powerful than the atomic bomb used in Hiroshima, and caused such catastrophic destruction that everything within a thousand-mile radius was wiped out almost instantly. Most of the dinosaurs and seventy-five per cent of life on earth died over the course of the coming years, as the fallout changed the earth's climate forever. Seas froze, volcanoes erupted, earthquakes split continents, and the poor dinosaurs couldn't keep up. Life retracted back into the oceans and for a time the planet was uninhabitable. But luckily for us, mammals emerged from the shallows once again, and a new form of existence began.

But it seems not all the dinosaurs died. Ten metres away, an iguana eyed me cautiously from his perch on a rotting log. Completely motionless, his grey scales gave the impression of a noble carving, rather than a living beast. He reminded me of a spirit animal on a totem pole. Up above flew a pelican. From a distance, its awkward shape resembled that of a ptero-dactyl and for a moment, I half-expected a plesiosaur to jump out of the surf. Who knows what's down there in the last bastion of exploration?

With my back to the water, I trudged up the beach, treading carefully to not break any of the beautiful shells, for fear that I would interfere with the natural order. With one last look at the frothy surf, I stepped over a gnarled root and into the mangrove swamp. At once I was engulfed by an oppressive heat. As soon as the sea breeze was blocked by the bushes, it was like walking into an oven; the air was stuffy and still and a cloud of mosquitoes rose out of the staid pools of rancid water. I was sweating like a pig and started to chug on the already tepid bottle of water I was carrying.

This is going to be a long journey, I thought to myself.

6

Yucatán

Sisal used to be one of the principal ports in the Gulf of Mexico. In the nineteenth century, steamships used to travel directly to New York carrying henequen fibre to make ropes for the industrial revolution. For a time, over twelve hundred haciendas churned out thousands of tonnes of rope a month, employing a majority of the Yucatecan population in the industry. It made a lot of landowners very rich, and gave work to the indigenous Mayan people.

Nowadays, there's nothing in Sisal but a few fishing boats and crumbling houses. The port is full of half-sunken vessels and the rotting guts of yesterday's catch. I didn't hang around. Having agreed to meet Alberto in Mérida at his home, I plodded along the empty main road for two days, barely seeing a soul. This was a one-way road from nowhere and aside from the occasional pig truck hurtling by, there was nobody around. On either side of the road the mangrove extended for miles, and the road cut through the swamp like a perfectly straight sword.

I don't like straight roads, because you can see too far ahead – they remove all sense of surprise and wonder, and you realise just how far there is left to go. Perhaps it was the searing heat, but even the occasional villages I passed by seemed empty, like the whole of Mexico was on a siesta. Perhaps it was. I walked, slowly at first, letting myself get used to the heat. I hadn't walked much in the last six or seven months, and from bitter experience I knew all too well the importance of acclimatisation. Every few miles, I'd stop and drink water under the shade of a thorn bush; my T-shirt was soon drenched with sweat, but the lack of wind meant that it barely cooled my burning skin.

I looked at the cold-blooded iguanas with envy, as they basked on the boulders that poked out from the scrubland at the side of the road. As I walked south, the mangrove steadily became drier and transformed into dense bush. It wasn't proper jungle, more a thick mass of vegetation barely three metres tall, but impenetrable to all, except tiny deer, wild pigs and the bizarre-looking armadillos, of which I saw two squashed as flat as a pancake in the middle of the road. Above, the only witnesses to the true scale of the vast, flat forest were the vultures as they circled in droves, waiting for me to pass so they could eat their roadkill in peace.

Occasionally there were overgrown paths with rotting fences and drystone walls that seemed to lead off, perpendicular to the main road. Some of the tracks clearly hadn't been used in years, as trees clamoured on their fringes to join up both sides, making them appear as tunnels of green fading into the blackness of the woods. These were the gateways into the haciendas, now deserted and derelict. Sometimes I could just make out the stack of a chimney poking out from the trees a distance away, its glory now faded and distraught, a symbol of changing times.

When synthetic rope was invented, the Sisal business went bust and the haciendas became obsolete. Apart from a few that eked out a living making specialist fibres for clothes, most of the ranches shut down, their owners fleeing to more lucrative trades in the cities, or moving back to Spain when Mexico became independent. I felt most sorry for the locals. Whole villages and towns had grown up surrounding these great houses, in a way not dissimilar to the coal and steel towns of northern England. But when things dried up the workers, who'd relied on employment in the fields and factories, were left with nothing but a crumbling monument to fleeting wealth and a big, expensive church that they could no longer maintain. The Spanish patrons were long gone and the jungle threatened to reclaim what was left of their memory. All that was left to do for the Maya was to sleep.

After two days, I arrived in Mérida. Suddenly the forest simply stopped and buildings began. First a flyover and a footbridge, then a factory, a business park, service stations, motels, fast-food joints and mobile-phone towers; all the trappings of a city that had sprung from nowhere. I followed the steady flow of traffic as it poured in from the ring road and found myself in another world. Despite the heat, the city folk were very much awake and before long I was sucked into a bustling, vibrant town. Storm clouds brewed overhead and as the afternoon wore on the sky became blacker and I waited for the inevitable rains to come. I smiled, it was like a homecoming, and I thought back to the last time I had been here years before and that fateful day I got my camera nicked.

The first droplets of rain came as I walked into downtown, the old colonial quarter, with its beautiful Spanish plazas and colourful churches and hidden gardens. The little *casitas* were as pink and yellow and green as I remembered them and I tried to recall where old Graciella's house was. I couldn't. Maybe she had left now, anyway. In the alleyways, old ladies in their *huipils* sat on doorsteps gossiping, and men in straw hats, with their brown, taut bellies hanging out, pushed rickety old bicycle rickshaws selling fresh bread, coconuts and ice creams. Sounds blasted from shuttered windows; the familiar trumpets and banjos of Mexican music. Cats stretched out on dusty old cars with no wheels and in the main square by the cathedral, horses stood idle, waiting for their carriages to fill. Cowboys rubbed shoulders with mariachis. The whole atmosphere was that of a frontier, a gateway into the Mexico of old.

But of course, it was an illusion; a bubble of tradition surrounded by modernity. Walk ten blocks and you're rapidly surrounded by McDonalds, Starbucks, and shiny new shopping malls. The contrast is hard to reconcile. Outside the downtown with its narrow alleyways and sixteenth-century porticoes are wide avenues filled with glass apartments and high-walled villas. Boys in rags on horses compete for tarmac with girls in Gucci driving the latest BMW. Thatched mud huts, the original Mayan abode, sit in all their timeless beauty next to concrete mansions. Old and new, the beautiful and the horrid, go hand in hand in Mexico.

'Eyyy, Levi,' beamed Alberto, as he stood in his front door. The following morning it had taken a while to find his house in amongst the modern apartments of the northern suburbs of Mérida. He buzzed me in through a security gate and I walked past a flash Mini Cooper with sparkling alloy wheels and bright-red trimmings.

'*Chinga!*' he said, hugging me. 'You're looking old, look at your grey hair. And a bit fat, too.' He looked me up and down. 'I thought you said we should be fit for walking, look at me, like an athlete,' he pushed out his beer belly as far as it could go, in fits of laughter. 'Come inside.' He patted me on the shoulder, ushering me into the welcome feel of his air-conditioned studio. It was like walking into an architect's showroom. It was the ultimate bachelor pad. The walls were white and minimalist. His monochrome photographs lined the hallway and a shelf displayed dozens of cameras, some modern, top-of-the-range types and other vintage pieces. All the furniture was designer, and plastic feature-plants gave the apartment a light, breezy vibe.

'Come, let me show you around. Here are some of my toys,' he pointed to a cabinet full of expensive photographic equipment: lenses, lighting, laptops. He had the latest espresso machine in the kitchen and a utility room stocked with models of *Star Wars* flying machines and film props, and even a very realistic-looking paintball gun. I remembered that I'd seen on Facebook that he had got married a year or so ago, but this didn't look like the house of a married man at all.

'Are you sure you want to do this?' I asked him. 'I mean, you realise what you're letting yourself in for?'

'Of course I do. This is going to be an adventure. And to be honest, I need one right now. You seem to turn up in my life exactly when I need to escape.'

'What do you mean?' I asked. 'The last time we went on an adventure, you lost your business.'

'Yes, and it was the best thing that ever happened to me, in the long run.'

'Oh. And what about your wife? I saw that you got married, she won't exactly be happy about you going off for four months, will she?'

'Well, we got divorced a couple of weeks ago, so now I'm single and I can do what I want.'

'I'm sorry to hear that,' I said, for having put my foot in it.

'It's OK. We were only married a year and it was all very sad, but everything is OK. I could just really do with an adventure, like I say.'

I didn't want to pry too much into the details and, anyway, I figured there was plenty of time for that later, so I changed the subject.

'Would you like me to give you your kit then?'

His eyes lit up. 'Yes, I want my toys! I feel like James Bond going on a mission.'

'I wouldn't get too excited, this is just the basics,' I said, handing him a pair of Altberg jungle boots, some Craghoppers expedition clothes, and a rucksack filled with socks, a first-aid pack and a water bottle.

'We'll get you a machete and a military hammock when we get to the jungle,' I said.

'Holy shit, a machete.' I could sense his genuine excitement for what lay ahead. I wondered how long he would last and feared that he was so unused to the rigours of life on expedition that he'd take something for granted and wind up getting hurt, or worse. He'd never been in the jungle, or walked further than a few miles. He knew nothing of first-aid, survival, or what to do in an emergency.

I thought back to our African trip together, when he'd driven with me from Syria to Malawi. It had been an adventure, for sure, but at least then we were in a vehicle with plentiful supplies. I had no idea how he'd deal with things this time round, but I reassured myself with the consolation that at least he had a good attitude and was up for a challenge, and I could deal with that in an expedition companion. The rest he could learn.

So we sat down and went through all the kit, I explained how stuff worked – the satellite phone, the GPS tracker, and of course, all the first-aid stuff. I showed him the first field dressing (FFD) and a tourniquet, and which antibiotics did what. He was an eager student, asking all the right questions and demonstrating that he'd taken it all on board. I thought back to when I'd first met him and he had lent me a camera and shown me how to use it. The roles had now been reversed and it felt slightly odd playing teacher to my former mentor. It boded well, though, that we'd get along just fine.

Having packed his rucksack for the third time and dressed him in his explorer's garb, boots and all, it was time to set off. So Alberto locked his front door, kissed his Mini Cooper goodbye, and we walked out into suburbia, heading south by south-east.

Alberto kept up. I was surprised. He'd actually trained for this, which is more than I could claim, and got himself relatively fit and healthy. I'd planned for us to have a short first day of walking, only ten miles or so, to make it to the next town out of Mérida, a quiet little place called Kanasin, which was basically part of the Mérida conurbation anyway. We walked along the main road most of the way, since there was no other option, and found ourselves battling with lorries hurtling past on their way to the coast.

Alberto didn't stop talking the whole way. He laughed and joked about how his life had suddenly got very simple and we agreed that despite the oppressive heat and aggressive driving, it was actually very good fun to be doing this journey together and that as long as we both kept a sense of humour, we stood a good chance of making it to Colombia.

By eight o'clock it was almost dusk and we'd walked enough for one day. We were both still acclimatising and thought a bit of refreshment wouldn't go amiss.

'Let's go get a beer,' I suggested to Alberto. We walked across the main square of the town, past a large Spanish church that was three hundred years old, and found a suitable place. An enormous plastic cockerel stood proudly on the roof of the saloon bar at the intersection of two roads. It protruded among the dangling electricity and phone wires that formed a chaotic web over all the Mexican streets.

The words *El Gallito* were written in black block lettering on the whitewashed walls below it.

'It's a cantina,' said Alberto. Like the village pub in England, every Mexican town has a cantina or two. In places like this, outside of the main towns, they were often fairly sordid abodes and El Gallito was no exception.

We walked through the swinging wooden doors, just as the starlings came in to roost on the telegraph poles and trees that lined the plaza. I immediately felt like we'd entered the set of a western movie. The interior was small and smoky. Filthy plastic tables and broken chairs were huddled around the spit-and-sawdust floor. Stained-wood panelling reached halfway up the dingy walls and above it was a veritable gallery of wretched art. Cheap paintings, antique posters of women in lingerie and sepia photographs lined the crusty paintwork. There were 1970s pin-up girls with their breasts out and cut-outs from dirty magazines all over the place.

The place lived up to its name. El Gallito – the cock – has the same connotations in Spanish as it does in British English, and as such, there were hand-drawn pictures everywhere of penises. One, in the style of a classical portrait, showed a penis with wings and a saddle being ridden by some sort of fair maiden. Blokes' humour, apparently, is universal.

Next to a broken jukebox was the 'Caballeros', the Gentlemen's bathroom, which consisted solely of a wooden plank only half-blocking a stinking urinal in the corner of the room. Naturally there was no Ladies.

'They don't let women in here. Not even the hookers,' said Alberto with an enormous grin.

An old photograph in a gold frame hung next to the bar. It was dated 1916 and showed the outside of the saloon. It seems little had changed in exactly a hundred years since the establishment was built. Behind sombrero-wearing cowboys in the wartime street scene, a large Coca-Cola emblem was emblazoned across the vintage wall.

'That's my grandfather,' said the fat bar-owner, pointing at the photograph with a chuckle. He looked like a jolly man, with a drooping moustache and his belly hanging out below a soiled T-shirt.

'I can't believe we were drinking Coke a century ago,' said Alberto. 'That's why Mexicans are all so fat.'

'What are you doing here?' asked the bartender. His name was Victor.

Alberto responded first.

'We're walking, amigo. All the way to Colombia. This is day one and I have my English friend with me, and we intend to get drunk tonight.'

'You've come to the right place,' said Victor.

Victor pushed two bottles of local beer across the bar, and with them two shots of tequila.

Alberto picked up the tequila along with some lemon. He dipped the lemon in a plate of salt and raised his glass.

'Tequila first, lemon and salt after – that's the proper way we do it.'

I raised my shot.

'To Mexico,' I toasted.

'To walking,' he replied.

And with that, we poured the liquid down our throats and felt the sensation of burning as the alcohol spread through our bodies.

Alberto then sucked his lemon clean of all the salt and winced at its sourness.

I did the same.

'*Otra*,' he motioned towards Victor, who poured another round.

'So, what happened with your wife?' I asked him.

'Ah, you know, it just didn't work out. She freaked out and didn't want the commitment and asked for a divorce. That was that.'

'It seems a shame, though, it was only a year.' I tried to offer some sympathy.

'Yes, I agree, but that's what she wanted, so screw it. Time to move on. Seriously, this trip couldn't have come at a better time. I've been really low the past few weeks and this is a new start. I've decided to give up on women, they've been nothing but trouble. Here I am, forty-two, and I spent sixty thousand dollars on a wedding and lost a house because of that woman.'

'How much on a wedding?'

'You heard. Sixty thousand dollars, for what? One night's party! Mind you, it was a bloody good party. We had five hundred guests and it went on for three days. There was enough tequila for every man to drink a bottle each. I had the best DJs, the best hacienda, the best cars, everything. What more could I have given her?'

'Not a lot, by the sound of things,' I agreed.

'Well, one thing is for sure, I never thought I'd be in a place like this, drinking cheap tequila and about to walk to Colombia.'

'Well, I hope you do believe it, because that's what we're doing.'

'I wouldn't change it for the world,' he said. 'That woman is welcome to my house. I'm here now, and we're going to have some fun.'

An old man stumbled in through the swinging doors. He was wearing leather cowboy boots with spurs, and a baseball cap. His face was weathered but, like the barman, it had a kind, friendly feel.

Without a word, he sat down next to us and Victor passed him a small bottle of vodka. He proceeded to pour its entire contents into a pint-sized glass, and without further ado necked the lot in one fell swoop. He smacked his lips and grinned.

'*Hola*,' he said, 'I'm Ramon.'

We introduced ourselves.

'Walking you say?' He pondered our journey, stroking a solitary hair that grew from his chin.

'You've got a long way ahead, may God be with you.'

'He's a church pastor,' said Victor, 'and the chief bell-ringer. He's been coming here every day for thirty years, and never once missed a bottle.'

With that, he got up and stumbled out as quickly as he came.

Victor handed us another tequila each, along with a slice of lemon. I wanted to tell Alberto how much I appreciated his enthusiasm for agreeing to come along, but I sensed that I didn't need to. He was a like-minded soul, and despite our different cultures, languages and backgrounds, I knew immediately that words weren't required.

I raised my glass of tequila and so did he.

'To walking,' I toasted.

'To adventure, the future, and lots more tequila,' he replied.

At that, I heard the church bell toll, chiming gracefully across the night sky, and echoing throughout the streets.

7

Ruins

The road was straight and cut through the bush like a knife. As we left behind the suburbs of Mérida, it wasn't long before Alberto and I found ourselves alone in the heat of the day with only the lizards and mad dogs for company. The villages were sleepy and quiet and as the day progressed, so did the beating down of the sun. On the long straight sections of tarmac, the horizon would be obscured by a haze of reflected heat. It was punishing and brutal and both of us were sweating buckets as we walked. Alberto never stopped talking the whole way. He told me about his life, and his businesses and his financial investments. He told me stories from his past and stories from his recent failed marriage. He told me about his ambitions to retire from the production business and live a nice life on the beach.

I listened, happy to let him talk for the time being. I enjoyed getting my body and mind accustomed again to the rigours of walking. I'd found that it takes a couple of weeks to really get into a rhythm and we were in no rush. So long as we made ten or fifteen miles a day to start with, we could cover more ground later on. I was just happy to be back in Mexico, trying out my limited Spanish, and taking in the wonders of a truly unique culture.

Wherever possible, we'd try and avoid the main roads and take the parallel rough tracks instead – they had far more shade as they wound between the little villages and were more interesting visually than the long, empty highways, even though they were sometimes longer. On walks such as these, with weeks and months ahead, I'd found it important that for the sake of morale, you have to take one day at a time; filling each day with as much joy and stimulation as possible. I'd much rather walk an extra mile and meet the villagers, than take a short but dull route along a main road. But that's what we were on right now.

'I see what you mean,' said Alberto.

'What?' I asked him, on one such stretch of road, my mind beginning to wander.

'It's quite boring, isn't it?' said Alberto. 'This walking.'

'Don't worry, you get used to it,' I replied. 'And you'll see, we'll have plenty to keep us interested, but you do have to expect that at times you'll just have to be happy in your own company.'

'But I like to talk,' he said.

I'd already gathered that, I thought to myself.

'And I like to listen, Alberto, but for the sake of the next four months, maybe spread it out a bit,' I said, punching him on the arm in a brotherly manner.

'OK, OK, I'll try,' he chuckled.

After we'd passed the town of Acanceh, with its looming Mayan ruin slap bang in the town square next to the church, we decided to take a small track away from the main road. The plan was to reach Tekit, where I knew of a hacienda we could spend the night in. It wasn't too far and we had some time to kill, so Alberto suggested we go and meet an old friend on the way.

'I've got an idea for something fun. I've not done it in ages, shall we go and explore one of the cenotes?'

It sounded like a good, if terrifying idea.

The rough trail led for three miles deep into the bush. It was flanked by an ancient drystone wall, the kind you get back home, except this one was doing battle with the jungle for its very survival. Lianas and vines threatened to entangle the pitted stones, and a vast network of roots from tropical trees pushed through the gaps. Evil-looking thorn bushes strangled the boulders, and in parts, it simply vanished.

'This way,' said Alberto, leading from the front as he swung his machete to chop away at the dangling leaves. I felt like we were entering another world, where nature was triumphant and the apocalypse had already happened. 'He's out there somewhere.'

Eventually the trail came to end in a small clearing, which had once been the entrance to a flourishing hacienda. A wall was almost completely covered with bushes, but a series of weathered steps remained and they led to what appeared to be a raised-earth terrace that surrounded a sprawling fig tree.

Aaron was already waiting for us under the shade of the gnarled branches. Here was the man we had come looking for.

'Welcome to San Antonio cenote,' he beamed, pointing at the base of the tree.

I looked down and was surprised to discover that he'd laid out all the gear that we'd need for our forthcoming adventure. But it was what lay beyond that caused me to feel a shudder down my spine. I peered into a dark abyss.

'Cenotes used to be regarded by the Maya as the portals to the underworld,' said the diving instructor with a smile. 'Look down there and you can see why.' I stepped carefully forward, avoiding the neatly placed oxygen tanks, wetsuits and diving masks that were laid out around the hole.

'Wow,' grinned Alberto. 'It's so deep.'

'Twelve metres,' said Aaron.

I looked down into the black crevasse. It was about the size of a grave, two metres long by one metre across, and only the faintest glimmer of light reflected from the pitch-dark pool of water below.

'There's, like, three thousand of them in Yucatán,' said Alberto.

'Six thousand,' said Aaron, correcting my guide. 'Maybe more. Only a few hundred have ever been explored. I've been into thirty or forty, but in my lifetime I'll never see them all.'

Aaron was one of the world's leading experts in cave- and cenote-diving and he'd offered to take us to see one of his favourite cenotes.

'This one is quite safe. It's only a small hole at the top, but when you get inside it's very big, you'll see. It's dark, but we will have torch lights so you'll see everything, so don't worry.'

I was worried.

'It's super dangerous,' whispered Alberto, nudging me as we looked down into the abyss. 'Ask him about the Japanese divers.'

'What Japanese divers?' I asked.

Aaron was quiet for moment. 'Well, some of them are dangerous, of course, the caves with no open water; you need to be experienced. A few years ago, some Japanese divers came and dived a new cenote, an unexplored one, but they got lost in the caves and must have run out of air. Nobody heard from them again.'

Cenotes are the result of a unique geological phenomenon meaning that there are almost no rivers or surface water-sources in the Yucatán peninsula. All the freshwater drainage systems are underground in a network of subterranean caves, linked by these sink holes. Some cenotes are vast open caves, others, like this, mere sockets into the underworld. This one had been used as a well by the Spanish hacienda owners. But even before the conquest and the dismantling of the Mayan cities, the ancient people used these holes as a means of sustenance for both this life and the next.

'Wait till you see what's down there, it'll be worth it,' said Aaron.

I gulped.

Alberto sweated.

'But be careful, don't touch anything.'

'Touch what?'

'Wait and see.'

'Any other helpful advice?'

Aaron raised his eyebrows. 'Yes, of course. Remember to breathe.'

'You first, my friend,' said Alberto, zipping up his wetsuit in the sweltering heat of the forest. 'You're the explorer, off you go.'

I couldn't quite believe what I was about to do. Here we were in the middle of the Mexican jungle, about to abseil into an ancient well that only a handful of people had ever been into, and what's more, it transpired that divers had been down into these things and never returned. But I couldn't back out now, we were here, and how many times do you get the chance to go diving in a black hole in the jungle? Plus, I couldn't lose face in front of Alberto, nope that wouldn't do at all.

I zipped up my wetsuit and donned the fins that Aaron had magically produced. First went Aaron and then my BCD and tank of air on a rope, lowered into the pit. After that went a small inflatable dinghy, and then it was my turn. Aaron had constructed a pulley system and employed the services of two local farmers whom we now trusted with our lives, not only to lower us down into the water-filled cave, but also to pull us up again in two hours' time.

Attached by a carabiner and a harness, I found myself being slowly shunted down into the grave-like hole, watching as Alberto's grin got smaller and the sunlight eventually became nothing more than a shaft of light.

As I wondered what I was letting myself in for, I began to think back to what had led me to this point in my life, holding on for dear life to a rope while suspended above a hole in the earth that promised to swallow me up.

'I'm down here. Keep coming,' echoed the reassuring words of Aaron. I looked down. He was floating in the water with all his gear on, directly below. Soon enough I was lowered into the cool depths, which was a refreshing change from the searing heat of the jungle above. Aaron swam over and unhooked me; the rope was immediately hauled back up for Alberto. I struggled to put on the diving tanks and lay there floating in the still water, waiting for Alberto to join us.

Attached to my wrist was a torch, which I turned on, and I had the chance to look around. Aaron wasn't wrong. We were now inside a vast cavern the size of a cathedral dome, surrounded by dangling stalactites. Bats fluttered silently in the crevices and the only sound was a constant dripping of water into the pool from the porous rocks above. I shone the waterproof torch down this time and to my astonishment the water was so perfectly clear I could see the bottom of the pool some twenty metres down. I could just make out rocks and stalagmites and piles of sand and centuries of debris that had fallen down the well into the watery pit.

'Yeeehaa!' yelled Alberto, as he slid down the rope.

I heard him shout out loud, 'Mum, Dad, forgive me, I'm sorry for all the bad things I did as a kid.'

And then as he splashed into the cold water next to us, his fear was gone. 'This is incredible,' he bellowed.

It certainly was. After a safety briefing and checking that all the kit was properly fitted, we began the dive, leaving spare gear and camera equipment in the dinghy.

Down we went, equalising our noses to the pressure as we descended. It didn't take long to reach the pinnacle of the sand mountain under the water. I saw bits of wood, unnatural in shape – clearly carved – perhaps planks used for the well of the hacienda that had fallen in over the years. Then there was what seemed to be the remains of a bucket – the same had happened. There were fragments of shells and odd-shaped stones, and then ... a ceramic bowl. What was that doing there? Aaron led me and Alberto closer to the ancient artefact. He pointed and spoke through the underwater radios that were built into the masks.

'Mayan sacrifice bowl,' he said in a crackled voice through the intercom radio. He then beckoned us to follow him. Kicking our fins, we swam through the crystal water ever deeper into the depths, following the course of the sandbank. Then I saw a huge horn poking out of the sand. On closer inspection, it seemed to be attached to a skull: it looked like a cow or a buffalo. 'Sacrifice,' came the crackly answer from our guide.

Further still and we came to something even more remarkable – and disturbing. There, on a rocky ledge, was another skull. But this time there were no horns. It was clearly that of a human being. Nearby, scattered around the bottom were the rest of the remains – thigh bones, ribs, spinal vertebrae, a pelvis.

I took a gulp of air. For a second I lost sight of Aaron, I was transfixed by the gaze of the eyeless sockets. I felt a tap on the shoulder. Aaron beckoned once again and I followed. Alberto was below now, motionless, staring at a rocky ledge and its eerie remains. I descended to get a closer look. There they were, dozens of them. I couldn't even count, there were so many. Dozens and dozens of human skulls and bones, scattered around the bottom of the cenote. Some were upside down, others sideways. Some had the bottom jaw still attached, others had been badly smashed. There were holes and fractures in several of them. It was undeniably murder.

'Sacrifice,' came the muffled voice across the radio, yet again.

The ancient Maya killed thousands of men, women and children every year as offerings to the gods. Some had their hearts and guts ripped out on top of the stone pyramids such as Chichen Itza and Coba, others were decapitated and thrown into the cenotes. Some, especially princesses and virgins, were simply thrown into the pits alive and left to drown. I couldn't imagine a more horrible way to meet your end than in this watery grave.

I looked at my air meter. I was almost out of oxygen. Thirty minutes seemed to have passed all in a few seconds, but that's what diving is like. Not wanting to suffer a similar fate to the victims of the Mayan death cult – or the Japanese tourists, for that matter – we ascended back to the surface. Thankfully, the farmers were still on hand to pull us up and out from the cenote.

The locals winched us up, chuckling to themselves. They couldn't understand why we had any interest in this old pit, full of heads and bones. They suggested we would have a much better time if we visited the local fiesta, where there was cheap beer and good horses, and maybe a bullfight if we were lucky. Did we want a lift? No thanks, I explained we were walking. They shrugged their shoulders and said they never walked anywhere unless they had to. Horses were much better. Pick-up trucks better still, but more expensive, of course.

As I looked up at the sky, the afternoon clouds were already dark and foreboding and in the distance the rumble of thunder seemed to shake the very heart of the forest. It was time to move and so I thanked Aaron for his introduction to the underworld and we set off to the south towards Tekit.

It was almost dark by the time we reached the town and the footpath that led into the village took us past a cemetery. I was all for carrying on and getting to the hacienda where we could find a bed, but this was no ordinary graveyard, this was a Mayan burial site. There is no human sacrifice anymore, but it seems the manner of bodily disposal wasn't all that different for some people, even in this day and age.

'Let's go inside,' said Alberto, 'I want to show you something.'

So we entered the walled garden though an iron gate. Inside were hundreds of mausoleums dating back a hundred years. You could tell the rich from the poor by the size of the gravestones, and the peasants again by the lack of graves altogether.

'The really poor people,' Alberto explained, 'get buried in a communal plot for two years. After that, the grave is dug up on the Day of the Dead and the bones are taken out.' He looked sinister in the half-light of the cemetery, a solitary streetlight flickered across the graves. 'Then,' he carried on, 'they are put in boxes, skulls and everything, and they're here.' He pointed to the inside wall, where I could see what looked like small pigeonholes less than a foot wide. Each of the dark crevices contained a rusty old metal box. We got closer. Some of the compartments had bars blocking entry to what lay within. Others were open. Many of them were filled with candles and offerings. The dead are venerated here in Mexico, and nowhere more so than by the descendants of the Mayans here in the Yucatán. I opened a creaky box and there inside, looking up, was the skull of a man, on a pile of bones. I closed it quickly.

'Let's leave,' I said to Alberto. 'We've seen enough death for one day.'

The next morning, we walked from Tekit to Mama in an hour and a half. Already we were managing to make four or five kilometres an hour, which was good going considering the immense heat and dripping humidity. Until now we'd simply carried what we needed for the day's walk in a small daysack. A litre of water, to be resupplied at every shop, our cameras and phones, with maps stored, some sunglasses to avoid the terrible glare of the Mexican sun, and the most important thing – a sweat rag. We'd left our main bags behind and arranged with Aaron the Divemaster to send them forward to Mama, where we would collect them later on. After that we needed a way of carrying them.

'They're too heavy to carry ourselves,' said Alberto. He was right, all the stuff we had came to over twenty-five kilograms. We used to carry much more than that in Army, but rarely for these sorts of distances, and almost never in this heat and humidity. I had already made my mind up that I wasn't in the mood to break any world records, and I had nothing to prove. This wasn't some sort of competition as to how much weight I could carry, so I agreed that we should find a way of transporting the bags as we walked.

'What about porters?' I suggested. It had been a reliable method in the Himalayas.

Alberto laughed out loud. 'Ha! Do you think you'll find a Mexican to carry your bags? No way, they're too busy sleeping under trees.'

'Even if we pay someone?'

'Not a chance. Anyone with that kind of a business mind has already left and gone to the USA. Don't worry, I have an idea. We can get a tricycle in Mama, I know some people there.'

Mama was similar to most of the villages we'd passed. It had an old Spanish church in the main plaza, which was dilapidated, its paint peeling off and with holes in the roof. Most of the houses were single-storey concrete blocks with small verandas and tin roofs, although there were many thatched mud houses as well, where the elderly and poor Mayans live.

The central square was nothing more than a waste ground, filled with feral dogs and boisterous chickens. Some children played football barefoot in the dusty park, as the old men of the village looked on saying nothing. A few teenagers trotted around on horses, doing nothing in particular. Only the women seemed to work, carrying baskets on their head.

'I like the old Mayan houses more than the new ones, I think,' I mused out loud to Alberto. It seemed a shame that they had traded in the beautiful traditional thatch for concrete and tin.

'Me, too,' he said, 'but that's what happens when they send money back from the US. They can earn good wages, sometimes six or seven hundred dollars in a week, especially if they have three or four jobs. All the money comes back to these villages and they upgrade their huts. You know what it's like when it rains, they'd rather not get wet, so they get the tin roof. It's seen as superior, so when one of them gets it, they all think they have to get it. If you still have a grass hut, people think you're poor and won't talk to you.'

'How many people from here have gone to work abroad?' I asked.

'I'd say four or five hundred men from this village alone. Almost half the population, I think.'

As the first droplets of rain began to patter on the floor, I could sympathise with the locals.

'This way,' said Alberto, as we found ourselves in a side street. We walked up the driveway of one of the more modern houses. It had a big gate and bright turquoise walls and a satellite dish for TV poking from the tin roof.

'These are my adopted family,' he said, waving as a group of young men bounded out of the garden where they had been drinking beer. A man called Fabian Tzib Tchu hugged Alberto warmly and shook my hand.

'We want to buy a tricycle,' said Alberto to his old friend.

'Of course, but first you must eat with us.'

We were taken into the garden, where six or seven women of all ages, all wearing *huipils*, were busy over a fire pit. Some were roasting a pig, others making handmade tortillas for the tacos. They were all chatting away in Mayan, not Spanish.

'I know a few words,' said Alberto proudly. 'But it's hard, it's almost like Chinese or something.'

'Go on then, tell me something,' I challenged him.

He paused. '*Pelaná*,' he said.

All the Tzib Tchu family began roaring with laughter. I guessed that it wasn't something pleasant.

'It means your mother's genitals. The Mayans use it all the time.'

We sat down and ate with the family. They never stopped joking and laughing the whole night. They weren't rich, but they weren't poor either. They had their whole family around them at all times and were hospitable to the point of it being too much. We ate more tacos than I could possibly imagine and drank an entire crate of beer, as well as several bottles of their home brew, so that we were unable to leave.

The next morning we forced ourselves to begin early, knowing that if we stayed for breakfast we'd never leave before lunch, and if that happened we'd be obliged to stay for dinner, too. But we had to push on, there was no time for a break this early in the journey.

Fabian had promised us a tricycle and went off to find one, but not before insisting that we take up the offer of a blessing for our journey.

'My uncle is a medicine man,' he said. 'He lives at the end of the road, go and see him while you wait.'

And so we did. I figured that after the past day and seeing so many skeletons, a bit of protection against the ghosts and spirits probably wouldn't go amiss. We knocked on the Shaman's door and found a frail, little old man sitting on a wooden bench in a dark room watching television.

'We've come for a blessing,' said Alberto.

The old man was called Don Theo. 'Sit down,' he said, almost imperceptibly in Mayan. He spoke only a few words of Spanish, so that Alberto had to use signs and break down his language to the basic form. Don Theo seemed to understand, though. He pointed to a chair that faced against the wall, where a sort of shrine had been erected. There was a framed painting of Mary, and another, slightly smaller one of Jesus, hanging from the wall right in front of the chair, so that you sat staring into the eyes of Catholicism. Also pinned on the wall was a crucifix, a wind chime and a garland of plastic pink-and-yellow flowers. Underneath all of that was a wooden trellis-table covered in a white sheet.

On the table was all manner of holy relics. A postcard of the Last Supper sat next to a melted candle. There, too, was a jam jar filled with spices of some description, and a statue of St John the Baptist. There were coins, key rings, and three plastic children's toys. Two superheroes and one dinosaur. But most prominent of all was the cut-off, bottom half of a Coca-Cola bottle, which formed a tray for the *Alux*.

'What is it?' I asked Alberto, as I sat down. I felt like I was paying a visit to the hairdressers as I made myself comfortable and stared at the paintings.

'It's like a little devil, or fairy,' he said. 'These people are very superstitious.'

The Shaman kept a solemn face, but touched the little stone idol that sat inside the Coke bottle on its head. It resembled a miniature Easter Island head.

'They find them near the pyramids and dig them up, they're meant to be lucky, and the Shamans worship them.'

I sat and waited for the magic to happen. Don Theo went to the corner of the room, where he picked up a handful of sticks with the leaves still attached. Then he stood behind me and began to chant. It was in Mayan for the most part, but I could just about make out a few Christian saints' names and he invoked Mary and Jesus repeatedly.

'It's a combination of Christianity and ancient Mayan religion. Same with Day of the Dead – the Mayans kept the ancient traditions and merely gave the old gods new names – the saints. But the black magic carries on,' said Alberto.

The Shaman then proceeded to whack me about the head with the sticks over and over, stopping only to take up a different and more effective angle. The ritual went on for a whole minute and then old Theo stopped to pick up something even more disturbing from the table shrine. In his fingers, I saw an enormous two-inch brown thorn. It looked like something from an acacia tree, except it had two spines so that it resembled a buffalo horn.

'What's he going to do with that?' I asked Alberto, who had been watching the whole process from a safe distance behind the flailing witch doctor.

'I have no idea.'

But the Shaman paid no heed. He took the thorn and started to stab me with short, sharp jabs in the forehead.

'Ouch! What the . . .'

He grinned for the first time, flashing a mouthful of glinting golden teeth. He laid a hand on my scalp as if in blessing and nodded, suggesting that it was over, and that now I was safe against whatever ill may come our way.

'Your turn,' I said to Alberto.

'You must be joking,' he laughed.

Waiting outside was Fabian with the ricketiest-looking tricycle I had ever seen. Once upon a time it would have been bright orange, but now the paint was peeling off and every inch was covered in rust. The seat was broken and the pedals were hanging off and the chain didn't look like it had seen oil in a century. But it did have a large frame basket at the front, even if the wooden floor was rotten and full of holes.

'It will have to do,' said Alberto. 'It's better than nothing.'

And so we loaded our bags into the basket, filled up a cooler with bottles of water from the village shop, thanked the Shaman and paid Fabian for our new trike.

I thought we would push it along the road, but Alberto had other ideas. 'You can walk if you want to, but I'm going to ride it,' he smiled, at which point he got on and wobbled off down the road.

8

Trouble in Paradise

'I'm going to call it the beast,' said Alberto as he rolled down a slope, the wheels creaking as they wobbled. 'After the train that takes all the illegal immigrants to America.' He was clearly enjoying himself on the downhill, as I jogged on behind. 'I know how they feel now. Walking in the heat, pushing their bags like this.'

'Except we're going in the wrong direction,' I said.

'True, we're getting some funny looks.'

I suppose we must have looked like a right pair of oddballs. There we were, two men plastered in sun cream, wearing Indiana Jones hats, walking down the road in the heat of the day. It wasn't exactly sane. As we trundled through the remote villages and past the isolated farms of central Yucatán, we were usually greeted with a curious wave or a grunt of disbelief. If we spoke to anyone, they would assume that our car had broken down and we needed help.

One day, as we were pushing 'the beast' down the main highway between Teabo and Xaya, a police car pulled over behind us with its lights flashing. Alberto was some way ahead and the policeman got out with his hand firmly gripping a black pistol. He looked like he meant business.

'Where are you going?' said the cop.

I'd learned from my years of expeditioning that it is best to not give too much away. People generally think you're mad or stupid if you tell them you're crossing an entire landmass on foot.

'We're walking to Belize,' I told him. I figured that he'd know the distance to the next country and it was something he could visualise, rather than confusing him with the concept of an 1,800-mile journey.

It didn't work. He just scowled.

Luckily Alberto had noticed and turned around to come and save the day. He did it with a charm and measured skill that I found impressive, and reassuring.

'*Hola, Señor,*' said my guide. 'I'm glad you stopped. Thanks for taking the time. We're a bit lost, you see, we're trying to get to Belize with this rusty old tricycle. This mad Englishman has decided to walk in the midday sun and is making me go with him. I felt sorry for him and so I couldn't say no.'

At that the policeman burst out laughing. He'd done it, I thought. He'd won the fella over in ten seconds flat. That was Alberto's gift, he could charm the hind legs off a donkey.

The policeman found him irresistible, and Alberto had sub-consciously made a plea by stating that we were lost.

'No, no, you're not lost, the border is that way, but it's very far.'

Alberto smiled and thanked the policeman profusely. Cheeky sod, I thought, we're not lost, I know exactly where we are. But his chat had worked and the policeman was on our side now.

He explained why he'd pulled us over.

'We got some reports. Someone said you're not from the Yucatán. People here are a bit scared and nervous, because last week in Cancún eleven inmates broke out of prison. They caught three of them, but the rest are still at large. We think they're armed and will fight to escape, so we were worried that you might be involved.'

Alberto laughed. 'This Englishman looks suspicious, I agree. I'd arrest him if I were you.'

The policeman pulled out his smartphone and scrolled through some pictures.

'You look like this one.' He pointed at one particularly nasty-looking criminal with a facial tattoo.

Personally, I couldn't see the resemblance.

The policeman eyed me up and down, as if looking to see whether I had any tattoos. He seemed confident that I was harmless, so he waved us on and said goodbye, with a warning for us to keep a vigilant eye out for the suspects as we walked.

In a bid to avoid further cases of mistaken identity, we once again took to the backroads away from the highway as we plodded ever further south. The tricycle was a godsend here in the Yucatán, since it was completely flat and for the most part the roads were paved, but we knew as we got closer to Belize the going was about to get tougher, and we'd probably have to leave it behind.

We'd spent the night at a small village called La Pantera, known for its juicy mangoes, and as we were packing up to leave the next morning, a man pulled up next to us in a pick-up truck filled with the fruits. Damian, a Mayan elder and community leader, who also happened to sell coconuts along with mangoes, asked us if our car had broken down and if we needed any help. We were used to it by now.

'No, we're walking, thanks,' said Alberto.

'What's your field?' he replied in a considered tone.

'What do you mean?'

'Well, you both look respectable. What is your field? You must have a field? Are you a doctor? An engineer, a scientist?'

'Ah, I see,' said Alberto. 'I'm a photographer.'

'And the gringo?' Damian nodded to me.

'He's a writer. He likes history,' Alberto answered on my behalf.

Damian's eyes lit up.

'Then come with me. I need to show you something.'

Intrigued, we followed the man, away from the main road down a small farm track for about three miles. It was in the direction we wanted to go anyway, so we didn't mind. As we progressed, the path got narrower and narrower and the forest closed in about us, until we were virtually covered by the canopy. The further south we got, the bigger the trees had become. No longer were we in the arid bush of the north Yucatán, but in the tropical south of Quintana Roo. Yet, it was still completely flat. We'd noticed holes as we'd been walking along, and signs for yet more cenotes, and thus far there had not been so much as a mound, let alone a hill.

We were somewhat surprised then, when Damian took us off the track and we found ourselves hacking through the lush forest and up the beginnings of an incline. It was impossible to see for more than a few metres, given the density of the vegetation, but our legs didn't lie, this was definitely a hill, and a big one at that. Up we went, following a natural path where steps seemed to be carved in a straight line. Surely it couldn't be?

I thought back to my inspiration – Stephens and Catherwood – the pair of unlikely explorers, who, in 1839, and only a couple of hundred miles away in Honduras, made their discovery of the ancient city of Copán. I already knew there were plenty of pyramids around in the Yucatán peninsula. In a previous life, I'd visited Chichen Itza, Palenque and Mayapan, as well as the coastal ruins at Tulum. And on this journey we'd seen the famous

Mexico, land of contrasts and a place close to my heart.

Alberto Cáceres, my old friend and guide for the journey.

Yucatán coast near Sisal. This stretch of coastline saw the first Spanish conquistadors and set the scene for the start of my journey.

Fiestas play an important part in Mexican life.

The ruins of Mayapan, Yucatán peninsula.

Ancient Mayans used underwater caves, called cenotes, as places of human sacrifice. There are over 6,000 in the Yucatán.

San Pedro. Hurricane Earl devastated the Belize coastline days before we arrived.

Belize is home to a variety of different cultures. The Mennonites arrived from Europe in the 1950s and still practise a 17th Century form of conservative Christianity.

In Belize I revived my old army instincts and trained in jungle survival.

The pyramids of Yaxha, Guatemala. This was an important city to Mayan culture and only rediscovered in 1904.

El Petén is a region in Guatemala notorious for its lawlessness and a base for the region's narco-traffickers.

The Rio Dulce river – largely seen as the gateway to Central America and the southern limit of ancient Mayan culture.

The Garifuna people are found only along the coast of Central America. They are the descendants of escaped slaves from St. Vincent. They still maintain their proud African traditions.

San Pedro Sula. Notorious for its gang lands and, for a time, the murder capital of the world.

A 'casa loca' or crazy house – where gangs take their prisoners to be tortured and often killed.

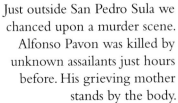

Just outside San Pedro Sula we chanced upon a murder scene. Alfonso Pavon was killed by unknown assailants just hours before. His grieving mother stands by the body.

Lake Yojoa. The Honduras landscape is beautiful and unexplored.

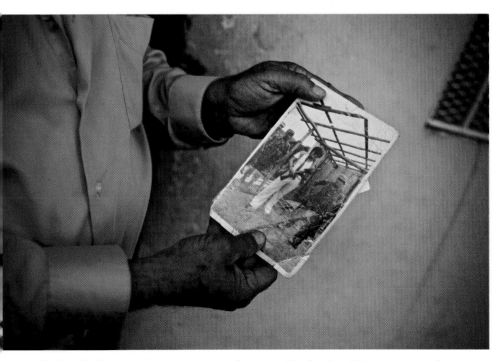

Pedro Pablo, a revolutionary, who fought with the Sandinistas against the brutal dictator Somoza in the 1970s.

Nicaragua is known as the land of volcanoes. Here, Masaya volcano is extremely active.

Granada has some of the best preserved Spanish Colonial architecture in Central America.

'Tony', a reformed people smuggler.

The 'other migrant crisis'. Thousands of migrants are making their way from across the world to try and get to the USA.

In Costa Rica we came upon a camp of 2,000 Congolese migrants.

Mt. Chirripó, the highest peak in Costa Rica.

Alberto with a three-toed sloth

Horses play an important part in Central American travel. We lasted all of four days with ours.

The Pan–American highway is the longest road in the world. Apart from the Darién Gap it spans 30,000 miles from North to South America.

The Panama Canal, one of the seven wonders of the modern world.

Yaviza – the end of the road.

'Jose', chief of the Wounaan tribe in Puerto Cara.

Wounaan ladies still wear traditional dress in some parts of Panama.

Our Emberá porters who trekked through the Darién Gap.

The Border Service (SENAFRONT) protects the Darién against rebels and drug traffickers.

The Darién Gap. The most inhospitable jungle in the world.

A Kuna village on the Caribbean coast.

'Puerto Escoces' or New Edinburgh, where the Scots tried to set up a colony in 1698.

Sapzurro in Colombia – gateway to South America.

The end of the journey in Colombia.

pyramid in the town centre of Acanceh, but I wasn't expecting this.

As we crawled up the mound, now on hands and knees amongst the tree roots and vines, I was sure.

'This is a Mayan pyramid, isn't it?' I said to Alberto.

'It must be,' he said. 'There's no reason there'd be any hills here.'

I looked down at the way the steps were evenly carved out of the stone. Most of them were covered in soil and grass, but they were almost certainly not natural.

Damian grinned. 'Write about this,' he said.

'What's it called?' I asked.

He shrugged his shoulders. 'I don't know. It doesn't have a name.'

How could it be true? I got out my phone as we stopped for a breather and searched the Internet. No name, no place mark on Google Maps, nothing except an obscure reference in a PhD thesis from a decade ago, which suggested there might be archaeological remains in the area of Nueva Joria, 'as yet unexcavated'. This was real exploration, and proof there are still wonders out there that lie hidden by nature.

As I clawed my way up the steps, following behind the man who was clearly pleased by his secret pyramid, I noticed hundreds of fragments of pottery poking out of the soil. I was astonished, but not as much as when we reached the top. As we emerged onto a small flat plateau, I was pleased to find that we were above the trees. The view was remarkable. Up there we had plain sight, for the first time on the journey, of the vastness of the landscape surrounding us.

For as far as the eye could see, it was nothing but a completely flat expanse of green, with the exception of three other mounds close by. They looked like pyramids too, but the one on which we were standing was the tallest of them all. I checked the altitude. We were almost forty metres high. That made it a clear ten metres higher the highest pyramid at Chichen Itza. If that was the case, then that made this unknown and unnamed pyramid one of the highest in the entire region, if not the country.

Alberto, huffing and out of breath, was equally impressed. 'Those Mayans must have had strong legs to get up these things. Why did they do it so steep?'

'Human sacrifice,' said Damian, who'd barely broken a sweat. 'This is where they beheaded people.' He patted a large boulder that sat on top of the rocks. 'People coming up here didn't need their legs for much longer.'

For a moment, we were all quiet. I simply wanted to enjoy the moment of discovery and imagine the joy the early explorers must have felt when they, too, found these monuments in the jungle. Of course, they would have also had their Damians: locals who knew that these wonders were here, but had half-forgotten who built them and why.

'We used to come here as teenagers,' he broke the silence and winked at Alberto. 'It's where we'd bring our girlfriends.'

'Poor girls,' was Alberto's reply, as we looked down into the vastness of the jungle below.

It took another three days to reach Chetumal. The further south we got, the darker the clouds became. Despite this being the rainy season, we'd been quite lucky. Apart from a few downpours in the evening, we had escaped without getting too soaked. But as we trudged past Bacalar and on towards the border with Belize, it seemed like a storm was brewing.

'Lev, wake up!' shouted Alberto.

I rubbed my eyes, but it was dark and I couldn't see anything. 'Is it morning?'

'No,' came the reply from outside the door of my hut. 'There's a hurricane coming. Come and see the news.'

I looked at my watch. I'd only been asleep for a couple of hours and it wasn't even midnight yet. As I pulled on my trousers and shirt, I listened to the hammering rain as it pummelled the thatched roof. Geckos flitted around the wooden frame of the cabana, escaping the wet, but the water was already flooding in under the door and seeping through the walls. I opened the door, but Alberto was gone.

'Over here!' he shouted above the din of the thunder. I saw him over at the main *Palapa*, a bigger, open hut, where there was a kitchen table and a TV blaring from the corner. The owners of the guest house were huddled around it, watching intently.

I darted across the garden barefoot, my toes squelching in the sodden grass, which was now just a vast puddle, to get to the hut as quickly as I could. There I joined the crowd as they stared at the screen. It was clear to see it wasn't good news.

'Hurricane Earl ... Dozens dead, thousands homeless. Entire coastlines destroyed,' said the newsreader in Spanish.

'It's going to miss us,' said Alberto, 'it is already going inland south of here.'

There was a sigh of relief from the Mexicans.

'Where is it worst affected?' I asked, as the images of decimation rolled on loop: flapping palm trees, cars overturned, homes under water, boats bashing against the piers.

'Belize,' said Alberto solemnly. 'Exactly over the water from here. The Island of San Pedro.'

I looked at the map. The obvious choice was to avoid the

coastline altogether and carry on due south to Orange Walk and through the central forests. But by serendipity rather than design we'd drawn closer to the Caribbean than we'd expected, and now we had just escaped a close call with a hurricane. If the weather girl was to be believed, then in a couple of days it would have transformed into a storm as it crashed inland over Belize City and into the jungle beyond. It seemed safer now to pass in its wake along the coast, rather than risk blocked roads and fallen tress inland. Also, a part of me couldn't resist wanting to see with my own eyes the destruction caused by this incredible force of nature.

So, after a short wait as the winds died down, we took the first boat from Chetumal to San Pedro – *La Isla Bonita* – the beautiful island. Now, it seemed, the storm had gone. The water was calm and the sky was clear. It was as if the news of the last few days was a mere story, designed to keep people watching.

'Goodbye, Mexico!' shouted Alberto, as the boat sped across the straits to the cays.

'I'm going to miss your tacos.'

I'd almost forgotten that this was his first time in Central America outside of Mexico, and he was as wide-eyed as I was.

An hour later the coastline of San Pedro came into view. As we approached the port, I noticed immediately the level of damage that Hurricane Earl had inflicted. It was real after all. Most of the piers and jetties were smashed beyond recognition, leaving only their skeletal remains jutting from the water. Emerging onto the gangplank and walking onto the concrete dock – the only part of the port that had survived intact – I looked around.

'*Chinga*,' said Alberto. 'This place has been fucked.'

Not one to mince words, he was, of course, correct. The beach was littered with debris: planks of wood, fallen trees, masonry and tonnes of plastic and corrugated-iron roofing. It was incongruous to see such wanton destruction in this paradise isle. Beyond the beach were the wooden houses where people lived. Fortunately, most appeared to have survived.

We picked up our bags and walked through the gate to where a customs official stamped us in.

'Welcome to Belize,' she said in English, with a flashing smile. After the weeks I'd spent in Mexico, it was strange to hear English again, but the warm Caribbean lilt felt welcoming. As we stepped onto the street, we were immediately reminded that this was a very different country. Almost everyone was Afro-Caribbean for a start, and their creole patois was almost unintelligible.

'What are they saying?' asked Alberto, as a bunch of young men hustled to get our attention.

'I can barely understand it myself.'

'I thought you said they speak English.'

'We're speakin' English, man,' said a young black man with dreadlocks down to his waist.

He had a beer in one hand and a joint of marijuana in the other. 'You wan' some special stuff?'

We politely declined. I was hoping we'd find a taxi driver so that we could send our bags ahead to a hotel for the night, but there were no cars in sight.

'Ain't no taxis 'ere, man,' said another Rasta, whose phone was blaring out a Bob Marley track from inside his pocket. 'Only carts.' He pointed to a row of electric golf buggies. 'Take one a dem.'

It turned out that there are no taxis allowed on the island, in fact there are almost no cars at all. It's so small that people walk.

So we walked along the beach, picking our way through the mess. Rotting palm leaves floated in the turquoise shallows as we stepped over the remains of someone's refrigerator, now half-buried in the sand.

'It's the price we pay for living on the Caribbean,' said Alberto. 'You just have to accept it as part of life.'

I noticed a group of men hanging around a half-destroyed house, its tin roof dangling precariously from the rafters. It was barely noon, but they all seemed drunk.

'Hey man, are you David Hasslehoff?' shouted one of the men towards us. I didn't ask if he was referring to me or Alberto.

'Where are you from?' another bellowed.

I told him.

'England? Alright mate. Lovely jubbly,' he affected his best cockney drawl whilst simultaneously taking an enormous swig straight from a bottle of hard liquor. 'My name is Joe.'

I asked Joe about the hurricane.

'I lost everything. We don't have nothing,' he said. 'Look,' he pointed to the ground. 'Look at my golf cart, it don't have no wheels.'

I looked down to see a small, plastic children's car which did indeed seem to be missing its wheels.

The men erupted with gin-fuelled laughter. The Belizeans, despite their misfortune, it seemed, still maintained a sense of humour.

I thought back to the last time I was in Belize with the Army almost a decade ago. I was reminded of that same black humour when I worked alongside the troops of the Belize Defence

Force. Laid-back to the point of being almost horizontal in their attitude to work, at least they saw the funny side to life and nothing seemed to bother them.

For some reason, Belize had been generally overlooked by the Spanish conquistadors and despite the fact that the Spanish officially laid claim to all of Central America, this little coastal region soon became a haven for all sorts of people fleeing their tyranny. It wasn't first settled until 1638, though, when it became a hideaway for pirates and buccaneers from England and Scotland, as well as escaped black slaves fleeing the islands of the Caribbean. A buccaneer and mate of Sir Walter Raleigh called Peter Wallace was one of the first Europeans to properly explore the mangroves and waterways in the area. Legend has it that when he built a fort and a few huts at the mouth of a river, the natives, who couldn't pronounce Wallace, called it Vallis, since they were used to hearing Spanish-sounding names. That, over time, turned into Ballis, and then of course Belize.

A hundred and fifty years later, the British had fully settled in Belize after fighting numerous battles with the Spanish fleet in the emerald waters. It wasn't gold that they were after, though, it was timber. The jungle provided a seemingly endless supply of teak, pine and mahogany, which was exported to fund the fledgling empire. The nation of British Honduras was created, the only English-speaking country in the entire region.

The British legacy wasn't confined to the humour and language, though. We arrived at Belize City a few days later and found ourselves in a place that felt at once familiar, yet also alien. There is the Anglican cathedral and the red postboxes; the Queen's initials standing proudly on street corners, and her head still adorning their dollar bills. Yet there is an unmistakable West Indian feel to the place, in the manners, the dress, the attitude of its inhabitants. Like much of coastal Central America, most of the population are the descendants of African slaves and their creole children. That said, there are plenty of indigenous Mayans and Spanish speakers, too.

The scene had something romantic in its vibrancy, like a pantomime, perhaps; there were Chinese shopkeepers with parrots for pets, and the melon-selling Mennonites with their pale skin and eighteenth-century German costumes. Filipino sailors jostled for pavement space with money men in Hawaiian shirts and panama hats. It looked like a theatre stage for a pirate adventure and I half-expected Captain Jack Sparrow to come swinging into the act. Every shade of skin colour was represented in the markets and streets of the ramshackle town. To call it a city would be an overstatement. Less than sixty thousand people live there, but it seemed that they did so in pretty decent harmony. For the moment at least, their biggest battle was against nature.

'Looks like that neighbourhood has been pretty badly smashed,' said Alberto, as we walked out of the town centre and into the Yabro district, south of the Belize river. Young men were busy clearing the rubble from a collapsed house as we walked by. There didn't seem to be any rhyme or reason as to how the hurricane had destroyed some houses and spared others.

'It must by the quality of the construction,' I said to Alberto, looking around. Most of the houses were made of wood with tin roofs, surrounded by concrete walls.

'I'm not so sure, they all look pretty shitty,' said my guide. 'I don't understand how any of them survived.'

'God!' shouted a young black man. He was tall and muscular

and had been throwing bits of wood into a pile. Across his chest, I could just make out a tattoo of some numbers, but he was black to the point of blueness. His dreadlocks poured down his spine like a cascading waterfall.

'God, I tell you. He's da one who saved us. Dis hurricane, it was punishment for de evils we bin doin'.'

Before I could ask what evils, he carried on, not really caring whether we listened or not.

'Dis place is like Sodom and Gomorrah. People out drinkin', girls out smokin' drugs, whores and de rich people goin' around corruptin'. Dis is what we get. God will smash dem houses of dem dat have sinned, an' save dem who ain't.'

'And what happened to your house?' said Alberto, although the damage was plain to see.

The man chuckled to himself. 'Ma house is smashed to pieces. I have most definitely been a-sinnin'.'

We left the outskirts of Belize City behind and embarked on a long slog towards the west. We should have been walking south, but the only border open with Guatemala was towards the setting sun. In the distance, as the highway disappeared in a straight line for as far as the eye could see, were the rolling hills of Pine Ridge Mountain, and beyond that, some of the toughest jungle in the world.

9

Boot Camp

It had been over nine years since I'd last been in Belize, but as I stepped into the little British Army camp the memories came flooding back. Above the corrugated-iron roof of the headquarters building flew the Union Jack. It was like every other Army camp in most respects. Cheaply built, grim-looking, functional, with those awful D-shaped barracks that hadn't changed since the Second World War. I was waved in by a Belize Defence Force sergeant, who pointed out the building where I'd find the Colonel. It was crammed behind the potable water tank and a few palm trees.

As I walked through the gate, I remembered the last time I'd been here was in the desperate search for my soldier who'd gone AWOL with a prostitute in Mexico, and was found after three days minus his shirt and passport. I wondered if the latest batch of recruits got up to such mischief.

'No R&R for this lot,' said the Colonel, a gruff Lancastrian who'd risen through the ranks over the course of thirty-odd years to the heady glory of running a ramshackle camp in a former colony that had been independent since 1981. 'They spent half of last week twiddling their thumbs in the hurricane shelter as Earl battered the place. They're behind on training and we've got a general visiting this week.'

I didn't envy him. Or the students for that matter. When generals visit anywhere, the whole place turns into pandemonium as careers are made or lost. Shouting gets louder and blood pressures rise. Nope, I was glad to be free of all that for now. Still, I'm not complaining. The Army had given me a good career and a hell of a lot of experience, and was ultimately the reason why I was now back at Price Barracks knocking on the Colonel's door. I wanted to use one of his men.

I'd met Aron Tzib nine years ago very briefly, but it was an experience I'll never forget. In between shooting targets and hacking paths through the jungle and firing blanks at a pretend enemy, we were treated to a two-day 'survival training package'. As a young officer fresh out of Sandhurst, with soldiers to entertain, this was where the real fun started.

Two days away from the bosses, where you get to make fires by rubbing sticks together, knock together snares and traps to catch food, learn how to chuck a spear, discover which mushrooms you can eat and which will send you loopy – that's the kind of stuff they don't teach you on Salisbury Plain, but we were eager to learn. It is the kind of training that civilians think soldiers do all the time, but the reality is that it's actually a once-in-a-career opportunity, although they don't tell you that in the recruitment centre.

Since I was passing through this way on my journey, I thought it would not only be a good opportunity to drop by the jungle school and say hello to an old friend, but also to refresh myself on jungle skills while I was at it. And more importantly, it would be an introduction to a brand-new environment for Alberto, who had never been to the jungle.

'You can have him for two days and that's it,' said the Colonel. 'Make sure you look after him.'

'Of course,' I promised, although I had a feeling that it would more than likely be the other way round.

We agreed to meet with Aron on Pine Ridge Mountain, to the south of the western highway on a plateau that was covered, appropriately, in Caribbean pine trees. To get there, we wended our way along a rough dirt track that had been almost washed away in the rains of the week before. Several trees had fallen so that anyone driving must have had to get out and chop them away with their machetes. By the time we reached the entrance to the forest it was almost dark and so Alberto and I set up our hammocks at the side of the road.

Aron arrived late in the pitch of night. He'd been dropped off by one of the forest rangers and appeared in his camouflage gear, ready for work.

'*Hola*, mate, been a bloody while,' he said, with the strange combined intonation of Creole, Spanish and estuary English. He'd clearly been hanging around British soldiers for far too long.

I greeted him and reminded him of our acquaintance from a decade ago.

'You probably won't remember me, but I came with the Paras in 2007,' I said, shaking his enormous hand.

He pondered a while.

'Hmmm, 2007. Yes, I do remember actually. Bloody Paras. Hang on, didn't one of your blokes do a runner with some Mexican prostitute?' He laughed out loud.

'That's the one.'

'Yeah, and another fella fainted when we slit the neck of that pig.'

I'd forgotten about that, but it's true.

The flames of the campfire licked the hanging leaves of a nearby tree as Aron stood there, as solid as a barrel, and about the same size. He was every inch the Mayan warrior, looking like the stone reliefs that I'd seen carved in the pyramids of the Yucatán. I imagined his forefathers, naked except for a jaguar skin and a bow, perhaps a feather in their hair. But this modern incarnation, in his camouflage pants and military vest, was just as at home in the jungle as his ancestors. Aron had been training British and American soldiers in the art of jungle survival most of his life. He'd been taught the ways of the forest by his father and grandfather before him, so that he knew every trick in the book.

'So, you've come for a refresher then have you?' he asked. 'The boss said you were heading south and needed me to tell you what bugs you'll need to eat.' He grinned.

'Something like that,' I said. 'Alberto here hasn't been in the jungle before, and it's been a few years for me, so we thought you could help us out.'

'Alright,' he said, 'I've got just the place. Get some rest tonight, because tomorrow you'll need all the energy you've got.'

The following morning, we set off into the forest. Pine grew with abundance here, the natural offspring from the British plantations all those years ago, and at first the trail led through the tall evergreen trees that grew in perfectly straight lines up to the cloudy heavens. I was reminded, somewhat unpleasantly, of a military training area. For some reason, wherever there's pine trees and the chance of rain, someone in a uniform will come along and decide that it will make the ideal place in which to dig holes and fire guns, and wherever you are in the world, whether it's the Brecon Beacons, the Cypriot highlands, or here in the tropics – they all instil the same feeling of foreboding. I think it's the knowledge that when you enter that realm, you're going to be pushed out of your comfort zone and experience things that you probably don't want to.

As we descended towards the Rio Frio – the cold river – the vegetation suddenly and unexpectedly changed. We took a right, off the track, and immediately found ourselves in thick, tropical jungle. It was as if we'd entered an entirely separate biosphere, in fact that's exactly what we'd done.

Aron led the way, hacking a trail with a black-handled machete. It was the sharpest thing I'd ever seen in action and put my jungle knife to shame. It cut through the jungle vines like a samurai sword, leaving a trail of destruction behind it. Aron seemed to move like some sort of spirit animal. His footing was always sure and I didn't see him lose a step once. Barely sweating, he kept a steady, deliberate pace as Alberto and I concertinaed behind him. We were in an alien environment now altogether, and I'd forgotten how particularly treacherous it could be. I'd traipsed through some rainforests along the banks of the Nile, and the foothills of the Himalayas, but this unfathomable bush was an altogether different beast.

To begin with, the fringes of the jungle were secondary jungle, that is to say forest that had once been deforested by humans, whether ten years or a thousand years ago. It's likely this area had succumbed both to the stone axes of the ancient Mayans who created the destruction of their own civilisation by destroying the environment to fuel their pyramid habit, and to the chainsaws of the British Colonial era. Most of the larger trees had been felled, meaning the undergrowth was much thicker, since it had been able to grow up in the absence of a full canopy. The primary rainforest was still some miles away, beyond the Rio Frio, but for now we had to hack and sweat our way through some of the thickest vegetation I'd ever encountered.

'This is a total bastard,' said Aron.

Alberto, for the first time on the journey, was totally silent. He was sweating buckets like me, and blowing out with every step.

'You're not wrong,' I huffed, remembering back to the last time I was here with the Army, although I was younger and fitter back then. Old soldiers call it the green hell. When you're hanging out in this awful humidity, and every branch and thorn seems out to get you, and every creepy-crawly wants to ruin your day, it's understandable that some people literally lose their mind in the jungle. It is an unforgiving environment, and unless you prepare, it's one that will easily defeat you. That's why we'd taken this detour, to make sure that for the rest of the journey we'd have the knowledge and skills to be able to survive – particularly in the Darién Gap.

'We're not going too far today, though,' said Aron. 'Down there is the Rio Frio, and where the lesson begins.'

He pointed into the wall of green. Visibility in this sort of bush is less than ten metres, so it wasn't until I'd pushed through a matted knot of palm leaves that I saw a steep cliff leading down to a gushing stream.

We slid down the cliff, grasping at vines and tree shoots along the way for stability until we reached the bottom, and with it, the crystal-clear waters of the river. By the time we'd got to the bottom, we were all so hot and sweaty that it was impossible to resist jumping into the refreshing pools. I went first, bags and all, sending the schools of fish darting across the water. Even though it was waist-high, it was utterly transparent to the very bottom. Aron jumped in after me, drinking straight from the water.

'It's perfect,' he said.

'Don't you need to filter it first?' asked Alberto.

'Not this. There's no people for miles around, and no cattle either. This water is the purest you'll find anywhere. It is filtered naturally by the rocks and the soil. Come and fill your water bottle.'

Alberto, unused to getting his feet wet, initially tried to balance on a rock, bending over to dip in the Army-issue water bottle I'd given him.

I was about to grab him and pull him in and tell him off for being a wimp, but nature beat me to it. The Mexican slipped and in a bid to avoid falling on the rock, almost did a backflip, ending up head first in the cool river, emerging like a flailing puppy who had been thrown into the water for the first time.

'*Chinga!* Its fucking freezing,' he shouted, gasping for breath.

Aron laughed. 'They don't call it the Rio Frio for nothing.'

After cooling off, we waded upstream for a couple of hundred metres, until we found the place where Aron had wanted to bring us.

Right ahead, in front of us was a glorious waterfall – the source of the river we had been seeking. But even more impressive was the fact that it emerged from inside an enormous cave. To the left and the right, the cliffs rose for twenty or thirty metres and were covered in creeping vines, ferns and sprouting palms. But there in the middle was the cave mouth, the size of an aircraft hangar, and inside the murky hole was the sound of a thousand bats, squeaking and squawking now that their morning had been disturbed.

We climbed up the side of the waterfall over the slippery rocks and boulders until we stood on a ledge from where we could see the interior of the cave. It was like the inside of a cenote, but bigger than any I'd been in before. You could probably fly a helicopter around the place with the right skills. Within seconds we were surrounded by bats, flying low, scooping and banking like a squadron of Spitfires on the warpath. Alberto and

I ducked as the flying monsters circled, but Aron just stood still and chuckled.

'Right. Time to learn about survival,' he said, with the authority of someone used to being direct and to the point. I remembered when I first came to Belize and he'd shown us how to kill and butcher a pig. The soldiers had been captivated by the little man and stood watching as he decapitated the beast and ate its liver raw. As he reminded me, at least one of my veterans had passed out with squeamishness.

He led us through the cave, where we sat on a boulder listening to dripping water from the roof forming stalactites.

'The first rule of survival is shelter,' he said. 'In any situation where you're lost and exposed to the elements, you have to get a roof over your head. That's why I brought you to this cave. If there was a thunderstorm or a hurricane, you'd be pretty miserable if you were stuck outside getting wet. And when you're wet and cold that is when you lose your morale, and eventually your mind. You'll lose your will to survive and then make a mistake. That's when you'll die. And I've seen it happen plenty of times.'

Alberto looked as white as a sheet.

'Get up,' said Aron. 'I was just teasing with the cave. You're not going to find one of these every time you get lost. So you need to learn how to make a shelter.'

We followed Aron back out of the cave, down the waterfall and back into the jungle.

'Here will do.' He dumped his rucksack on the floor, and we did the same.

'When you choose a place to camp, you need to be near a freshwater source.' He pointed to the river ten metres away. 'That's the only thing that matters. But it's best of course if it is flat, and away from any dangers like wasps' nests.'

He gripped a tree and shook it.

'Now check for deadfall. That's the biggest killer in the jungle. When you get dead trees or branches, when it rains or if it's been windy, they come loose. And if a big fucking branch comes down and hits you on the head, it's game over. Same with coconuts.'

Alberto gripped the nearby tree and shook it vigorously. 'No coconuts here.'

Aron carried on, he was being serious. 'My mate once had a branch fall on him when he was putting up his hammock.'

'What happened?' I asked.

'It went in through his mouth and straight through his jaw, came out into his shoulder. He lost all his teeth, but luckily survived.'

'Fuck,' said Alberto.

Aron took out his machete. 'Let's chop down some trees. We need about twenty saplings. As long and straight as you can get them. And some vines for twine, as well.'

'I feel a bit bad chopping down all these trees,' said Alberto.

'Don't worry, stuff grows back quickly here. Literally in a couple of weeks nobody will know we've ever been here. We never cut down the big ones though – only the Guatemalans do that.'

So we went off and spent two hours collecting materials to give to Aron, who showed us how to make an overnight shelter. It was remarkable how he wound the branches together with bits of grass and twine. Everything he used was natural and by the end of it he had built a three-metre-long raised platform with an A-frame roof, which we then finished off with palm leaves to create a woven roof. It was just in time.

'It's raining,' said Aron, 'quick, get the bags inside.' We got all the gear and placed it in the shelter. Within ten seconds of the first drops of rain, it began to pour down in a way that I had never seen before. The rain came down like bullets, painful to the skin, creating enormous splashes, and before long the whole jungle floor had become a muddy bog. 'That's why we do it on a platform,' said Aron, pleased with his creation. 'Right. Next stage of survival is warmth. We need a fire.'

'How the hell are we going to make a fire in this rain?' said Alberto.

'Come on, you'll see,' replied Aron.

'What? You mean we have to go out in this?'

'Of course. If you don't and you're in a real survival situation and you can't get warm, then you'll die.'

Not wanting to risk it, we thought it best to follow our jungle man. We didn't need to go far.

'Look, the insides of these logs are dry, you only need to chop off the wet bits. Look underneath the foliage and there will be dry sticks, too. Just watch out for snakes.'

So we collected as many dry-ish sticks as we could and took them back to the camp.

'You need one bit of hard wood for a base, and a soft stick to rub into it.' Aron took out his knife and whittled a bow, and, using some string from his survival tin, started to drill the two bits of wood together until a little plume of smoke magically appeared.

'Wow, so the shit you see on TV is real after all?' said Alberto.

'Kind of. This bit takes forever.'

Aron spent about twenty minutes drilling away on the wood before there was enough heat in the embers to catch on to the tinder. But as soon as he had it, that was that. He transferred the flame onto some grass, and then into some kindling and it wasn't long before we had a roaring fire under the shelter. 'That'll be enough wood to keep it going for an hour.'

'Now stage three,' he said. 'We need to eat.'

Alberto pulled out a bag of M&M's from his pocket. 'I'm good, thanks.'

'No. Not today, we are going jungle shopping. The forest is like a supermarket. I'll show you, you don't need that shit.'

We didn't have to walk far before Aron pointed to a bush. It looked like a palm tree, but a small one with the leaves growing straight out of the ground. 'This is good stuff. Help me chop off the branches.'

So we all unsheathed our machetes and hacked off all the leaves until it was a bare stump. Since Aron had the sharpest machete he then cut away at the base of the shaft until all that was left was a kind of green log. Using his knife, he then pared away the outer layers until he found what he was look-ing for.

'It's called heart of palm. Exactly what it says on the tin. This white pulp in the middle is edible. It's pure starch, like rice, full of carbs.' He pulled away at the white stuff and ate a chunk. 'Mmmm,' he licked his lips.

'Look,' he said with excitement, 'over there.' He bounded over to another tree, where a large brown tumour seemed to bulge out from the bark of the tree.

'What is it?' asked Alberto with wonder.

'A termite nest,' said Aron, clearly delighted with his find, 'I'm gonna see if it's alive.' He took his machete and gouged off a chunk of the crumbling nest.

'Oh, it's lovely, it's alive. That is food right there. That is survival!'

It was crawling with thousands of little white and brown insects.

'You can stick your finger in like this,' he prodded his index finger into the nest and waited till a few of the beasties crawled onto it and then sucked them off.

'How do they taste?' asked Alberto.

Aron licked his lips, 'It tastes like fish and chips.'

Alberto did the same and winced as the animals scuttled round his tongue.

'What does it taste like?' I asked.

'Like shit,' came the inevitable reply.

'Just shove your tongue in there,' said Aron. 'You'll get more.'

So I did. I let the termites crawl onto my tongue and felt as they got trapped in the saliva. They tasted bitter and woody. I swallowed them without chewing and it occurred to me that if you were in a survival situation, you'd need a bloody lot of termites to stop you feeling hungry. 'Let's stick to the heart of palm,' I suggested.

It stopped raining just as we got back to the camp and we laid out our sodden clothes next to the fire to dry, as Aron boiled up some water to make the tea. It was late afternoon now, and in the jungle it gets dark early.

'There's plenty more food out there, of course. If you need to hunt then you can set traps, or make a spear, but it's all very time consuming, and plants are much easier. They don't run away.'

'What's the biggest danger in the jungle?' asked Alberto.

'Like I say, you've got deadfall from the trees, and then the risk of flash flooding. Don't put the camp too close to a river. And then there's the animals. Don't worry about the big ones – you won't even see a jaguar unless you're very lucky. Spiders won't hurt you too much. It's the snakes you've got to worry about.'

He drew us closer as he told his story.

'It was on a Sunday evening in October 2003. It was a night like tonight and I was walking home through the forest with my friend. A tree had fallen across the path. He was at the front and climbed over the log and carried on. I went to do the same, but just as I was raising my leg, a snake jumped out of a hole and bit me on the thigh.'

Aron rolled up his trouser leg to reveal the puncture marks.

'At first, I didn't feel anything. But after my friend came back, I realised how serious it was. It was a fer-de-lance – the deadliest snake in the Americas. My heart was racing and I knew that if the venom got all around my system, I'd be dead in a few hours.'

It was almost totally dark now, with only the glow of the fire and the dancing shadows to protect us from the night. All around the jungle seemed to come alive. Fireflies jigged around the trees and the reflection of a hundred spiders' eyes glinted back at us from the darkness like droplets of dew. The noise was deafening as the crickets began their nightly call.

'My friend helped me up and I stumbled for two miles back to my village. My leg was in agony. I'd never felt pain like it before. It was as if someone has pushed a hot knife into my skin and was twisting it around.'

Aron lifted the boiling water off the fire and poured us all a tea.

'It took an hour to get to Belmopan City, but by that time my leg was completely black. I was bleeding from everywhere, even my eyes. I was vomiting and shaking and I thought I was going to die.'

We huddled closer to the fire.

'And when we got to the hospital, guess what?'

'What?' we said in unison.

Aron let out a roaring laugh. 'They didn't have any bloody anti-venom. I had to go round all the hospitals in the bloody country and go to Belize City and break into a pharmacist in the middle of the night to find some. It took seven hours in all.'

Aron stood up, patting his lucky thigh.

'Now, let's sleep. It's getting late, and tomorrow, we have a jungle to get across.'

10

Borderlands

I woke to the sound of rustling. I looked at my watch, it was six a.m., I'd slept solidly for twelve hours straight. Aron was already up and about, making tea and sharpening his machete.

'How did you sleep?' I rolled over and saw Alberto still lying down.

'Terribly,' he said. 'I couldn't stop thinking about snakes.'

'Come on, you two. It's time to get up,' said Aron. 'Make sure you shake out your boots before putting them back on. Check for scorpions and tarantulas.'

Neither of us needed to be reminded of that.

We washed in the cool water of the Rio Frio cave and dismantled the camp. Aron took out his map and showed us where we were aiming to get to.

'We want to get back to the main road, which is here,' he jabbed the map with the blade of a knife. 'It's about five or six kilometres, three-and-a-bit miles from where we are now.'

'So on a road that would take an hour,' I said. 'How long do you reckon it will take through the jungle?'

'Six hours,' he replied. 'At least, maybe more.'

We were heading due north, and after crossing the Rio Frio, there was no path whatsoever. We would walk on a direct bearing, and it looked like there would be lots of other rivers to cross as well.

'Ready?' he said, tightening the straps on his rucksack. 'Let's go.'

We stepped off and followed Aron. Like yesterday, he maintained a steady pace, slicing through branches and ferns. In the jungle it is hard to keep your bearings, and easy to become very disorientated. There's no such thing as following intuition here, as that will get you lost, so you have to trust in your compass and GPS.

Throughout the morning, the terrain was brutal. Sometimes we'd get completely stuck in matted entanglements of lianas and vegetation so thick that it seemed impossible. When it became too thick, we would have to crawl on our hands and knees to try and get under the branches. When that happened, we'd cover less than five hundred metres in an hour. The worst bit of going through uncleared forest, though, was the spider webs. Especially if you found yourself at the front, sooner or later you'd walk straight into a huge silken tangle and find yourself face to face with a grizzly looking, golden orb spider that looked like something from a horror movie.

'Is that what I think it is?' said Alberto, as a tarantula crawled up my arm.

'Yep,' I said in horror, even though I knew they were fairly safe.

'Watch out for the chichen trees,' said Aron.

Alberto had told me about them before. 'They are toxic – the stems, the leaves, everything. If you touch them, it's said to be so painful that people would rather take a knife and cut away the skin than have to deal with the pain of the sting.'

Everywhere I looked there were evil-looking thorns and spikes and oozing pustules erupting from the bushes. On the ground as we crawled were scorpions, hairy centipedes with bright-red bodies, and beetles that I was certain had never graced the pages of any books before, they were so ugly.

Around noon, it started to rain. We hadn't eaten anything and we were hungry. 'We've only managed two kilometres,' said Aron, shaking his head.

'What?' said Alberto. 'We've been going for four hours already.'

'We need to get a move on, then.'

We tried to pick up the pace, but with the wet ground under foot we found ourselves slipping and sliding and making mistakes. I grabbed onto a branch to stop myself falling and tore the skin of the palm of my hand on a vicious thorn. Alberto had already been bitten by a spider and his fingers were swelling like balloons.

To make matters worse, we'd had to walk along the streams instead of cross-graining the ridges, which was exhausting and slow because of the thick vegetation. 'We're already wet, so it doesn't make any difference,' I said to Alberto.

We waded along the creeks, which were sometimes shoulder-deep in water. We were soaked through as the rain got harder, and with it we got colder and colder. Even Aron slipped over a few times in the river. I noticed the water levels were rising.

'We need to get out of the water now. If there's a flash flood, we'll drown,' said Aron.

And so we tried to follow the course of the stream downhill along its banks, but there were times when the undergrowth was so impenetrable that we'd have to simply jump in and swim to the other side. I'd noticed that Alberto hadn't said a word for at least an hour and I was concerned.

'Are you OK?' I asked him, worried that he was losing confidence and morale in equal measure.

He looked thoughtful.

'You know what, I'm cold, I'm wet and I'm tired. I'm also the hungriest I've ever been in my life.' And then he smiled. 'But I can't remember when I was this happy. It's hard work, but I've learnt that I can eat termites and swim across rivers. I love it.'

And with that, he pushed on ahead to the front and began chopping away with his machete.

'Hurry up, *muñeco*. We haven't got all day!' he shouted back at me.

Given the fact he'd never been to the jungle before, I thought he was doing pretty damn well, and I knew then that I'd made a fine choice of guide with my Mexican fashion photographer.

It took another three hours to climb up and out of the jungle. It was late afternoon by the time we reached the trailhead. It was time to say goodbye to Aron.

'I'm heading back to the city. I've got soldiers to train,' he said. 'I'd love to come with you, but I think you'll be fine without me. Just remember what I told you. And stay away from the snakes.'

He hugged us with his little barrel frame and walked off to the east to find the nearest village. Alberto and I walked the other way, towards San Ignacio and the Guatemalan border.

The western highway was as straight as the pine trees that flanked it. But as we carried on along it, the forest grew thinner and thinner until we reached an area of farmland that stretched out for miles around. It reminded me of the vast fields of central Europe, or the corn lands of Bible-belt USA. It felt like we'd been transported into another world. There at the side of the road was a sign, welcoming us to 'Spanish Lookout'.

Gone were the potholed roads and the ramshackle wooden huts of coastal Belize, with their rickety tin roofs. We suddenly, and unexpectedly, entered the first world.

'What on earth is this place?' asked Alberto, as we stood gazing up at an enormous grain silo. Next door was an industrial-size dairy farm with its own attached ice-cream shop. Everywhere there were top-of-the-range shiny tractors. The homesteads were beautiful and clean, and well made. They all looked like the Little House on the Prairie, each with its own windmill and horses, fat cattle and white picket-fences.

But most remarkable was that the population were all white-skinned Europeans, and what's more, they were dressed like something out of a period drama.

'Mennonites,' scowled Alberto. 'They're all over the place in Central America. We have a few of them in Mérida. I never knew there were so many here, though.'

This community at Spanish Lookout, it seems, were pretty well established. 'They came from Germany originally. That's why they dress like sixteenth-century farmers.'

I looked at the women in their long dresses and bonnets as they strolled along carrying wicker baskets, and the men in their overalls and straw hats. Whole families trotted by in horse-drawn carriages, in perhaps the most surreal scene I could have imagined.

'They sell melons and make cheese,' said Alberto.

The Mennonites – an ultra-conservative Christian denomination – left Germany in the 1600s, having become a persecuted minority. They went to Russia, where they could enjoy religious freedom. But in the early twentieth century, when the communists came to power, they fled in their thousands to the Americas. Many went to Canada, and groups like the Amish went to the USA. Yet more went to Mexico and from there found themselves in British Honduras, where land was plentiful and they could enjoy their freedom under a tolerant British administration. Nowadays, despite living in isola-tion up here in the highlands, they effectively kept Belize afloat.

'They make millions with their massive farms,' said Alberto, 'but they still dress like hobos and never wash. I don't get it.'

A horse cart came past, and its ginger-bearded rider doffed his wide-brimmed straw hat as he passed.

'They speak in German, too. But not modern German that we can understand, it's some weird old language.'

'There's another one,' Alberto whispered. 'They all look the same, because they're so inbred.'

He was right. An almost identical-looking man was walking along the roadside carrying a huge watermelon under each arm.

We waved and smiled to the Mennonites and at best they touched their caps, not a one would speak to us or even smile. We thought it best to carry on towards the town of San Ignacio. The shortest way, according to the map, was along a little farm track towards the Belize River.

'Fancy a short cut?' I asked Alberto.

'Of course,' he replied with his usual enthusiasm. 'We can put our jungle skills to the test.' I couldn't tell if he was being sarcastic.

So we left the main road and followed what seemed to be a little trail through some fields. The grass was long and the meadow hadn't been grazed in a while. It was very beautiful and the landscape reminded me a little of England on a summer's day. Wildflowers grew up and the occasional gnarled tree stood testament to man's selfishness. Even a hardy farmer needs shade from the sun. To the west, not far away at all now, I could see the rolling hills and mountains of Guatemala. I was excited by the journey ahead and even though the jungle had been hard work, I felt prepared and happy that Alberto had got through it.

We had left the Mennonites behind, but we were still in the vast farmland areas, although the closer to the border we got, the rougher it became. It was deathly quiet and we hadn't seen a soul for hours by the time we reached the banks of the river. There were a few farms dotted around and soon we found ourselves on private land.

'We're going to have to climb this fence,' I told Alberto, 'to get down to the river.'

He shook his head. 'I knew I'd have to do some illegal fence-climbing at some point. You just want to see the Mexican in action, don't you? But because I'm Mexican doesn't mean I should have to climb fences, you know!' he said, with joking disdain. 'Still, one day I may need to use these skills to get over Donald Trump's wall if he gets elected.'

Alberto hauled himself over the eight-foot fence, trying to avoid the barbed wire at the top, where he very nearly snagged his crown jewels.

'Ouch!' he wailed.

'Hurry up,' I told him. 'We might get seen, and I don't fancy being on the receiving end of a German's shotgun.'

We made our way down to the river. It had looked narrow on the map, but up close was a different matter. It was brown, dirty, and at least thirty metres wide.

'And full of crocodiles,' said Alberto. 'What are we going to do now?' he asked.

'Swim across,' I told him.

'I thought you might say that.'

The alternative was a six-mile detour to the nearest bridge at Santa Elena and neither of us fancied that. And anyway, the jungle had prepared us. We put our valuables in waterproof bags and swam with the current through the murky waters as fast as we could, in case there were indeed any crocodiles.

Luckily, we made it in one piece, wet and covered in weeds, but in good humour.

'Look at me!' said Alberto. 'It's complete. Now I look like all the other wetbacks – that's what the gringos call the illegals who swim across the border to get to the States.'

We trudged up the far bank. There were more fences to scale, it seemed. And hedges, and walls. It wasn't long before we realised we were inside someone's private estate. We ambled like a pair of sodden tramps through an orange orchard and then, at last, out onto a perfectly manicured garden.

'Oh shit,' I said, noticing that up ahead, in between us and the outskirts of the town, was a rather large, twelve-foot brick wall, covered in razor wire. It was topped off with broken glass and I saw at least three CCTV cameras. 'Get back in the bushes,' I whispered to Alberto. So we both retreated to the safety of a large rhododendron bush, where I reviewed the situation.

'There's a gate over there,' said Alberto.

'Yes, but it'll probably be locked.'

'What about the house?' He pointed to a large white building surrounded by trees and yet more razor wire.

'It looks like it belongs to a drug lord, never mind a Mennonite,' I said.

'It probably does. This region is the way all the drugs come on their way from Colombia.'

'Now you tell me.'

'Shall we just run for it across the garden?' Alberto asked.

'No, there's only one thing for it. Let's just stroll over towards the gate and see what happens.'

So we did. In situations like this, I'd found it best to be bold. If we sneaked around or ran looking suspicious, then we'd likely be arrested or shot, whereas at least if we strolled about we could play the 'lost tourist' card.

We walked along the path towards the fence in the hope that

we'd either find it unlocked and simply walk out and leave, or else get spotted by the owner of the white house, who could let us out. Halfway across the lawn, I noticed something over by the house on the far side of a fence: three large and very vicious-looking Doberman guard dogs.

'Maybe they won't notice us,' whispered Alberto, his pace picking up slightly. It was too late.

Suddenly there was an almighty noise as the three beasts started barking, they were clawing away at the fence, and then they started to run. They bolted around the right-hand side of the fence, where there must have been a hole, and they were now bounding across the lawn towards us.

'What do we do?' asked Alberto.

'Just stand still,' I said. 'Whatever you do, don't run.'

The Dobermans were still racing towards us, as we froze, terrified; their white teeth bared and with terrible snarls erupting from their slobbering mouths. I remembered that I'd heard once from an Army dog handler that no matter how loud and nasty a dog is barking, so long as its tail is upright and wagging, it won't attack. 'Show no fear, pick up a stone or a stick to show you mean business, and it won't bite,' he said. Easy to say that when you're covered in a padded suit, but when the hounds have been released and their teeth are inches from your bare ankles, it's a different story.

The animals came on, snarling and growling and snapping all around us, but they didn't bite, thank God.

There was suddenly a whistle emanating from the direction of the house a hundred metres away. I saw a man walking down the driveway. The dogs were still snarling, but I thought it best for us to be polite and introduce ourselves. I walked over with Alberto in tow. The man stood still at the edge of the lawn and waited for us to reach him, his dogs still snapping at our heels, clearly annoyed that their fun had been spoiled. The man was tall, white-skinned, and European looking. He might have been a Mennonite, or else one of the few hundred other European descendants that ran the large fruit farms. Thankfully, he didn't look like a narco-trafficker, but he was rather large and did not look best pleased.

'Hello,' I said. 'Terribly sorry, but we're a bit lost.' Remembering how Alberto had charmed the policeman in Mexico and blamed it all on me, it was payback time. 'I'm with this Mexican guide and he's got no idea where he's going, and we ended up having to swim across that river down there and found ourselves in your garden. Would you mind letting us out?'

He snarled like one of his dogs.

'Didn't you see the sign?' he said, in English with a thick Belizean accent. 'It says no trespassing. I should have you arrested. You're lucky I didn't shoot you.'

I nodded. Alberto gave me a look of malice.

'Where are you from?' the large man asked, his bushy eyebrows twitching as he leant forward to inspect his intruders.

'England,' I replied.

Suddenly the man's demeanour changed entirely. He stood up straight and smiled.

'Oh well, that explains everything,' he said, offering me his hand to shake. 'You buggers are all mad, walking about every-where in the middle of the day in the heat. The gate's unlocked, you're welcome to stay as long as you want. Don't worry about the dogs, they won't hurt you.'

We thanked the man for not shooting us and hurried off through the gate in the direction of San Ignacio.

The Guatemalan border lay a few miles to the west of the

town, so we spent the night at a small hotel on the outskirts, eager to see what lay beyond the following day. For both of us, Guatemala would be a new country and a new experience. We were both much fitter physically than we'd been when we started and I think Alberto was slipping into expedition life very well, considering the fact that he'd never walked further than to the shops before. He was as strong-willed as any soldier and had the humour to match, and I wasn't surprised when he told me that he'd much rather swim through crocodile-infested rivers than have to go through another failed marriage.

'Give me a pack of bloodthirsty dogs over my ex-wife any day,' he joked, as we stamped out of Belize and into our third country. We left the English-speaking world behind for the last time and entered a very different place. Gone were the friendly smiles of the good-humoured Caribbean nation. Here in Guatemala, there seemed to be an altogether tenser and more uptight atmosphere. The most noticeable difference was the prevalence of guns at every turn. Armed police and soldiers picketed the street corners in the grubby town of Melchor de Mencos, and there seemed to be private security guards outside every shop, all armed to the teeth with pistols and menacing pump-action shotguns. People didn't say hello here, and it was the first place I'd noticed that drivers didn't stop and offer us a lift.

The landscape, too, changed dramatically. We had entered El Petén, a region once notorious as a great wilderness filled with dome-shaped hills and great valleys. It was described by John Stephens as a mosquito-filled hellish jungle:

> enclosed on all sides by a forest wall, but the river, although showing us no passage, still invited us onward. Could this be the

portal to a land of volcanoes and earthquakes, torn and distracted by civil war? ... The woods were of impenetrable thickness ... and there was no view except that of the detestable path before us.

Nowadays, the dangers come in different forms. El Petén, which means 'the bush', has been deforested throughout the last couple of decades and transformed into grazing and pasture land, the expensive timber being sold off and great herds of cattle taking the place of the trees. The vast mounds, once covered in teak, mahogany and ceiba, are now bare, giving the illusion of a limitless sea of green hills carved into lush meadows by the natural streams and man-made fences.

Despite its environmental taming, the notoriety remains. Because of its location, far away from the capital, and next to the fluid borders of Belize and Mexico, the whole area has become synonymous with lawlessness, drug-running and human smuggling. Bandits operated freely here, and it was where the rich narcotic-traffickers came to evade capture and live in hidden ranches and villas among the knolls. The tracks and trails of El Petén were off-limits to all but the most corrupt policemen. The soldiers we'd seen in the town shook their heads with disdain when we told them where we were going, and wished us a solemn good luck.

Five miles west of Melchor, we took a small dirt road south, directly into the heart of narco-land.

II

El Petén

Every few miles we encountered small hamlets and farmsteads just off the side of the trail, but for the most part the road was empty. Sometimes we'd see herds grazing on the hillsides and occasionally horses munching away in the fields.

'It's beautiful, isn't it?' said Alberto.

There weren't many people around, but the few old ladies we saw selling snacks from their front yards, gave us glaring glances. The first few days in El Petén passed without incident. We'd walk, stop to eat some plantain, walk some more, and then find a place to string our hammocks. We were in a comfortable routine and almost forgot that we also happened to be wandering through the drug lords' backyard.

We walked deeper into the bush, following the course of the dirt road. The hills seemed to roll on forever. On the morning of the twentieth of August, after waking up in our hammocks, strung between some trees at the side of the road, we found ourselves in a tricky situation. As usual, it took some time to decamp. Having said that, Alberto had learnt a lot during our jungle boot camp and was a naturally quick learner. He took his hammock down in only a few minutes and was, for the first time on the expedition, ready to go before me.

'Hurry up, *muñeco*,' he said, tongue in cheek, as ever.

It meant little doll.

We had grown accustomed to calling each other by anything other than our actual names by now, but his Spanish repertoire of name-calling was far more prolific than mine.

What took the most time was arranging breakfast. Sometimes we'd skip it entirely and plod on till we found a village for lunch. This day, however, lunch found us.

We were walking past the small settlement of El Naranjo. As we crested the hill, we spotted a large mansion about half a mile away, sitting on a mound and surrounded by rows of razor wire. 'It's a Narco Finca,' said Alberto in a whisper. 'Look at all the land they own.'

It would have looked like any other ranch we'd seen along the way, except for the security. At each corner of the property there were watchtowers and even some spotlights.

We looked back along the road, but there was no one. It was spookily quiet.

'Do they actually grow drugs here?' I asked.

'No, these are the Guatemalan middle-men from the cartels, the guys that make all the money arranging the drugs to get from Colombia to the US. This is where they come to hide their money and their families from the government.'

The road had been quiet for the past two days apart from the occasional lorry, but all of a sudden we spotted five or six brand-new 4x4s with blacked-out windscreens speeding by in quick succession, without so much as slowing down.

'Narcos,' said Alberto, with a nervousness I hadn't recognised in him before.

'You reckon?'

'For sure. Who else can afford these brand-new Land Cruisers and Mitsubishis? They're this year's model! You think this money came from growing beans and bananas?'

Speaking of beans and bananas, it reminded me that it was late morning and we hadn't eaten anything yet. So far we'd passed one village shop, but they had sold only bags of crisps and fake cola. Hardly the diet of professional walkers, I thought to myself.

'I could eat a whole donkey,' said Alberto, salivating at the thought.

'A horse, you mean?'

'No, a donkey, balls and all,' he laughed out loud, as we passed a braying beast. Fat pigs, too, wallowed in the muddy ponds that lined the roadside on the far side of the barbed-wire fence, and skinny cockerels vied for pride of place with the feral dogs to perch on the piles of sand and bricks that signified work would get done one day.

As we approached the junction of a lane, I heard the roar of an engine pull up behind us as we walked. Alberto was busy photographing a horse tied to a tree (presumably contemplating how it tasted), when the horn beeped and he turned around. I couldn't see who was driving because, like the pick-ups we'd seen drive past twenty minutes earlier, the windscreen was blacked out. But as the car pulled to a halt, the driver's window rolled down to reveal a chubby-faced Mayan man, with a shaved head and dark rings round his eyes.

'Want a lift?' he said in Spanish.

'No, thanks, we're walking,' replied Alberto, walking up to the window.

'Get in,' the man said. He grinned with a flash of stained teeth.

I walked back to the car to where Alberto was standing. Forcing my own best smile, I was desperately hungry and the temptation to risk it and jump in the car was overwhelming, but as I peered in and saw three rough-looking men sitting there, I thought better of it.

'Have you eaten?' asked the driver, clearly a mind-reader.

Before I could answer, Alberto replied, 'No.'

'Get in,' repeated the man. 'You will eat with us.' He motioned toward the lane. 'There's a village that way, not far. You can walk from there.'

I looked at my map. He was right. The village was level to the road we were on and if we carried on walking from there, we weren't actually skipping any distance from the route. I looked at Alberto. He looked at me. I could sense his reticence, but I also knew he was as hungry as I was.

Without a word, we got in the back of the car and immediately sped off.

Never get into a car with a stranger. I'm pretty sure every schoolboy and girl was warned of that. I remember the lessons, the posters and the government-sponsored advertisements back in the 1980s, when it seemed that all the world's ills were finally realised.

Well, stupid or not, I clearly wasn't listening, because I've hitchhiked in pretty much every country I've ever been to and I haven't come to much harm myself. So long as I exclude a couple of car crashes and one pointed gun and two attempted robberies, but out of eighty countries that's not bad going, I suppose. The point is, I thought nothing of getting into the car. When you make a living out of travel, you have to put your faith in the kindness of strangers, otherwise you'd never leave your hotel room.

I sat on the right-hand back seat, with Alberto in the middle next to me, and on his left was a man in his forties, the oldest of the three locals. He wore a dirty checked shirt and was smoking a hand-rolled spliff. The sickly-sweet smell of marijuana wafted through the car. In the passenger seat was another man wearing a baseball cap. He didn't say a word. The pot smoker did most of the talking, and the driver occasionally asked questions.

'Where are you from?'

'I'm Mexican and he's from England,' said Alberto.

'You came from Belize? Why are you walking?' asked the driver.

'The gringo likes to walk. I'm his guide,' Alberto laughed.

I smiled. The pot smoker laughed. Here we go again, I thought to myself, Alberto's turn.

'What's the camera for?' I saw the fat man's eyes glancing at the video camera on Alberto's lap.

I thought it was best to tell the truth rather than continue with the daft-tourist routine, which they clearly weren't buying anyway.

'I'm a writer, and we're also making a documentary,' I butted in, before Alberto could reply.

He nodded discreetly and continued.

'All about Central America. We're walking to Colombia.'

The fat man turned around and looked us up and down as he drove.

'Colombia has good ganja,' said the pot smoker next to us. 'Gives you good energy for making love to the ladies.' He made a lewd motion with his hands.

The driver and the man in the passenger seat looked at each other suspiciously.

'Are you working for the government?' he asked, suddenly agitated.

'Hell, no,' said Alberto. '*Chinga*. We're just travellers.'

'How much is the gringo paying you?' said the fat man.

'Not much, I'm doing it for fun.'

'If you're walking, what is your route?'

Without thinking, I told him my plan – following the road south through El Petén to Rio Dulce, then down the river to Livingston and Puerto Barrios, and onward to Honduras, through San Pedro Sula . . .

Shit. I realised what I was doing. I was telling a complete stranger, no, three strangers, who could be anyone, my itinerary and plans for the next weeks. I stopped abruptly.

'But of course, we sometimes change our plans,' said Alberto. 'Where is the rest of your team?'

I butted in again, 'We're meeting them ahead, later on today. We've just spoken to them on our phones and they're tracking us on our GPS anyway. They'll be wondering why we're going off route.' I nudged Alberto discreetly.

'Yes, these TV people don't give us a moment's rest,' Alberto interjected, playing the game.

'They're going to buy drugs from Colombia,' said the pot smoker, bursting into uncontrollable laughter, as we pulled into a village. The car came to a halt outside a small shop that doubled up as a restaurant.

The fat man got out first and motioned for us to follow.

We all stood around the car and there was an awkward silence. Alberto grasped my arm and said in English quietly, 'Have you any photos of your book on your phone? Hurry, they don't believe us.'

I didn't see the immediate danger, but I trusted Alberto's instincts and got out my phone, scrolling through the camera roll until I found a shot of my Nile book cover. I handed it to the fat man, who looked at the picture, spelling out the words, 'WALKING THE NILE.'

'*El Nilo,*' nodded the pot smoker, looking over the fat man's shoulder. '*Es muy falta.*'

He was right, it was very far, the memories hadn't escaped me yet.

'How many books have you sold?' he asked me.

'Erm, I don't know. A few thousand, maybe.'

'Ah, good money, eh? You must be very rich.' His eyes widened and the other men grunted with agreement.

'No, no, books don't make him any money. He's really poor, look at his clothes, they're so dirty.' Alberto patted me on the shoulder.

The fat man didn't look convinced, but at least now they believed we were who we said we were, and relaxed a little. We sat down at a table and waited for the pork and tortillas to arrive.

'So, you're going to Honduras next?' said the fat man, whose name it transpired was Hugo.

The pot smoker, Walter, winked at Alberto. 'Good ganja there, too.'

'Yes, we are, any advice?' said Alberto, as a waitress poured fresh lime juice into plastic cups.

'Yes,' said Hugo. 'Don't film or ask too many questions to the narcos. They don't like it and you'll get into trouble.'

'OK.'

'If you want, I can help you. I know people there, they can get you across the border in a truck, if you like?'

'It's OK, we're walking and anyway we have passports, so don't really need to be smuggled.'

Hugo looked a little disappointed.

'So, what do you do?'

I asked the men, before realising it was an inappropriate question as Alberto's knee slammed firmly into mine.

The men looked down at their plates and started eating. 'We grown beans and corn,' said Hugo in a mumble.

'I'm a policeman.' After a moment of silence, the third man who'd been in the passenger seat spoke up. He hadn't said anything until now and we hadn't caught his name. 'Be careful in Honduras. There are American DEA officers everywhere. Their spies are in all the villages. Even here in Guatemala, they work on the border. I thought maybe you were one of them, filming things.'

'No, they're not,' said Walter, who had stubbed out his joint in favour of eating. 'They're looking for drugs.'

'No, we're . . .' I was about to protest, before the policeman carried on.

'Want to see his house?' he pointed at Walter. 'It's just next door. You can film his house for your film and make us famous.'

'Erm, OK,' I agreed.

After finishing up the pork, we walked out of the shop and went to the house next door through a little garden. Rows of holey underwear were strung from a washing line, under which a five-foot-high cannabis plant sprouted from the flower bed. Walter, who was almost certainly a bachelor, had torn a piece of paper and was busy rolling another joint as he led us into his house. It was nothing more than a tin shack with holes in the walls. The floor was filthy and a fraying hammock dangled loosely from the termite-infested beams.

Inside the tiny hut was a small stove, a chest of drawers, and bags and bags of dried marijuana. He lit the roughly rolled spliff and handed it to Alberto, who took a drag out of politeness. The policeman smiled and shrugged his shoulders. Hugo, the fat man, made a gesture and we knew it was time to leave. Before they could change their minds, we shook their hands with big smiles, thanking them all for their advice and promising them we'd send copies of the film and book, and keep them all updated on the journey. Then we walked, and kept on walking as fast as we could.

'I'm not sure what I made of them,' I said to Alberto, as he caught his breath.

'I reckon they were narcos,' he carried on.

'Do you think?'

'Of course. One hundred per cent. Remember when you asked them what they did and they said they grew beans and corn?'

'Yes.'

'Well, I looked at their hands. They weren't dirty. Their clothes, everything about them, made me think they weren't farmers. I think they wanted to check us out. That's why they stopped. They wanted to see if we had any money, that's why they kept asking how much I got paid and how many books you sold; whether we were worth kidnapping or not.'

'What about the policeman?' I asked.

'Maybe he was, maybe he wasn't. Even if he was, and the DEA story was true, it doesn't mean he's not a narco. Here they're all in on it. You don't think all these mansions were built right under the noses of the army and police without them knowing? And the fat guy, Hugo. He said he'd been to Honduras, right? Why would a simple farmer go to Honduras? And the fact that he offered to smuggle us in a truck? You know what I think?'

'What?'

'I think they were low-level smugglers. Not the bosses, but the meat heads. They were too stupid to be top bad guys, since they let us film and ask questions. They let their vanity get the better of them when they thought they could get on TV. Lucky for us we had the camera, eh, otherwise they would have taken us to their hideout and we'd be sat on our knees with a blindfold on by now.'

Alberto was right. We'd had a lucky escape. I'd made the mistake of underestimating the environment. I think I'd got sloppy after walking through the Yucatán and Belize, which for the most part were safe, but here was a different story. I could have slapped myself now. As we headed south on the deserted road, I realised that I'd told those men our exact route, so that if they changed their minds and fancied kidnapping us after all, they knew exactly where we'd be; regardless of how stupid they might be, it didn't take a genius to work out that one loose word to their boss, or another gang member, could end up with us in deep trouble. It was a lesson learned for both of us, and one that couldn't have come at a better time, because where we were going, we couldn't afford to take any chances.

South of La Cumbre, El Petén closes in, and the rolling hills slowly transform into a series of looming karsts and mountains. The road snakes through the jungle-clad gorges flanking the main valley. We had left the dirt track behind and found ourselves on a busy highway full of trucks and motorbikes, and yet more shiny 4x4s, as they went about their business. A further three days' walking brought us to the Rio Dulce – the sweet river – at the point where an enormous sky bridge had been built to intersect the great lagoon. We'd finally reached the gateway to Lake Izabal, which stretched out for twenty miles to the west.

But we were heading now in the opposite direction, to the east, back towards the Caribbean, where we would be able to cross into Honduras. It was here that Stephens and Catherwood had entered Guatemala and begun their epic voyage in search of the Mayan lost worlds, all those years ago, and I imagined the intrepid pair on board a steamship as it chugged along the Rio Dulce, and the wonder in their eyes as they set forth into the unknown.

I wondered how much had changed in reality. I was well aware that life for the early explorers was far more perilous than it is for us now. For Stephens, there was no communication other than the occasional handwritten letter. The telegraph hadn't reached Central America at that time. There were no trains, cars, or paved roads. Each day was a struggle for survival and life was cheap on the road. Caste wars between the races in the Yucatán and a civil war in Guatemala made journeying impossible for all except the bravest, and only then with a diplomatic passport, aristocratic connections, and a saddlebag full of gold. Oh, and half a dozen rifles, just in case.

These days anyone can travel anywhere, and that's part of the privilege of living in these times. A plane ticket and an Instagram account are all one needs to justify a trip, if you even need that. Of course, there are risks and hazards, you only have to turn on the news to see that, but what I'd come to realise is that even in the most dangerous places in the world, there are still thousands, if not millions of people living out their daily lives in relative peace.

Even in a war zone, not everyone is getting shot at all the time. I'd been in enough war zones to understand that ninety per cent of the time, nothing happens – merely the humdrum daily chatter of people going about their business, hoping that infernal politics will settle for long enough to allow them to go to the shops, or visit their sick aunt, or celebrate a friend's birthday. We sometimes forget that, when we're fed a constant drip of bombs, bullets and terrorism on the popular news. The truth is usually a lot less dramatic than first appears, and it's only by visiting those sorts of places that you can understand that for yourself, and in doing so, gain the experience and wisdom to make the right choices along the way. While you need to be prepared for the worst-case scenario, and accept a certain level of risk, more often than not, things work out OK in the end.

Alberto and I followed the course of the Rio Dulce east, past engulfing canyons and thick forest, watching as Mayan fishermen cast their nets into the deep brown waters below. Pelicans glided low against the lapping waves and herons perched in little crevices in the cliffs, watching us with marble eyes. We emerged at its estuary in the town of Livingston, where a few hundred Garifuna people live. They are the descendants of African slaves who escaped the island of St. Vincent in the seventeenth century to form their own unique, African communities along the Caribbean coastline to this day.

Out of El Petén, with its suspicion and paranoia, we were welcomed once again into people's homes and lives and given a glimpse into a world inside a world, where the rhythm of west Africa still thrives. Among the ramshackle wooden houses, we were greeted by trinket-sellers offering turtle shells and conch. Stalls laden with all kinds of colourful fruits from the surrounding jungle filled the narrow streets. Every house seemed to be a restaurant, where little hatches revealed old men with dreadlocks and gargantuan women too big to leave the house, instead putting their culinary heritage into practice. All the while, a familiar and constant drumbeat blasted from their radios.

It was a scene I'd seen a thousand times along the Nile and it was easy to forget which continent we were on. These proud people, isolated from the rest of Guatemala by the colour of their skin, their language and their culture, live out on a limb like a tribe apart. Whereas in Belize, Africans had mixed with Europeans and Indians alike under a remarkably open and tolerant society, the same could not be said here.

We followed the Caribbean coast south, walking along the beach with the emerald water lapping against our feet and the sun beating down. Our only shade was the spindly leaves of the palms overhead that fringed the edge of the mangrove swamps. For a while we found ourselves in paradise, but it was a short-lived vision, because up ahead we knew the hardest part was yet to come.

The past month had given us an insight into life in this distinct region. For both of us, we'd learnt how to get along in some tough circumstances, very much outside our comfort zone. It was a challenge, though, that we'd come to relish, as each new day brought with it incredible wonders, and for me at least, this was the first expedition that I'd embarked upon safe in the knowledge I was walking with a companion who could guarantee to make me laugh, no matter how hard things got. As we arrived at the Honduras border, I was glad that I wasn't doing this alone.

12

Barrios

It was almost the end of the first week in September when we arrived at Corinto, the gateway to Honduras. Hardly anyone was crossing at this border and except a solitary official in uniform, the offices of the immigration post were empty and bare. The pavements were overgrown with weeds and rusting trailers that hadn't moved in years gave the whole place an almost apocalyptic feel. A limp Honduran flag dangled in the oppressive afternoon heat; the only suggestion that we had entered Central America's poorest country.

Plodding on towards the east, we skirted the Caribbean coastline along a main highway. To the left stretched the last flat lands that we'd encounter for a long while, and to the right, looming some two miles distant, were the Merendón mountains. At two and a half thousand metres, they formed a natural barrier to the comparatively flat Petén that we had spent the past weeks walking, and it came as no surprise to learn that this was the extent of the ancient Mayan civilisation. Beyond this wall of almost vertical green rainforest, we would be leaving behind a familiar culture and entering somewhere altogether wilder.

Honduras means 'the depths' and was named by Columbus as he sailed past the country in the deep water, but decided against disembarking. Perhaps the ruggedness of the country put him off. As we stared up at the vast mountain range, I could hardly blame him.

At Cuyamel we stayed for a couple of days to stock up on provisions before setting off into the hills. For this we'd need some local help, as there didn't seem to be any clear trail, so we employed the services of two local lads who knew the way over the passes to San Pedro Sula twenty miles away.

'What are your names, *chicos*?' asked Alberto, as the pair of scruffy teenagers stood to attention before us. I'd found it remarkable how a border can change so much, including it seems, national character. Whereas in Guatemala we'd been greeted with nothing but insolence and disdain, there was a totally different atmosphere here. The locals were smiling and seemed happy; the kids, in spite of their all-too-apparent poverty, were all very willing to help out, or maybe they were just a bit more entrepreneurial? In Guatemala, you couldn't get decent service even if you emptied your wallet. The shops were empty, the people cold, and the atmosphere indifferent. In Honduras, people genuinely wanted to help out a couple of foreigners, and we had no trouble finding willing volunteers.

'I'm Jose,' said the older of the two. 'I'm Darling,' said the younger. They were brothers.

'Darling?' asked Alberto.

'Si,' said Darling, clearly unaware that there were any connotations to his name.

'That's, erm, unusual,' said Alberto, suppressing a giggle.

'Right, come on then, Darling. Let's go.'

And so we followed the likely lads up a dirt track and into the Merendón mountains.

Despite the dark clouds overhead, it was hot and sticky. The humidity was oppressive and though it threatened to rain, I had a hunch that today it wouldn't. As we trudged up the hill, the track got narrower and before long it had petered out to nothing but a footpath. We passed by Jose and Darling's family home. It was a little wooden hut with a tin roof overlooking the valley below. Darling ran in to fetch a machete, while we caught our breath outside.

I'd forgotten what proper hills were like. I hadn't climbed uphill for months – excluding the little jungle hike we'd had in Belize – probably since leaving the Himalayas behind a year before, but until now I'd taken it for granted that sooner or later we'd be faced with real mountains. In my own mind I was mentally, if not physically, prepared. I had forgotten, it seems, about Alberto.

'*Chinga*,' he said, blowing out after just twenty minutes climbing through the banana and coffee plantations. 'This is horrible. You didn't tell me we'd be climbing mountains, you bastard.'

'Think of it as training,' I said. 'There's a few more ahead.'

The further south we got, the more mountainous it would become, and although I hadn't broken the news to him yet, there was one particular mountain that I was hoping to scale – Cerro Chirripó in Costa Rica. But that could wait, it was still a long way off, and in between here and there we still had two full countries to get through; for all I knew, Alberto may have decided that the beaches of Tulum were a far more appealing prospect, so best not to scare him off too soon.

Jose and Darling giggled as we plodded uphill. They found our slow movements pitiful. 'How often do you walk this way?' asked Alberto, in between breaths.

'Once a fortnight these days, but when we were children, sometimes more,' said Darling.

I laughed. He couldn't have been older than fifteen.

'Why don't you go more often?' I asked.

'It's too dangerous. My mother won't let us go to San Pedro Sula.'

'Why?'

'Because of the gangs. She's scared that they will kidnap us.'

At that moment we found ourselves at the bottom of a small but beautiful waterfall. The trail had taken us into thick woods, and the path was covered almost completely by the canopy, so that only a few shafts of light penetrated the ceiling of leaves. It was a welcome bit of shade and we took the opportunity to jump in the water and cool off. As we lounged in the refreshing pool, listening to the sounds of the jungle, I heard the noise of hooves.

Twenty metres away, where the path curved a bend, two men appeared riding horses. They looked to be in their early twenties and were wearing singlets, baseball caps and heavy gold chains. They looked more like rappers than cowboys.

'Good morning,' we all said to the horsemen in unison, particularly since the lad in the lead had a Smith and Wesson pistol poking from the waist of his jeans.

He stopped and greeted us and asked us where we were going.

'San Pedro Sula.'

He nodded and gave us an upturned smile as if to say rather you than me.

'What about you?' asked Alberto.

'A party,' the man replied. 'A birthday party.'

It seemed like an odd response given that the nearest hut was miles away, but I supposed that even in the jungle the villagers must have birthday parties.

'And what about the gun?' Alberto pointed to the pistol.

'What about it?' The man shrugged his shoulders as if it was a daft question.

He grinned and handed it to me like it was a prized possession.

'What do you use that for?' I asked.

'Just in case.'

He took back the weapon, shoved it down his pants and rode off, waving goodbye with his friend in tow.

It was a stark reminder, as is often the case in expeditions like this, that beauty and danger go hand in hand.

Five hours and several ridges later, we arrived at a small village called El Zapotal, exhausted, hungry and soaked through with sweat. It had been one of the most punishing days of the journey so far and it was a welcome relief to be able to look down from the top of the hill onto the tropical savannah below and in the distance, nestled in the valley, our objective: the city of San Pedro Sula.

Jose and Darling said that they couldn't come any further and would now go home. It was gone four o'clock in the afternoon and would be dark soon, but they assured us that up here in the hills they would be safe and make it home in time for the evening.

'It's you who should be careful,' said our wise young guide. 'Don't go through the Barrios alone.' So we paid them a good wage and then they were off, jogging back to the west. He was referring to the lawless districts and suburbs that were run by the gangs.

Until just over a year ago, San Pedro Sula held the dubious honour of being known as the murder capital of the world. Between 2011 and 2015 the city bore witness to six thousand homicides. At its height, killings averaged three a day. It was with some trepidation, then, that we proceeded to follow the trail down the mountain into the outskirts of the infamous town.

Alberto explained, 'A few years ago, the United States started to deport a lot of the gangsters back to Honduras. In the eighties and nineties, loads of Latin Americans went to find work in LA and ended up in the gangs. They worked with the Mexican drug cartels and basically ran the show in Central America. But for the last ten years, since getting thrown out of America, they've brought the gang culture back to these cities, and now this is one of the worst.'

He continued, 'There's two main gangs that live here. You've got Mara Salvatrucha, or MS-13, as it's called, and then there's Barrio 18, who are even worse. They both hate each other. They're like two tribes, yet they're the same people. It comes down to money and drugs and whoever pays them.'

After an hour, we reached the suburbs of the town and found ourselves on a congested street flanked by factories and bus stations. This was, after all, Honduras's second-biggest city. The cars buzzed past as we picked our way through the busy pavements. It felt bizarre to be in the jungle one minute and in a city the next, but it had become the norm here on this journey.

'And how do we know who's in the gangs, and where they operate?' I asked Alberto, not wanting to accidentally offend a gangster if I could help it.

'Well, you can't always tell, of course. A lot of the thugs have got tattoos, sometimes on their face. And look over there ...' Alberto pointed to a concrete wall surrounding a trailer park. Scribbled on it with black paint was the unmistakable number 18.

'Looks like we're in one already.'

I felt a shiver of nervousness run down my spine as the sun set behind the mountains we'd just left and the smog of the town filled the streets in a red haze.

'I think we should hurry and find somewhere to stay, before it gets dark,' I suggested.

So we plodded on along the main street towards the town centre. The noise of car horns and the chatter of pedestrians was at least reassuring. There were old ladies and children in the streets, and what's more, this wasn't a filthy shanty town, of the kind of which I'd seen in Guatemala. No, the roads were clean and there were fancy hotels as we approached the main plaza. Chain restaurants filled the avenues, and our hungry stomachs grumbled at the sight of Pizza Hut, KFC and McDonalds. This didn't resemble the ganglands of my imagination. There were boutique fashion outlets, shopping malls and posh coffee shops. Given the fact we'd been roughing it for quite some time, we decided to treat ourselves to a good hotel and found a shiny glass building right on the main strip. It even had a little swimming pool on the roof. As we stood on the terrace looking down at the city as night fell, it was hard to imagine that it was also the scene of so much horror.

'Where are we heading from here?' asked Alberto, looking out towards the horizon.

I pointed towards the south, past the airport, where a rocky escarpment rose out of the flat darkness. 'That way, towards Rivera Hernandez.'

We both looked at each other in silence. We both had a feeling that it was only a matter of time before we encountered the reality of life in the world's most dangerous city.

The next morning we'd agreed to meet Daniel Pacheco, a local pastor, community leader and carpenter. Rivera Hernandez, we'd discovered, was one of the most dangerous neighbour-hoods in the city, if not the entire Americas, and we knew that it would be foolish to attempt to walk through it alone.

A short, jolly man with dark black hair and a smart polo shirt greeted us outside a kids' playground, where a band was playing. It was mid-morning and the sun was beating down over a bright, jovial city. It was 'children's day' and the whole population was out in their finest clothes, shopping, eating and generally making merry.

'So, you want to walk through Hernandez?' he asked with a large smile. 'No problem. Let me make some calls.' Our new guide walked away a few metres and began speaking with someone on his mobile. Alberto, I could tell, was straining to eavesdrop.

'He's talking to a gang boss, he's telling them we are coming,' he whispered. 'Shhh.'

Daniel walked back over with a grin on his face. 'It's sorted, we have permission.'

'Who did you speak to?' said Alberto.

Daniel was upfront and honest.

'I won't give his name, but rest assured he's in a position to make sure we will be safe. I spoke to the leaders of both gangs, MS-13 and Barrio 18. I said which route you wanted to take and they will make sure nothing happens to us.'

'So we will meet the gang bosses?' Alberto expressed his surprise as well as I hid my own.

Daniel laughed. 'No, of course not,' he said. 'They're both in jail.'

'What?' I said, unable to hold back any longer. 'How are they able to give us permission if they're in jail?'

'It doesn't stop them running the gangs. It's the safest place for them. They get treated like kings in there. And anyway, if they want to leave they can. The police are so corrupt here they do whatever the bosses say, otherwise they know their families will be killed.'

'Well, that's reassuring,' I said, half-joking.

'Really, you mustn't worry,' said Daniel. 'I've known these people all my life. I started off growing up with the gangs, but luckily I escaped and got educated. I wanted to come back and save my people, so I became a pastor to try and teach them about God and the value of life. They're not all bad people, they've just lost their way. They send their apologies by the way.'

'Who do?' I replied.

'The bosses. They said if they had more warning they would have had the streets cleaned up and the graffiti removed.'

Daniel patted me on the back. He seemed genuine and loyal and I felt like he could be trusted.

'Come on, let me show you the way.'

So we followed Daniel off the main street, down an alleyway and into the heart of Rivera Hernandez. It was clear which side of the gang-divide this neighbourhood was. The walls were covered in the words MS-13 at every turn and razor-wire topped the fences. Each house resembled a mini-fortress, with high metal gates and concrete sangars. I was reminded of the Taliban compounds we used to storm in Afghanistan.

Each step took us further into the ghetto. Unlike the city centre, this area wasn't busy. In fact, it was eerily quiet. A few old men sat on rocking chairs smoking cheap cigarettes on their verandas, watching us through the bars. A woman carried her shopping down the street, followed by a nervous little girl. There seemed to be more feral dogs than human beings, sniffing around the piles of garbage. One thing was clear, though, we were certainly under observation. Teenage boys lurked on every corner, some sitting on windowsills, eyeing us with suspicion.

Daniel's smile never left his face. He'd wave enthusiastically to every man, woman and child that passed by.

'Don't worry, they're keeping an eye on us for our own protection,' he said through the corner of his mouth, all the while scanning the horizon.

'This is where I grew up and have lived all my life. It's not often we get foreigners here, so people are a bit wary. They all know not to mess, though.'

We were inside the middle of MS-13 territory now. There were no police, only gang kids patrolling here.

'Saul!' bellowed Daniel, as we rounded a corner and bumped into a young man in a basketball shirt, his cap facing backwards, and a stream of tattoos covering his skinny arms, chest, all the way up his neck like a black snake. His face was downturned and he looked like a rampant school bully.

'This is Saul, he's like a son to me.' Daniel put his arm around the boy's shoulders and told him that we were passing through the neighbourhood. The lad said nothing, he only scowled at us.

'How old are you?' said Alberto, grasping his hand to shake.

'Twenty-one,' he said, without making eye contact. He was evidently a gang lookout. I was surprised. He looked sixteen at most.

'I try and get these kids off the streets and into education. But sometimes they have nothing and can't afford to eat, so what can I do except give them love and try and encourage them to live in peace?' said Daniel, still holding the young man.

Alberto was intrigued and asked the reluctant Saul more questions.

'How long have you been in the gang? What's your job? How do you make money? What about your family?'

Saul stood there in silence, before looking to Daniel.

'Go on son, it's OK, tell them, they are friends.'

'Six years,' he said with a fragile voice. It surprised me a little. Here was a gangster who looked like evil incarnate, yet the voice was that of a nervous child. 'They killed my brother, so I joined MS-13 to get revenge.'

'Who did?'

'Barrio 18. The enemy, of course.' He showed us his hands. The name 'Vilmer' was tattooed across his knuckles. 'One day I will find who did it and kill them.' He said it without any emotion. There was only a quiet sadness.

'My mother is dead. My father, I don't know who he is. Mara is my family. I make my money in drugs, of course, how else? And sometimes I have to kill people. I'm a *sicario*, it's my job.' He shrugged his shoulders and carried on looking up and down the street.

I'd watched gangster films before. This wasn't what I had come to expect at all. The lad wasn't boastful, just direct. For him, there didn't seem to be much choice in his decision to become an assassin.

'Do you ever go into Barrio 18 territory?' I asked.

He shook his head. 'Not unless it's war. Now is not war, so I don't go. But maybe soon I can go and take revenge.'

Barrio 18 territory was where we had to pass through next. Saul walked away without even a goodbye, he just nodded respectfully to Daniel and made off down an alleyway. I think perhaps I was expecting some sort of fortified wall, or a water-filled moat, or at least a desolate wasteland between the two gangs. Instead, the two neighbourhoods backed right up against each other, separated by only a narrow street. There were no walls or barbed wire. It seemed that people could come and go as they chose. Except, of course, they didn't choose. Only the changed graffiti on the walls signified that we were crossing into a new area.

'Now we must be very polite,' said Daniel, his permanent smile wider than ever. As we crossed the invisible line, it became clear we were being followed. I turned around and noticed a pick-up truck with two men sat in the front and one stood in the back, edging slowly behind us at a distance.

'Don't worry,' said Daniel, 'they're with us. One is my brother, the other is one of their leaders.'

My heart raced faster, the further down the road we got.

'These are the most ruthless gang.'

'What would happen if we tried to come in here alone without you?' I asked.

Daniel flashed a grin, showing off a glinting gold tooth.

'A van would come, and they'd put you in it and take you to a place called a *Casa Loca* and torture you until you tell them what you're up to. They have hooks that hold and cut out your tongue.' Alberto winced. So did I. But Daniel carried on, keen to tell us about the brutality of Barrio 18.

'Many people have been killed. They hang you up in the house naked ...' he motioned by raising his hands in the air, wrists together, '... and with pliers and clamps, they squeeze your balls until you die.'

Ahead we spotted more of the spies. Kids, some no older than ten or eleven, stood around chatting into mobile phones, reporting on our every move.

We carried on walking through the streets, slowly and deliberately saying hello to everyone we met. There is no rushing a danger zone; this was no gauntlet to run, better to rely on a bit of charm and manners. Daniel was clearly a respected figure on both sides of the divide. He was non-political and, like a holy man, held the confidence of all sides. As the afternoon wore on, we got closer to the edge of the neighbourhood, until at last we saw the fields and the hills that lay beyond the city limits. It was getting late and we needed to make it out before dark. The past few hours had been surreal and eye-opening in equal measure, but we didn't want to push our luck, and I think both Alberto and I were keen to leave.

'There's one last thing you should see,' said Daniel, as we walked into what looked like an abandoned council estate. A long block of flats, three storeys high, presented itself as the final building in San Pedro Sula before we could escape into the countryside. It was painted in pink and yellow and stood out against the high concrete wall that surrounded it. Outside there was an open yard in front, where a group of men were playing football. The flats looked fairly new, certainly not more than a decade old, but they were unfinished and bare. There was no glass in the windows or any furnishings. It reminded me a little of those purpose-built houses the Army would construct, so that soldiers could train in urban warfare.

'What is this place?' said Alberto, as we walked past the footballers and into the black doorway of the house. There was broken glass all over the floor and smashed tiles and bits of burnt wood were everywhere. Weeds grew in the cracks of the bricks and the whole interior smelled of piss.

'It's a Casa Loca,' whispered Daniel. 'A crazy house.'

My heart sank. Surely not. After all that, was Daniel about to unleash the fury of the gangs on us and string us up by our wrists and clobber us around our testicles until we died?

He clearly noted the shudder down my spine and chuckled.

'Don't worry, I just want to show you the place so you don't think I'm making it up. It is important people know how terrible the situation here is so that the government will do something about it. With education and help, these kids wouldn't need to join a gang. Go inside and have a look.'

I took a step and heard the crunch of glass underfoot. I shone the light from my phone against the walls. There was Barrio 18 graffiti all over them. Spiders' webs filled the corridors and there was an overwhelming smell of urine. I followed the warren of empty rooms that were linked in the pitch black. There was no electricity in here, only dangling wires from the sockets.

'Lev,' whispered Alberto, in the dark, 'look at this.'

I walked over to where I could hear his voice and shined my light against the wall. It was pockmarked with bullet holes.

'Let's get the hell out of here,' he said. But as we turned a corner, trying to find a way out of this house of horrors, I felt Alberto recoil with terror. There was the sudden and overwhelming stench of death. I've smelt it before, I knew it could be nothing else. I lifted my phone as quick as I could and there, in the corner of a room, was a rope dangling from the ceiling. I lowered the phone light and to my disgust saw the figure of a dead dog hanging by its neck.

Alberto put his hand to his nose, trying not to vomit.

'What the fuck?'

Behind it was a message to the Mara not to mess with Barrio 18.

You will die like dogs.

I felt sick. 'Let's go,' I said again to Alberto.

Daniel was waiting outside and a pick-up truck had appeared. It was Daniel's and it was time for him to get back to his side of the border. It was dusk now, and this was no place to be hanging around. I thanked Daniel for helping us though Rivera Hernandez and we shook hands before he got into the car. I noticed that the driver's door had a bullet hole in it.

'It's a nine millimetre,' said Alberto. 'Who shot you?'

Daniel, still smiling, shrugged his shoulders. 'I don't know.'

'It's a dangerous business being a pastor round here,' was all I could reply.

I wished him luck in his crusade against the gang wars and we left the Barrios behind, glad to have made it out of the place safe and in one piece.

13

The Ascent

The next morning we made our way past a great swathe of sugar-cane plantations that filled the flat expanse of the San Pedro Sula valley south of the city for as far as the eye could see. We walked along the main highway towards El Progreso, and then south along a smaller road passing by a village called San Manuel.

'Yesterday was pretty intense,' said Alberto, wiping the sweat from his brow as we plodded along a country lane. Fields rolled away on either side and we both felt glad to be back in the countryside.

'You're not wrong,' I replied. 'I'm just glad that we were in Daniel's safe hands. I feel like he showed us just enough to scare us, but not quite the whole story.'

'What do you mean?' asked Alberto.

'I mean, since we warned off the gang bosses that we were coming, it felt a bit sterilised, like we didn't get the big picture. I don't know, it was just a hunch.'

Perhaps I'd spent too much time in war zones, but having walked through San Pedro Sula, supposedly one of the most dangerous cities in the world, and to have come out without having seen a shot fired, well, it came as a relief, but also left the nagging feeling that we'd only scratched the surface. A maso-chistic part of me wanted to stay and talk with more gangsters and find out what life was really like.

That was the hard part of these expeditions: no sooner had you arrived than you must leave again. You meet amazing people and build connections, and then before you've even discovered a fraction of their story, you have to carry on. With such a long journey, you simply can't hang about, otherwise you'd never get there. The journalist and explorer inside me wanted to stay, to better understand the torment and motivation behind these tragic people, and to get to grips with why violence plays such an important part of their lives. The adventurer in me wanted to push the boundaries, and embed myself on the frontline of this unseen war. But then the realistic, sensible part of me said that we should be grateful for what we had got and be glad that we were sufficiently removed to be able to walk away.

'Be careful what you wish for,' Alberto raised his eyebrows.

'I know, I know. We were lucky that nothing bad did happen, let's keep our fingers crossed it stays that way. I feel like yesterday has prepared us for the rest of the journey. Nowhere else we go can be that bad, surely?'

But of course, things always happen in the places you're least expecting them. We'd come to the end of the village and found ourselves in a beautiful lane. Cows munched away on the long grass in the meadows and we were looking forward to seeing the positive side of Honduras, when all of a sudden I noticed a crowd up ahead. Figures seemed to be milling around, loitering under trees. Some of the men were smoking cigarettes and the women were hugging children. As we got closer, I noticed that a part of the track had been taped off with yellow police tape.

The crowd ignored us. They were all looking at what lay beyond. There, at the bottom of a wooden fence, lay a dead body.

It was motionless, covered in a bloodstained jacket and swarming with flies. The man was face down, but I could just make out that it was a man by the short curly hair and the size of a foot protruding from a trouser leg.

I'd seen dead bodies before, of course, and it's never pleasant. They always assume a position that only the dead can manage. It's the awkward, uncomfortable angles; the terrifying stillness and the smell. But there was something about this one in particular that was altogether more gruesome. Perhaps it was the juxtaposition of a corpse lying against such a panorama of beauty, or simply the knowledge that the man had been murdered, killed in cold blood.

'Who is he?' I asked a waiting policeman. He shrugged his shoulders in disinterest. I almost forgot; for him this was nothing new. He probably came across a couple of murders every night. I looked around to see whom I could ask. Most of the crowd were youngsters, apparently unmoved by the sight of the cadaver. Some were even taking photos on their phones. But there was one old lady who did look moved. She stood there, gripping onto an umbrella, just staring at the body.

I asked her name.

'Maria Teodora Pavon,' came the reply. She wiped away a tear. She looked ancient, a lady of seventy-six, but could have easily been a hundred.

The body was that of her son.

'What happened?' I asked the poor woman.

'Who knows?' came her response. 'He liked to steal.'

'He was a robber?' asked Alberto.

'Yes. He'd broken into this property before, and they'd shot at him. Last time he escaped, but now he is dead. I'm ashamed of him. He deserved it.'

I looked at Alberto as Maria shook her head and closed her eyes. They aren't the words you'd expect to come from the mouth of a mother.

'He tried to kill me before.' She grasped at my arm, and stared at me with piercing eyes. 'He threw a pan of boiling water at me once. And then he hit me with a machete. No, no. He deserved to die, and I'm not surprised.'

'What was his name?' I asked.

She grimaced as if it was painful to say. 'Alfonso Pavon.'

I didn't know what to do except put a hand on her shoulder and offer her my condolences. It seemed a futile gesture. She was angry and bereaved and full of disappointment.

'I just want his body back so I can bury him and forget it.'

She walked off into the crowd, alone, muttering to herself about what shame he had caused. Alberto stared at the body.

'This place is full of horror. It's tough, life here is tough.'

What more could either of us say? Death is so commonplace here as to be almost insignificant. Life is indeed tough, and cheap, too. Just as more police arrived, we left and carried on, leaving the crime scene behind.

The road began to climb up into wild forest as we left the towns and villages behind. The country grew more beautiful by the day, and before long we were following the spectacular ridge-lines of the central Honduran highlands. Up here, the landscape was stark and powerful; Caribbean pine trees silhouetted against a brooding sky that warned of forthcoming rains. The only people we'd see were occasional farmers, eking out a living from plantain, and a few old merchants selling weird-looking fruits from the roadsides. We met one character who had attempted a new life in the United States, only to be deported after thirteen years.

'I was living in Minnesota,' said Enrique. 'That's where I learnt my English.'

He stood proudly, wielding a large machete that he'd been using to cut vegetation from the roadside.

'I was there for thirteen years, but I got in trouble and got deported. I was there illegally, I just went over the border when I was younger. They caught me once in 2000 and I went right back. I got married over there to a Native American woman from South Dakota, but now I have to wait ten years before I can return.'

'Ten years!' I said. 'What are you going to do? What about your wife? You're not going to see her?'

'I've got no choice, so no. I'm not gonna go back there illegally again.'

'Why not?' I asked, surprised.

'It's too expensive. It costs ten thousand bucks to do it illegally, and for what? I'll tell the people something. Don't do it. Don't go there. You need to pay for everything. Look ...' he pointed up to a tree that he'd been working under, 'right here we got guayabas. We can eat guayabas in the wild. Over there you have to pay for guayabas.' He laughed. 'No, it's too expensive. My wife can wait.'

We shook his hand and let him get back to the business of honest work.

'Can you imagine a woman waiting ten years?' said Alberto, as we carried on along the road. 'Ha! Not in Mexico, that's for sure.'

Wherever we went it became a familiar story. From where we had started in Mexico, throughout Belize and Guatemala and now in Honduras, people were chasing the American dream. Thousands of men, women and children were making the perilous journey in the opposite direction, hoping for a chance to make it to the golden streets of the United States. But it was, of course, an illusion, and untold numbers like Enrique had either been deported, given up, or perished along the way.

Having seen the violent ghettos of San Pedro Sula, and the terrible consequences of living amongst the gangs, it occurred to me that no one should be surprised that people are willing to stake it all on the chance of a better life in the States. But I also wondered how many people like that man had come to realise that the proverbial grass wasn't always greener.

As we skirted the beautiful shorelines of Lake Yojoa, where the grass really could not have been greener, I realised that in spite of the natural splendour we were both beginning to struggle a bit.

'How do you stop the blisters?' said Alberto.

'You're still getting them?' I asked.

'Yeah. I put the tape on like you said, but some days they're still painful.'

I didn't know what to suggest. I'd made him strap up his feet with zinc-oxide tape, which stops the rubbing and hardens your feet, but sometimes there's not a lot else you can do other than grin and bear it, which until now he'd done remarkably well. The past day or two, though, I'd noticed a limp and he'd fallen behind a little.

'How do you do it?' he asked.

'Me? Well, we're wearing the same boots, so it's not that. Sometimes you just have to ignore the pain and your feet will stop attention-seeking.'

He smiled and kicked me up the backside.

But the truth was, I'd found myself slowing down, too. It wasn't blisters, though. Maybe it was the oppressive air and the humidity, or the fact that my mind had been dwelling on the events of the last few days – the horror of San Pedro Sula and the aftermath of the murder we'd stumbled upon. Whatever it was, I'd become sullen and quiet, and I realised, probably terrible company.

'You haven't spoken all day, and that's the best advice you can offer, you bastard?' said Alberto, mocking.

We'd rejoined the main highway that led to the town of Comayagua and it was all uphill. The mountains seemed to get bigger, the further south we got, and it became impossible to avoid the main road altogether, so eventually we had to resign ourselves to trudging up it. It was a shame, because the beauty of the hills was alluring, with their pine-clad furrows and crashing waterfalls. But the fact remained that the rainy season was looming fast and we still had a long way to go, and if we had any chance of making it through the Darién Gap, we had to get a move on.

Each step became a chore as the road wound its way through the hills. The Pan-American Highway was some distance away yet – off to the west, and we would join it in Nicaragua – but nevertheless we were still on a main road, filled with dirty lorries, and the road itself could not have been less inspiring. It cut a great tarmac swathe through the hills, with quarried cliffs on either side and piles of rubbish that had been thrown out of passing cars.

'Why is it that people can't see the fact that dumping a huge bag of baby's nappies at the side of the road is a terrible thing? The selfish bastards.'

Alberto laughed. 'Where else are they going to throw it?'

'Why do they drive all the way out here to throw away diapers? Why can't they throw them out at home?'

'Well for a start, it's not like in England, where you have the council coming round once a week. It's not that developed here.

Secondly, they're probably the diapers of an illegitimate kid, so they don't want people finding out. And thirdly, those things stink like shit, so of course people throw them out.'

'Well, it's still damned selfish, and bad for the environment,' I said, unconvinced.

'Yes, well so is this road. Look, it cuts this national park in half like an orange. Surely that's worse than a few dirty rags? Or what about the cities, all the crap that people build and dump? You know, I agree with you on littering. It doesn't look nice – but poor people don't think like that.'

The real problem, we both agreed, was quite simply a booming population. Only sixty years ago, the population of Central America was fewer than 40 million people. Now it's in the region of 175 million.

'That's a lot of mouths to feed,' I suggested.

'And a lot of diapers,' Alberto nodded. 'And a lot of trees chopped down. To give everyone fuel and food.'

'Well, maybe if people didn't have so many children, then it wouldn't be such a problem,' I said.

Alberto shrugged. 'What can I say? We Latin Americans like to have sex.'

We arrived in Comayagua to discover an entirely different Honduras. Its colonial splendour was akin to Mérida and it had a completely different feel to the 'Americanised' vulgarity of San Pedro Sula. Here there were no chain restaurants or flashy hotels, only cobbled streets and ancient fountains. Like everywhere else in Central America, dodgy wiring hung from the telegraph poles like a tangled spider's web, but that didn't spoil the charm of the place.

The cathedral stood as a proud monument to the Spanish legacy. We took the opportunity to climb up a narrow staircase into the bell tower, where we were treated to a view over the valley. The red-tiled roofs and the pretty little courtyards had an almost Mediterranean feel, especially against the backdrop of the pine-clad mountains in the distance. I was perhaps not as surprised as I should have been, then, to discover another, even more impressive monument to the past, hidden away in the bell tower.

'What is that?' asked Alberto, as we entered a small room with arched windows overlooking the central plaza. There, in the middle of the old room, was a giant glass case. But it was what it contained that was remarkable. There, in the middle of a sixteenth-century church in Central America, sat an enormous brass clock.

It looked like something out of one of Leonardo da Vinci's sketch books. There were wheels and cogs and brackets every-where, all moving in perfect unison. Imagine if you ripped the guts out of a grandfather clock and made them all ten times bigger, so that they could fill an entire room – that's what it looked like. But this was no ordinary clock; this was apparently the oldest clock in the whole of the Americas, and in fact, the second-oldest clock in the world.

'It was built by the Muslims in 1100,' said the church caretaker, a burly man with a pistol holstered on a large belt; not your average warden, but he seemed to know a bit of history. 'It's nine hundred years old! That's older than a lot of the Mayan pyra-mids. It was originally built for the Alhambra in Spain when the Moors ran the place, but when the Spanish retook it, the King gave it to a bishop to celebrate the discovery of the new world, and he brought it here.'

The caretaker showed us the mechanics of the brass dials. 'This is all done with weights, and it links the bell to the clock face.' He led us around the safety barrier so that we could sit in the nave of the window with our legs dangling out of the ledge, three storeys high over the square. From there, holding tight, I looked around at the wall where a big clock face was ticking away, as it had done for all those centuries.

'What do you make of it?' I asked Alberto.

'The clock? It's incredible. I've never seen anything like it,' he said, admiring the awesome handiwork of those old Africans.

'No, I meant the Spanish legacy.' It had occurred to me that I should probably get my guide's insight into the single most unifying culture in the Americas.

We sat outside in the main square, looking back up at the cathedral with its ancient secret hidden inside, and Alberto replied.

'Well, maybe I'm biased. Look at me, I'm white. I'm basically Spanish. Maybe there's some Mayan in there somewhere, but we don't really think like that in Mexico, and probably not across Central America. I'm Mexican and that's all that matters. It just so happens that most of the brown people – the Mayans and the indigenous – are poor. Look, the Spanish came and invaded at a time when everyone was ignorant. There was no technology, and people until then thought the world was flat. They didn't care about Indians in the jungle, they wanted gold and power and, well, they found it here. If they didn't come, somebody else would have. And of course, when you throw religion in there, there's bound to be bloodshed.'

He went on, 'I think the Spanish conquest was inevitable, and to be honest, it wasn't all bad. Look at the beautiful cathedral and that amazing clock. If the conquistadors hadn't found this place, we'd still be living in the jungle and throwing innocent people down into cenotes. I mean, I'm not saying that everything they did was good. Of course not, there was slaughter and entire civilisations were destroyed, but I think that's part of life. Things come and go, places change.'

There was an eruption of music just as darkness fell. The plaza came alive with youngsters and old people alike. Some began to dance under the street lights, others sat and drank coffee in the cafés. A band marched through the streets dressed in red; it was the Honduran national anthem.

'I'd forgotten,' said Alberto, 'it's Independence Day here. When Honduras and other countries became free of Spain.'

It was indeed. Behind the band was a procession of children in all kinds of uniforms and fancy dress and the noise of the brass trumpets was calamitous.

Suddenly there was an ear-cracking explosion right outside the cathedral. Instinctively I ducked for cover. 'What the—' I kept my head low as more bone-shaking explosions erupted around the square. Hundreds of car alarms were going off simultaneously and I could hear the screams of children, but as I emerged from underneath the bench where we'd been sitting, expecting to see carnage, instead I found Alberto doubled over with laughter.

'It's just firecrackers, Lev, don't worry!'

I breathed a sigh of relief. 'That was the biggest bloody firework I've ever heard,' I said, as the ringing continued in my ears.

'You've spent too much time in war zones,' said Alberto, still chuckling.

Two more days brought us to the capital of Honduras, Tegucigalpa. For the most part we walked along the highway, but took shortcuts where we could, on one occasion finding ourselves stuck with a huge dam barring our way. Alberto charmed the security guard, who let us climb over the fence and trespass a while, but we were used to that now, and Alberto was beginning to take it all in his stride. Since my remonstration, he'd stopped complaining about his blisters and we just got on with the task in hand.

We passed a large American airbase, testament to the ongoing influence of the United States across the region, but especially wherever there was a 'fight against drugs'; as well as the state prison, testament to those who were on the receiving end of that fight. We left the pine forests behind and descended into the valley of the city itself, as the smoke from the shanties rose above the afternoon mist. Along the roadside, in the gutter of the pavement, we spotted a handful of empty 9mm pistol cartridges.

'I don't see any target practice around here,' I said to Alberto, as he held them in his hand, letting them clink between his fingers. A drive-by shooting was the likely explanation.

Tegucigalpa unfolded before us, and in every way it was a bigger, grittier, dirtier version of San Pedro Sula. For miles, favelas were stacked high on the hillsides and a glum aura of stricken poverty hung in the air. It was a depressing sight and neither of us wanted to hang around. So we stayed for only a couple of nights, to restock with food and supplies before pushing on, ascending towards the hills of Nicaragua. The last two days in Honduras were through some of the most beautiful scenery we had encountered yet. It is perhaps best described straight from my journal entry:

20/9/16 – Spot the looming mountain range ahead, twenty miles distant. Scenery is dramatic as we walk through a nature reserve of bush. Glad to leave the city behind and be back in the wild. It reminds me of a mix between Africa and Greece. There's every kind of flora; palms and pines, oak and beech. Take a shortcut through the forest up hill. It's hard going and Alberto blowing out, but he's revived somewhat when we get to the town of Aluaca and a pretty local girl proposes to him. He says he's not interested in marriage anymore, and tells her no thanks. He got the wrong end of the stick – she actually said massage, not marriage, but by then it was too late ... Rolling hills, feels like the world is nothing but this; an endless expanse of green. A white stallion bolts down a lane; wildflowers and roses grow in the hedgerows and farmers are sat milking their cows; the people are friendly. I'd almost forgotten about home until now, but it reminds me of England on a summer's day and it's hard not to miss it. Tomorrow, Nicaragua.

14

Escape to Nicaragua

Unlike the entry into Honduras, with its ghost-like border, walking into Nicaragua was a very different matter. A line of trucks tailed back for a solid two miles along the highway and crowds of people clamoured to get their papers stamped. Armed border-police and soldiers patrolled the road, trying to manage the chaos. Getting out of Honduras was the easy bit, getting into Nicaragua was somewhat more of an ordeal.

'Turn the camera off now,' shouted an angry soldier, pointing straight at Alberto. 'Who are you?' he growled.

Before either of us could answer, three or four more turned up and surrounded us in the no man's land before we had even attempted to show our passports. 'Over there. Stand against the wall,' said the boss of the soldiers, before he disappeared off with our passports. He was swarthy and weathered, and looked like he'd killed men with his bare hands. We stood and waited for what seemed like an eternity under the watchful gaze of the armed men.

After about two hours, the boss returned and said something to his soldiers. The men then picked up our bags and emptied them upside down all over the floor. Clothes, water bottles and spare batteries fell onto the concrete veranda outside the office. There was me thinking we'd left the danger zone, but by the attitude of these officials, it seemed nothing could be further from the truth.

'What is this?'

The corporal picked up my satellite phone.

I explained that I had it in case of an emergency in the jungle. 'Which jungle?'

I told him our route and our plans to walk to Colombia. He did not look impressed. They confiscated all our electrical gear, as well as our machetes, before marching us before an official wearing a suit.

'You,' he pointed to me. 'Are you Americano?'

'No, I'm from Great Britain.'

He didn't seem to know much about Great Britain, and couldn't care less.

'You're not CIA then?' he barked, in a final effort of pitiful interrogation.

'Nope, afraid not.'

He squinted at me and waved me away with a dismissive flick of a wrist.

'They're completely paranoid here,' said Alberto, as we hauled our bags back on and trudged off up the road that led towards Ocotal.

I suppose it's not all that surprising, given Nicaragua's history. Ever since Nicaragua became independent from Spain in 1838, the Americans have been involved in one way or another. In the 1850s, a mercenary called William Walker invaded and conquered the entire country for his own glory, then in 1912 they sent the Marines in to keep an eye on things – and ended up occupying Nicaragua for over twenty years. The US carried on supporting one side or another throughout the twentieth century, as politics often descended into civil war. They installed and funded a dicta-tor family called the Somozas, who ruled until 1979, when finally the locals had had enough and the revolutionary Sandinistas kicked them and the Americans out.

I knew that Nicaragua was known as the land of revolutions and rebellion, but I wasn't aware of how deep a legacy it had clearly left.

Because we'd been detained for two hours crossing the border, it was late by the time we arrived in Ocotal. We spent the night in an old guesthouse on the main square. It was a dilapidated, peeling old place, centred around a courtyard, where an old lady sat in a rocking chair throwing things at the lizards that scuttled around. She barely acknowledged our presence as we walked in and asked for a room, simply lobbing a set of keys in our general direction. After the pleasantries of southern Honduras, with its smiling country folk, I felt like this was a return to the reception we'd got in Guatemala. It was an uneasy sleep we had that night.

After two days, we reached Estelí. It was a place I'd been a bit worried about. It was here that the 1979 revolution against the Somoza dictatorship had started, and by all accounts it had been a bloody war.

As we walked into the bustling market town, it was clear that the memory lingered. Murals of masked men with pistols and machetes covered many of the outside walls. Statues of heroic figures with rifles and bandoliers guarded roundabouts and children's playgrounds. They were celebrating the Sandinistas' struggle even now. The black-and-red flag of the FSLN party still fluttered above shops and government buildings. As the home of the revolution, this wasn't a place where the past was laid to rest: it was here, living and breathing. Estelí's main square still had its old church in the middle, but all the other buildings were new.

'Everything was destroyed,' said the voice of an old man sitting in his doorway. He'd been watching us take photographs of the bullet-scarred facades. 'Everything was bombed by Somoza, the bastard.'

The man was in his seventies, with white hair and a purple shirt. His name was Pedro Pablo and he was eager to talk.

'Come and see my house. I want to tell you about the struggle.'

We followed the old man away from the plaza to a quiet little street full of colourful, one-storey houses. I'd always found time to listen to veterans, no matter which country or side they were on. It was a matter of respect.

'This is all new, too,' he pointed at his home as we entered. 'My house was on the same spot, but when the army came, all of this was smashed.'

'Why?' asked Alberto. 'Because you were a communist?'

'Because we were rebels,' Pedro laughed. 'We were fed up of Somoza and his dictatorship. He wanted to keep us poor while he lived like a playboy, paid for by the gringos. It wasn't right, so I felt like I had to fight.'

He didn't look much like a fighter now. He was podgy and frail, but in spite of that, there was no avoiding the glint in his eye.

'I was twenty-six.' He showed us a black-and-white photograph of a man holding a rifle outside in the street. The bearded, scruffy man in the picture looked like Che Guevara in a mid-action pose, as if he was either in the process of getting up or falling over whilst being shot at.

'That was me,' said Pedro, 'in 1976. It was taken by a war reporter and I think they used it in a magazine.' He was clearly proud to have served his cause.

'I was a young man and did as I was told, but I reached the rank of captain before I was shot in the leg and had to demobilise.' Pedro rolled up his trouser leg to show a neat bullet scar that looked like an inverted thumb in his thigh.

'But I lost a lot in the struggle. My house, many of my friends who were killed. And my wife. She died in childbirth with my son when I was away fighting.'

'What about the child?' I asked.

He frowned. 'The church came and took the child. They said he was an orphan and stole him away to take to the United States. It took me a very long time to find him, but he is alive and well. I last saw him eleven years ago.'

Pedro motioned for us to follow him and walk down the street towards a little stone war memorial that had been erected in memory of the Sandinistas who had fallen. 'But if I hadn't been shot, and had my wife not died, then I wouldn't have met the nurse who saved me. I married her in the end, so it's a happy story.' He forced a smile. 'I did my bit. I feel proud to have served and now there is peace and tranquillity, and places for the children to play and have fun.'

I found it hard to imagine that this street had once been the scene of so much killing. It was a theme that plagued Central America's chequered past. But for now, at least, there was calm.

After two months of walking on the byroads and intermediary highways that criss-cross the forests and hills of Central America, we'd finally joined the longest road in the world, the Pan-American Highway.

It stretched out before us in a line that crested hills for as far as we could see to the south, like a giant anaconda surfing the waves of a jungle river. It was a mighty sight to behold, and an even mightier one to imagine. This road (although it isn't, of course, a singular road, but rather many) reaches from the northernmost tip of Alaska, all the way through Canada, the United States and Mexico, then all through Central America to Panama. It begins again in Colombia and spans the whole of South America to the southernmost point in Patagonia. At almost thirty thousand miles long, it has to rank as one of man's great masteries over nature. Almost. There was of course the Darién Gap, which, as we were soon to discover, has a very good reason for having the ultimate victory.

For now, though, we had no choice but to follow the road south along the spine of the country. I mentioned at the beginning that I wasn't a huge fan of straight roads. They're bad for morale if you can see too far ahead. It means you know how far there is left to walk, and sometimes ignorance is bliss.

We plodded on along the highway for an eternity. The flanking hills had a raw beauty in them, but also, something else, more sinister and malevolent perhaps. I couldn't put my finger on it at the time, but there was something quite terrible to the jagged crags and jungle escarpments. The air was still and black clouds hung low above the horizon to the south. Every so often there would be the rumble of distant thunder heralding the coming of the rains.

Alberto walked in silence. His feet were clearly in pain, but he'd chosen to try and ignore it. There was no other choice. We were making twenty miles a day on average, but each day seemed to bring with it more niggles and pain.

I was lucky, I didn't get any blisters, but sometimes merely the weariness of muscles aching was bad enough to make me reconsider my career options.

Both of us had to dig really deep into our reserves of energy and morale to carry on at times, and it wasn't made any easier by the presence of so many roadside memorials. Every few hundred metres there were crosses; memorials to the hundreds killed in car crashes along this perilous road.

Alberto shook his head. 'They drive too fast, or drunk, or just being stupid.'

Entire families had been claimed by this road and all that was left to show for them was a rotting cross and some plastic flowers. It brought back memories of a year ago, when my own car had sped off a cliff and into a jungle ravine in the Himalayas.

We reached the top of a hill, and for the first time for weeks we were able to look down across a flat expanse towards Lake Xolotlan and Managua, which lay some eighty miles distant. The nearby village was called San Isidro. I looked at my map.

'This is it,' I said, trying to muster up some excitement to take Alberto's mind off his blisters.

'What is?'

'We've reached the halfway point. How does that make you feel?'

'Really? You didn't tell me that.'

'I wanted to surprise you. We've done nine hundred miles.'

He played the game and did his best to look chipper.

'Only three more countries left to do. Not far at all.'

He nodded and forced a smile.

As the rain clouds gathered, we descended into the plain towards Puerto Viejo, towards the great lakes of Nicaragua.

That afternoon it rained like I've never witnessed before.

'Run!' shouted Alberto as we darted for cover under a tree at the side of the road. There was nobody else around, clearly they knew best and stayed inside on days like this. We should have taken heed of the clouds, but because we'd been focused so much on reaching the lake, now we were caught in a thunderstorm of epic proportions.

The sky suddenly went as black as night and cracks of lightning whipped across the darkness, exploding on some distant mountains, but they were getting closer to us. The rain slashed down, hacking into the puddles on the road with such a ferocity that it felt like we'd be torn apart by the onslaught if we were to leave the shelter of the tree. Rivers formed in the drainage channels and the gutters overflowed, so that within a minute we were ankle deep in brown water. '*Chinga!* This is fucking miserable,' said Alberto, shivering in the wet.

We had no choice but to make a dash for it and endure the bullet-like raindrops, so on we plodded. If it had been clear, we would have seen what lay ahead, but with the darkness and the rain our only interest lay in getting to the town of Masaya, where we could find shelter for the night.

The next day it was clear and bright. It was almost as if the rain never came, such was the fickleness of the weather around these parts.

'Look at that,' pointed Alberto. In the distance, the cloudless sky revealed a plume of smoke bellowing from a volcano that rose from the plain some five miles away.

'It's one of Nicaragua's most active volcanoes,' I told him. I'd read about Masaya volcano in the guidebooks and had wanted to visit it for as long as I could remember. 'It's known as the mouth of hell,' I said.

Local tribes used to believe that the volcano was home to a lava-spitting devil and would appease it by sacrificing women and children to it. Rumour has it that during the civil war in the 1970s, Somoza, the military dictator, would have rebels thrown from his helicopter into the crater of the volcano. Hellish, indeed.

'It's becoming more and more active,' said Maria, a local woman. 'The government says we shouldn't live here anymore.'

Security for visiting tourists had been stepped up, but in spite of this, locals still lived and worked in this perilous region. As we walked closer to it, I wondered what life was like for those who made their homes in the shadow of such a devilish place. I had bumped into Maria Morales in the street outside her home and we'd got chatting.

The village of Salgado, home to a couple of hundred people, sat right in the lava flow of the volcano. As we peered towards the smoking mountain, puppies frolicked in the mud and Maria's daughters eyed me with shy curiosity. It was a surreal sight to behold.

Grey smoke loomed over the village. 'Aren't you scared to live here?' I asked Maria.

'Well, of course', she said, 'but I don't have the money to buy a piece of land, so we are stuck here. We live here out of necessity. The ground here is not bad for farming, but when the gas comes out of the volcano, it causes problems. It damages our crops and makes the children cough.'

'And do you think it will erupt again?' I asked.

'I think so, yes. There was a big eruption in 2012. We have evacuation drills every so often and the government has warned us that it will erupt again soon, but we cannot leave.'

I glanced at a nervous-looking little girl, who had wrapped herself around Maria's leg. She peered up at us, examining her mother's face and then mine. Around me, her children played, gathering in earnest at the sight of a stranger in such a small settlement that tourists don't visit.

We said goodbye and left the village. It was saddening to think that this family and their fellow villagers lived every day in danger, left with no choice but to live so close to this powerful force of nature, which at any moment could spell their doom. If

Masaya were to have a similar eruption now, molten rock would course down into the villages at speeds of up to 450 mph, destroying everything in its path. In less than a minute, Maria Morales' little village could be totally wiped out.

We carried on south, passing a vast and fertile lava field. It extended three miles into the distance, up towards the peak of the volcano – the remains of an eruption that took place centuries ago. Underneath our feet were the sponge-like black rocks, full of holes in weird and twisted shapes; the result of pockets of gas escaping the solidifying lava. I couldn't help imagining what might have existed here before the burning-hot magma ironed out every rock, tree and settlement in its way.

It was a bleak and humbling reminder that the force of nature in a place like this is not to be messed with.

15

Land of Fire

We set off early from Masaya, heading east towards the old colonial city of Granada. The temperature was steadily rising and with each day it got hotter and more humid. Howler monkeys barked down at us from their shady spots in the trees and I envied their protection from the sun. I've found on these long expeditions that there sometimes comes a point when you grow tired of walking. Until now, I'd enjoyed the comforting routine of putting one foot in front of the other, taking it slowly and observing the world around me. Alberto's company had kept me in good spirits for weeks on end, but when the sun is beating down and the air is thick and sticky, even a sublime view and good chat isn't always distraction enough. Today was one of those days. We'd been searching for something to eat for hours. Alberto had gone quiet and we trudged along in sullen, hungry silence.

At around eleven o'clock, we saw a little stall at the roadside, only a few wooden planks with a rickety tin roof. But the sight of the makeshift restaurant was enough to make us pick up the pace and perk us up a bit.

There was a woman serving up quesadillas.

'It looks different,' he said, 'not like the Mexican ones.'

I had to agree, the contents did look a little mushier than usual. But when you're hungry and don't know when the next meal is coming, it doesn't pay to be fussy. And anyway, whatever it was, it couldn't be worse than bush rat in Uganda or termites in Belize. I'd chowed down far worse.

'What's the meat?' I asked Alberto, out of interest, while the lady slopped it onto the tortilla and grilled it over an open barbecue.

'It's pork,' he said. 'A local delicacy. She says that they make sure to waste none of the pig at all.'

The lady noted my question and with a smile she handed me a plastic bag with what looked like liquid offal and blood.

'It's exactly what it looks like,' she said. 'It's blended pig's head. Bones, cartilage, blood and brains. This is what we put in it.' She laughed. 'Brain quesadilla.'

It would have to do. We wolfed it down, trying to disregard the contents, which can only be described as tasting like a black-pudding paté with a hint of crème fraiche, and then we carried on.

It wasn't long till Granada came into view. We walked into the town, which seemed to have defied the passing of time. Old Spanish-era buildings and cobbled streets made the scene look like something from a period drama. Narrow alleyways led to garden courtyards and wooden street-carts overflowed with handwoven shawls, cashew nuts and pet iguanas.

We walked through the maze of alleyways with their terraced porticos and pink facades. It was a beautiful place and we would have liked to have stayed for a few days, but there was something else that really fascinated me. On the eastern edge of the city, we came to a lake that stretched out as far as the eye could see: Granada sits on the shores of Lake Nicaragua – the largest in Central America. In the distance, in the middle of the lake, a volcano jutted from an island created by ancient eruptions.

Eagles soared above us and waves lapped against the grassy beach.

'You want to go see it?' a voice came from across the road. Two young men introduced themselves as fishermen. 'We have a boat. We can show you the islands and you can meet my family,' said Alex, a stocky lad with the look of an entrepreneur. 'We don't get many visitors and my grandfather would love to meet some gringos.'

I'd wanted to see the famous lake for as long as I could remember.

'It's one of the only places in the world where you get sharks living in freshwater,' he said.

The sharks were the reason I had wished to see it and so we agreed to go on a little day trip. It would be a nice break from the walking for a few hours.

'For years the scientists didn't know how the sharks had got here, and how they ended up being able to live in the freshwater. They thought that they must have got stuck here hundreds and hundreds of years ago. But then they worked out that the sharks had jumped upstream, like salmon, along the San Juan river up the rapids, all the way from the Caribbean Sea,' said Alex, clearly knowing his stuff.

I peered down at the murky water. This made it one of the only places on the planet where there were sharks and crocodiles in the same place. I'd had my fair share of close shaves with oversized reptiles along the banks of the Nile, and even in the rivers of Nepal. As for sharks, well, I think I was subjected to the movie *Jaws* by my grandfather at far too young an age.

'Are you sure it's a good boat?' I said to the eager captain, as we clambered onto the little fibreglass vessel.

We set off and rattled past dozens of islands, the result of a volcanic splurge millions of years ago, which spewed molten lava into the lake creating four hundred islets, some barely a few metres across, and yet others the size of a football pitch.

'Nowadays they're all being bought by rich Nicaraguans from the big cities, and gringos, too. These millionaires come, they go past in their boats, then point at an island they like the look of. Then they build their mansions there,' Alex told us. 'My family have been living here on the lake for hundreds of years, but our way of life is changing now.'

After an hour, Alex's home came into view, an island no more than twenty metres wide with a couple of rough shacks nestled between the palm trees. The whole family was there, his mother and grandmother, his grandfather and brothers, and dozens of children, not to mention several dogs.

'My family have lived here for five generations now, or maybe six, and all the men are fishermen, although sometimes we have to go into the forest on the mainland to fetch fruit.'

'What about the sharks?' I asked, still intrigued. 'Are they dangerous?'

'The best person to talk to is my grandfather,' Alex told me. 'He's ninety.'

He was called for and an old man with leathery skin appeared, looking every inch the fisherman with his bare chest and blue cap. He introduced himself as Simon Canales.

He welcomed us and invited us to eat a lunch of tilapia fish and rice while he told his tales of fishing the waters of the lake. He regaled us with stories of storms and men lost to the waves.

'And what about the sharks? Have you ever heard of one eating someone around here?' I asked him.

'Of course, I'm more than ninety years old now, and have lived here and worked these waters for my whole life so I've seen a lot of things. It's been a long time, I think maybe fifty years, since that happened. Some people were bitten by a shark at Playa Grande. The shark was *this* tall.' Simon motioned to a point on a pillar about a foot above his head.

'So what happened?' I asked him.

He launched into his tale. 'There were two men in the water, swimming. One of them saw the shark, you hear me? One of them saw the shark. He warned his friend, then jumped back into the boat. As soon as he was in the boat, he reached for his friend's hair, to pull him in. But the shark ripped him to pieces, there was only his head left.'

'The sharks aren't the only problem around here,' Simon told me. 'There are many things that are dangerous for my family. I've got fourteen children and forty grandchildren. Can you imagine? It's impossible to keep them all safe all the time. There's crocodiles who hide in the shallow water and I'm always worried when they swim in the lake. And then there are hurricanes, flooding during rainy season, the volcano erupting and also earthquakes.'

Despite the idyllic beauty of Lake Nicaragua, its seemed as if the people were in a constant battle with nature just to survive.

That evening, the boys dropped us off on the shores of an empty beach to the south of Granada where we'd been picked up. In the distance, a volcano churned out dark smoke that merged with the clouds. I looked around and it seemed we had nothing but palm trees for company. It felt as if we'd stepped into the world of Robinson Crusoe. It occurred to me that apart from a couple of tins of beans, we didn't have any food left, so, remembering our training from Aron in the jungles of Belize, we quickly hung our hammocks and set about lighting a fire before going in search of food.

The only fishing to be had was on some rocks at a nearby headland, so we left our gear and picked our way through thorn bushes and rockpools. Just before reaching the place, I slipped on the rocks and bashed up my shin as well as slicing open the soles of my feet on a razor-sharp piece of coral. Alberto ran over.

'Are you OK?' he asked.

I was in agony, as blood poured out into the brine of the rockpool.

'Dammit,' I said, plus a bit more I would imagine. It was the worst place to get an injury. Tomorrow I was going to have to walk on that foot and I could only imagine what might happen if it got infected. I quickly wrapped up the wound with my neck scarf and hobbled after my guide.

We tried to fish and ended up a with pathetic catch of five microscopic tiddlers that wouldn't even make a single meal. But it was late, so we wandered back to the camp site. To make matters worse, we arrived to find an aggressive-looking man in a filthy uniform poking around our camp. I was hungry and needed to dress my leg properly and was in no mood for placating security guards on the make. But as we got closer, I noticed that he was carrying a shotgun and realised that my exhaustion would have to wait – this situation would require patience and some diplomacy.

'What are you doing here, this is a restricted area,' he barked at Alberto and me.

'But the people we spoke to in Granada said that this beach was permitted, that it is not a problem if we camp here, and anyway we'll be gone by tomorrow, you won't even know that we were here,' I reassured him.

But he wasn't giving in.

'No, you will need to pay me a fine so that you can sleep here. Otherwise you leave.' He patted his shotgun and I looked at Alberto. With the sun already setting, it was unlikely that we would be able to find anywhere as good as this, so reluctantly I handed the opportunistic security guard a few of my dollars – pretty sure that they would go straight into his pocket.

After a sleepless night plagued by sandflies, we set off along the coast. I soon realised that although the beach was the easiest route in terms of navigation, we were going to have to cut through the jungle in parts where the rocky headlands became too steep. We followed the jungle trails parallel to the shore, but my foot and my shin were giving me grief and slowing us down considerably. I was trying to keep the sea in sight, but eventually the thick undergrowth scuppered my tactic. I recognised that we were in deep jungle and soon enough I hadn't the faintest idea of which way to go. I was reluctant to tell Alberto that we were lost, but I was slightly starting to panic. If we didn't reach a village by nightfall, we were going to be very hungry indeed.

'Lev, why have you stopped?' Alberto was on to me, and I thought I may as well own up.

'Well, to be honest, I think we are a little bit lost. Let's have a rest and then we'll look for a stream to follow out of here. It's already taken us a few hours to get this far and I don't know how long it will be before we find the shore.'

After a few swigs from our water bottles, we set off again, keeping our eyes peeled for water sources that might be flowing towards the lake. Thankfully, we soon heard a rustling and a little boy appeared from behind a tree.

'*Chico*,' Alberto smiled. The boy was nervous. This was a known drug-trafficking route and he probably thought we were smugglers. But Alberto gave him a friendly handshake and offered him the last of our emergency biscuits. It did the trick and he pointed us the way to get through the jungle and back onto the beach.

Luckily, when we emerged from the trees, I could see that there was a small settlement. This must be San José del Mombacho, I thought, looking at the map. We were saved. Alberto was relieved, but it seemed that for the first time on the journey he was also pretty pissed off. I hoped that it was only the hunger and that he hadn't entirely lost confidence in me.

We carried on south, following the coastline. One day we were having a rest on a beach and filling up on some much-needed food, when a young man approached us.

'You need anything?' He was selling knick-knacks from a board: handmade jewellery, necklaces, sunglasses, keyrings and the like.

As he crouched down next to us, I had a chance to look at the dodgy street vendor. He was covered in tattoos and had a shaven head. I knew at once that it wasn't only trinkets that he was trying to flog.

Normally I would have politely declined and got back to the task in hand, but there was something about him that exuded a sense of positivity and he had a generous, kind smile, with a cheeky glint in his eye. There were no tourists around and he didn't have anyone else to sell his stuff to, so I let him continue with his patter.

'Where are you from?' he asked. We told him, and he immediately started chatting to Alberto in Spanish.

'I used to travel to Mexico all the time,' he said.

'What for?' I asked.

'Work,' he winked.

'What kind of work?' I asked, before getting a sharp look from Alberto.

On second thoughts, I realised I ought to have known better.

'You aren't journalists or police, are you?' he said.

'No, we're just walking, but I am writing a book.'

He breathed a sigh of relief. 'OK, well I'll tell you, but you can't know my real name.'

'Sure,' I said. 'What shall we call you?'

He thought for a moment, then smiled again.

'Tony,' came the response, 'like from *The Sopranos*.'

'Tony' was twenty-six years old and had grown up in the shanty villages around Granada. He told us about his brother and how he got to be a drug dealer.

'It all started when we were both just young boys. Our father committed suicide after our mother found out that he was sleeping with another woman – he shot himself in the heart. We had no money, and we had brothers and sisters who needed to eat, so I started selling marijuana on the beach. I was aged twelve then, I guess. I only did it sometimes, and only when I couldn't get other work. But soon, it wasn't enough money for all of us to live. Someone told me that I should sell cocaine. I would make more money, that guy said. Then by the time I was sixteen, I was taking it to El Salvador and Honduras and even all the way to the Mexican border with the USA.'

'How did you get it across the borders?' I asked him, fascinated by all the smuggling techniques that I'd heard tales of over the years.

'We'd take it on boats mostly. Two hundred and fifty kilograms of cocaine inside bicycle frames, or sometimes in fake medical kits. We had a boss, "El Doctor", and he thought it was funny.'

Tony continued: 'But then I got busted doing a deal in El Salvador and got sent to jail. It didn't last long, though. The wardens were so stupid. One of my guys smuggled in a nail file and every night when the Christians would do their hallelujahs and sing from the Bible, we would saw away at the window bars. Eventually we got completely through the window bars and nine of us got out.'

'So, you've been a free man since then?' Alberto asked him.

Tony shrugged. 'Nah, a few months after we escaped I was caught on the beach in San Juan del Sur – they gave me four years, because I was selling drugs there. It was good money, and it helped send my brothers to school. But unless you pay the police big bribes, they will always get you. But when I was in jail that time, I met my girl and now we have a daughter. My baby is three years old.'

'So, is that what made you change your life?'

'Yeah. Well, not just that. I was released last year and when I got out I found out that my other brother had killed himself, 'cos he didn't have any money. His wife had stopped him from seeing his kid and said he had to pay more to support the child, but he didn't have the money. He shot himself in his heart, just like our dad. So that's when I decided that even if I had a job that paid less money, I would find a job to change my life and keep my family safe. So now I'm trying to stay straight and sell this stuff on the beach instead of drugs.'

Tony pointed out across the water, 'This used to be a big smuggling route for all the crack coming from the south. Not just drugs either. People too. There's thousands of immigrants coming from everywhere that have to come through Costa Rica and Nicaragua in their journey to the USA. I used to help smuggle them, too.'

He shook his head. 'When I think about it now, I feel so sad for those people. They come from Africa and India and Cuba

– all over the world. I guess they just want to pay for their families, too. I would smuggle them in boats across the lake, or put them in trucks and take them to Honduras. They paid good money sometimes.'

'Sometimes?'

'Well, some didn't have any money.'

'So what then? I suppose you didn't help them for free.'

'Of course not. It depended if they were nice or not. If they were nice, we would just take their phones and whatever cash they had.'

'And if they weren't nice?' said Alberto.

Tony sighed. 'Then we'd beat them up and steal everything they had and leave them at the roadside. I didn't want to, but that's what the gangs used to do. Poor people.'

Human trafficking and kidnapping had always been the sort of thing that I'd been horrified to read about in the news, but felt completely disconnected from – unable to imagine the reality of it. But as it turned out, these things were an everyday reality for the people who live throughout Central America. Tony had done some bad things, that's for sure, but he also seemed genuinely remorseful for his actions and I believed him when he said that he'd changed.

'And what will you do with your life now?' I asked him, before we left.

He grinned. 'I'll take my family and try to go to the United States.'

Smuggler, it seemed, would now become smuggled. Let's hope his karma had already been served.

A few days later, we crossed the border into our sixth country, Costa Rica. I was excited to be making progress, in spite of the fact my feet were still painful and Alberto and I were now mainly walking in silence. Costa Rica prides itself on being one of the happiest countries in the world and famously peaceful amid Central American civil struggles. It's so peaceful, in fact, that the nation doesn't even have an army. Perhaps we'd have an easier time of it here? Our route was going to take us off the tourist trail, but our first taster of this lesser-known side of the country came sooner than expected and was a stark reminder of the realities of 'the other migrant crisis' that Tony had warned us of.

Peñas Blancas is home to one of the biggest official migrant camps in Central America. As we passed through, it was home to more than two thousand people trying to reach the USA. They'd been trapped there since the Nicaraguans closed the border eight months ago.

Just outside the village where the main approved facility was, we stumbled upon a makeshift camp where several hundred migrants lived in abject poverty. They were all black Africans, it seemed, although there were some Haitians in there, too.

We met a twenty-two-year-old lad called Nickelson Augustave. 'Call me Nicky, for short,' he said in perfect English. He agreed to give us a tour of the muddy campsite.

'Where are you from?' I asked him.

'Me, I'm from Africa; Brazzaville, in the Congo,' he said.

'How the hell did you get all the way here from over there?' Alberto asked him. 'How many kilometres have you travelled so far?'

'Whoah, I can't count. But I can tell you the countries. I fly to Brazil, then from Brazil I pass to Peru, from Peru I go to Ecuador, from Ecuador I get to Colombia, from Colombia I go to Panama, from Panama I walked to here. It's been three months since I left Africa,' Nicky told us.

We followed him into the camp, where it quickly became clear that the conditions were really bad. Hundreds of cheap tents were pitched haphazardly under a main shelter. There were rags and clothes hanging from poles and people lying around half-naked. Mothers suckled babies, men lay asleep amongst squalid filth, and children were left to fend for themselves. Nicky's friend came with us, another Congolese, watching in suspicious silence as Nicky did all the talking.

'So, why did you leave Africa?' I asked him.

'I left Africa because there was no opportunity in Congo. I used to paint houses back there, but I want to study, I want to study in West Beach, in Miami. Some of my family is still at home, we had to leave them behind. Maybe one day they can come to the US with us. My sister is coming, she is behind me, in Panama.'

'Is it worth it? To get to the United States?' I asked.

'Yes, of course. I mean, it's a serious struggle. We still have more than two thousand miles to go before we will get to America. And then we have to deal with the border police, or with the US asylum people. I have no money left, I had fifteen hundred dollars stolen a few weeks ago. But I don't care, even if I dead, I die, because in my country, it's bad. I cannot live.'

The further into the camp we went, the more obvious it became that it was utterly unfit to support the number of people living there. Thousands had been stranded at Peñas Blancas, some for more than six months. More migrants were arriving daily, stuck at the border, making the camp increasingly overcrowded.

'People find space to sleep where they can,' Nicky told us. Tiny little tents were all pitched side by side, with almost no space to walk between them. It reminded me of some sort of apocalyptic music festival, except here the only music was the cries of babies and abandoned women.

'We have no space, no privacy,' he said. And very few possessions, I noted to myself, as he showed Alberto and me his tent.

In the next-door tent, a baby suckled on a sleeping mother and her children played outside in the dirt. One of them was waving a rusty knife around in the air. Another woman sat with an uncast broken leg sticking out of her tent. Makeshift huts were dotted around the camp, surrounded by ditches filled with putrid water. A stale smell of human faeces and sweat lingered in the air.

The dream at Peñas Blancas was to reach the United States and secure a better, safer future. But the truth was that these people faced overwhelming odds. Nicky was travelling alone, but as we wandered around the camp, it was plain that hundreds were braving this journey with children. Some children were even travelling alone after getting lost from their parents.

'No one is providing any aid for us yet. There is no support from the government, or any NGO yet, and no one is sending food.' Unlike most of the camps I'd been to, there was no security or army to be seen. I knew that organisations like UNICEF were trying to help in other places, but the scale of the crisis was reaching unprecedented levels and there was only so much that they could do.

The only positive thing that I could see was that everybody seemed to be helping each other out with food. We met a man feeding a little girl, who was about three or four years old. I asked if she was his daughter. She wasn't and it turned out that her mother had gone out and although he didn't know her name, he was looking after her as if she was his own.

I knelt to take a picture of her, and she scowled at me, out of shyness and probably nervous about what this strange white man was up to. I quickly turned the camera around to show her a picture of herself. With a little chuckle, her face broke into a huge smile – her beautiful eyes lit up, and I almost cried for the first time in a very long time.

I came outside to find Alberto choked up and silent. Having spent far too much time in migrant and refugee camps around the world, I'd forgotten quite how harrowing it is to see such horrible conditions for the first time.

'Lev, I mean, it's really shocking, what you see on TV is nothing like the reality. You can't feel the smell, you can't see everything. You can't hear every story of the people here. And it's really, really, really tough. I can't imagine how difficult it must be for these people, I can try to understand, but I think it never will be enough, you have to be in their shoes to really see how shitty is this place.'

A small part of me felt guilty for having shaken him up quite so much. But that's the thing with travelling like this. There is good and bad, you can't simply expect to saunter along down hill roads and for everything to be just dandy. For every sublime mountain view, there will be a harsh reality – and some of these experiences were big, and often life-altering firsts for Alberto.

Before we left, I had something that I wanted to ask Nicky. On his route, he must have passed through the Darién Gap.

'How did you get from Colombia into Panama, because it's very difficult there, isn't it? Isn't it just thick jungle?' I asked him.

'Yeah, we walked through the jungle,' he told me. 'It's a very dangerous place. There are bandits along the road who stop you and ask for money. I had my passport stolen, by guys with their faces covered. They held a knife to my throat. Some guys who were ahead of us had everything taken, and when they asked for their money back, they were killed. And you can't trust the police, they are even worse. They treat the migrants like scum and they are bandits themselves. I saw a lot of people dead, a lot of people dying. I seen some death, but I couldn't do nothing.'

It sent a shiver down my spine, thinking not only what these poor people had been through, but selfishly, what lay ahead for us on our own journey.

'Did you ever want to turn back?' I asked him, wondering why he hadn't given up and gone home.

'Nah. We can't go back, only going forward, 'cos if we go back, they're not going to let us past the border.'

'So, now you're stuck?'

'Yes, we stay here to die.'

I was in awe of the courage that it must have taken to embark on a journey like this. Whatever the rights and wrongs of illegal immigration might be – and it must be said that I didn't meet a single migrant fleeing war or persecution, only economic hardship – the desire to better their own circumstances and seek a better life is something that the world can't ignore. I suddenly felt that my self-indulgent mission to walk for the sake of walking paled into insignificance in comparison with the expedition that these people were on – adventurers of an altogether different kind.

16

Chirripó

We left the horrors of Peñas Blancas behind us and set off into Costa Rica walking in silence down the quiet roads. There was an air of despondency – maybe it was the humbling experience of meeting the migrants – many of whom would have walked this same route in the opposite direction, or the reality that we still had a mammoth nine hundred miles left to go.

Everything had taken on a wilder appearance here in the rugged tropical highlands of Costa Rica. The trees were taller and the bush thicker. Our route had also taken us into an altogether different climate. Here the rainy season had arrived in full and we spent day after day trudging along in pouring rain, soaked through to the skin. With the rain came the challenge of keeping morale high. The sides of the roads had turned into slippery quagmires and by night, the continual downpour would hammer down on the feeble roofs of the lodges and houses we slept in, keeping us awake. It was even worse when we were under canvas in the hammocks, with the incessant inundation making sure that we never got properly dry.

We decided that for the first hundred miles we would buy some pack horses to help us with the trek across the country's northern region. It would be good to have these four-legged porters to help us with our bags. Ever since leaving Mexico, I'd harboured a slightly romantic vision of walking across the

Americas with horses, just like the cowboys and conquistadors of old. Mules been a great success in my previous journeys in the Himalayas, too, so I suggested to Alberto that we find somewhere to buy a couple of the beasts.

An old farmer suggested that his neighbour had four horses that he'd be willing to sell for the right price. 'I've never looked after a horse in my life,' said Alberto, dubious about my plan. 'I mean, I've ridden one a few times, which Mexican hasn't? But looking after them is a different matter.'

I bought the lot for an extortionate sum, hoping to be able to sell them for the same price later on.

'How hard can it be?' I said to him.

With four horses we'd be able to give them light loads each and carry extra food and water for the high passes and the jungle valleys ahead, where villages were sparse, and I was confident that with a bit of research on the internet we could look after them between us.

I thought the two smaller animals could be called Stephens and Catherwood, after the explorers who'd inspired me in the Mayan world. As for the big white one, I optimistically named him Pegasus.

'What's yours called, Alberto?'

He pondered for a while.

'Mine is Pancho. It's a male, it has big balls and it's Mexican,' he said with a grin.

We set off south towards San José, and beyond that Costa Rica's highest peak, Cerro Chirripó, with the horses in tow.

But it wasn't long before I realised that perhaps we'd bitten off more than we could chew. Over the course of three days, the horses became slower and more temperamental. They tried to kick us and bite us whenever we got close and the bags kept falling off the saddles, so we'd have to walk alongside constantly shifting and shoving our packs onto their backs. We'd been slowed down to a fraction of the pace we could walk without them and soon they were more of a hindrance than a help.

'We've been sold the worst horses in America,' said Alberto. His patience had been wearing thin since we got lost in Nicaragua and the horses were the final straw.

'Look, admit that this was a bad idea. These are shit horses and if we carry on going this slow then we'll never get home,' he snapped at me. I hadn't seen him lose his rag before. But I was adamant at the time that we could learn.

'Give it a few more days, I'm sure we'll get the hang of it. Come on, have some patience.'

He huffed and stormed off, dragging poor Pancho by the bit.

At about five o'clock on the fourth day, Pancho, who was already moving achingly slowly, lay down. He was refusing to move and it was starting to get dark. The prospect of having to camp on the side of this muddy track, exposed to the elements, wasn't particularly appealing, but try as we might, Pancho wasn't going to budge.

'Right, I guess we might as well start setting up camp here,' I said to Alberto.

As I pulled at the ropes to remove our packs from Pegasus, I heard an engine in the distance. The headlights got closer and soon a 4x4 car had pulled up next to us and a man leaned out of the window. He looked sympathetic enough, if a little puzzled.

'What are you doing out here in the middle of nowhere, are you out of your minds, it'll be dark in ten minutes.'

We told him we were fine. 'Just a bit of trouble with the horses. They don't want to move.'

'I'm not surprised. They're skinny beasts and look like they've never carried anything heavier than a kid. Also, it's not safe here, you're on the main track and anyone could see you and decide that they liked the look of your stuff, all your kit, or you.'

'Well, where are you going? Are there any villages along this road?' I asked him optimistically.

'It's a long way to the nearest village, but I'm a research ranger and work at the biological station a few miles from here. If you're really stuck, I might put you up in our hut or something. Do you want to get in?'

Alberto and I looked at each other. Nothing was more tempting than the idea of speeding along this road, away from the rain, driving to a shelter with a reliable roof. But we had Pancho, Pegasus, Stephens and Catherwood to consider.

'Thanks, mate, but we've got to deal with these horses, so we'll have to do it the slow way.'

He shrugged his shoulders. 'OK. Well, don't camp here. Keep walking and you can't miss the research centre. It's on the right-hand side in just over three miles. You'll see lights and there is a hut, set back from the road. You can stay in the samples shed tonight. Put your bags in the back of my truck and it'll make you faster with the horses.'

So that's what we did, carefully and politely making sure we kept our valuables with us, and thanked him profusely, watching as his taillights disappeared into the darkening night.

We had a few more miles to cover and then we might get some good sleep. Alberto rode ahead of me, chasing the car to make sure the stranger didn't disappear with the bags, and I dragged Pancho through the darkness. The rain pelted down relentlessly for the hour and a half it took to get there. The whole thing was completely surreal – like some horrid nightmare. We finally arrived at the hut in the pitch black. It certainly wasn't much to write home about, but it would do. We put our sleeping sheets on the floor below rows of hanging plastic bags full of mushrooms and plants and weird-looking specimens that were dangling from wires and strings. Under the shelter we made a fire from some dry kindling to boil water, so that we could drink tea and get warm before dozing off to the sound of the pelting rain and the deafening bullfrogs.

Sometime before dawn, my fitful sleep was interrupted by the rumble of thunder and the incessant flashes of lightning. I could hear the horses neighing and snorting, terrified by the storm. Suddenly I heard an almighty crack and the whole sky lit up. It was like being in the middle of an explosion. The lightning must have struck a nearby tree, as I could smell the stench of burning and feel the electricity still in the air. As if my ears weren't ringing enough, the dank atmosphere was filled with the buzzing of mosquitoes whining around my head. It made me nervous about what other bugs and creepies might be crawling around beneath me. I wished I'd not been lazy and had bothered to string up my hammock. What if there were snakes around? What was I thinking? Of course there were snakes around!

I tossed and turned to the sound of Alberto's contented snores, and the endless torrential downpour. I could make out a shadow of some sort, not too far away, of what must be a deer, and then a pair of eyes. Of a jaguar, perhaps? I wished that dawn would come faster, so that we could get going and I wouldn't be at the mercy of Costa Rica's wildlife.

We woke up at first light, but still tired. I resolved to be more patient with the horses; maybe they needed a few days to get used to us and they'd probably had a worse night than us in fairness. The ranger came back and helped us to load them up, securing the bags and fastening the ropes so as to avoid the previous day's struggles. We set off along the muddy track and for half an hour I was feeling vaguely optimistic.

But soon enough Pancho was playing up again. He kicked and snorted and refused to move.

'Walk, you *pelaná*, piece of shit,' Alberto screamed at the animal. He was at his wits' end, and to be fair, so was I. I'd blown an enormous chunk of money, almost two thousand dollars, on these horses and they had reduced us to covering less than ten miles a day.

'Lev, this is a complete joke.' I turned around to see Alberto attempting to feed Pegasus. 'He just won't eat. We have to get rid of them.'

I was beginning to agree. The novelty had worn off after only four days. The animals were refusing to cross rivers, bucking and rearing every time we tried to lead them through water, of which there was increasingly more, the higher we got into the hills.

That night we found a little hotel where we could stay and feed the horses properly and give them some shelter. Perhaps they were just tired? The following day we started to saddle up early, hoping that we could cover some ground. We left the hotel heading south, but we had gone no further than two hundred metres when Catherwood started to have a mega-fit, shying and thundering across the road. He kicked out, trying to hit Stephens, and ended up booting my rather expensive Leica camera in the process. It was the final straw.

'Alberto!' I yelled, 'Get Stephens. Let's take these bloody creatures back.'

I led a whinnying Catherwood back in the direction we had come. As well as having wasted more dollars than I cared to think about, the horses had left us woefully behind schedule. Luckily, the owner of the hotel agreed to buy the beasts. Unluckily for us, we got less than a third of the money back that we'd paid for them, although to be fair, she didn't charge us for lunch.

Costa Rica is home to five per cent of the world's biodiversity. To all intents and purposes, this stretch of our walk should have been paradise on earth. But instead, for days and days, we would start walking just as the heavens opened, trudging past endless banana plantations on the muddy hillsides. No views, no people, and constant pelting rain.

One day we approached Arenal volcano, supposedly one of Costa Rica's most spectacular sights, but we got there to discover a complete white out – there was nothing but fog and clouds to be seen. We were cold, wet and miserable – and pretty tired of walking. The reality of walking in the rainy season had finally caught up with us. Boredom was setting in as well. With nothing to look at, there was little to distract us from the repetitive grim slog of putting one foot in front of the other. It reminded me of my time in the Army slogging across the Brecon Beacons and the thought sent a shiver down my spine.

The fields around us had turned into filthy brown ponds, and raindrops dripped down the back of my neck. The more it rained, the heavier our packs became. What on earth am I doing, I thought to myself. I swore I'd never do a walking expedition again after the Nile and the Himalayas, and yet here I was getting cold, wet and miserable, when I could have been at home with my feet up in front of the fire.

I'd spent so much time away the past three years that people had stopped inviting me to weddings and birthdays. My social life had turned to shit and I couldn't manage to hold down a girlfriend for more than a few months without them realising what they'd let themselves in for. And worse still, I was being thoroughly selfish to my family and loved ones; never committing to anything or anyone, because I knew that I wouldn't be able to confirm that I'd be there for them. It was a depressing thought and the more I walked, the more I wanted to pack it all in and get a normal, nice nine-to-five job.

Mosquitoes became a feature of most nights, and enormous spiders a big part of our days. We'd stay in tiny lodges with limited electricity, which meant that at any point after dusk we could be plunged into darkness. One evening, a venomous coral snake got into the toilet while Alberto was answering the call of nature. Though they're small, their venom is lethal, and sends a powerful poison round your nervous system that paralyses the breathing muscles. If he hadn't been wearing his head torch, he might never have seen the slithering little beast and might have spent his final moments in agony on a public latrine. Luckily, he had a very narrow escape.

The road weaved south and we passed briefly through the capital of San José, where we were able to have a last-minute reprieve before tackling Cerro Chirripó and the southern mountains. After two days of confinement to a hotel, due to the heavy rain and storms, we set off, determined not to let the weather and conditions beat us.

The following morning we met up with Mari, a local young guide. We were heading along a stretch of road that weaved its way south through the cloud forest and then into Chirripó National Park, in order to summit Costa Rica's highest peak. As we ascended, a thick mist was rolling in and the road ahead of us was shrouded in a dense, grey fog. The visibility wasn't more than twenty metres. Mari was one of Costa Rica's new breed of young environmentalists. At just twenty-four and as fit as us, she had already explored much of her own country and seemed like a good choice to get us over the mountains.

'We call this road the road of death,' said Mari. 'It's often like this and the people drive like crazy, so there's a lot of car crashes around here.'

But we hardly needed to be told. As Mari said this, a car hurtled around the corner behind us, as if by divine example. It overtook the truck that was passing us, despite the ludicrously narrow gap. It was as though the driver couldn't see the vertical precipice to the left of him. The roads were slippery and muddy from the continuous storms and rainfall and I could imagine a car skidding on a hairpin bend. I'd had my own close shave with death in the Himalayas when my car had lost its brakes and plunged into the jungle. I did not want a repeat of that. Nor did I want to be squashed by an oncoming lorry appearing out of the mist, so the sooner we got up and over these mountains and away from the main roads, the better.

'It scares me. It worries me a lot,' said Alberto. 'One of these guys in these big trailers, they don't see us and they might just drive on top of us.' Alberto was right. Walking along these roads was one of the most dangerous things that we do on these sorts of expeditions. People worry about snakes and crocodiles and getting shot at, but the most common cause of death and injury is always going to be road-related.

'Let's stop for some food as soon as we can, and get out of the elements. Maybe we can wait for this fog to clear a bit,' I suggested.

We found a roadside café, which reminded me of the truck stops back home. But it did nothing to calm our nerves. We certainly weren't going to get any distraction or respite from the horrors of the road of death here. The walls were covered in photographs of car crashes – hulks of vehicles wasting away in valley floors, trucks that had collided with trees, cars that had spun off the road – everywhere we looked, crumpled metal adorned the walls, contorted and deathly. It was an eerie place. I dreaded to think how many casualties the photos represented.

Alberto looked anxious. 'It's like a scary movie. I really hope that we don't end up a part of it.'

A truck driver came in for a coffee break, and even though we might have been keen to avoid hearing more stories about the road, we asked him to join us out of politeness.

He told us his name was Jair.

'There are so many turns,' he told us, 'and the weather up here means that it gets very slippery.'

'Have you ever seen any accidents up here?' I asked him.

'Plenty. Many. I have seen dead people. People drive very fast in their cars here. They're not conscious of what they're doing. They are trying to get to where they want to reach, but they never get there, because they are driving too fast.'

'So you've never had an accident?'

'I'm very careful. I take a lot of precautions. That's what keeps me alive.'

The mist didn't look like it was about to clear any time soon, so we decided that the best thing to do would be to get off the main road, where there would be less risk of being smashed into by a lorry. A narrow, steep path led us ever upwards in the direction of the country's highest peak.

The next day we finally reached the montane forest of Chirripó National Park. At almost two hundred square miles, the park is one of Costa Rica's biggest, highest and most remote jungles. As a result, it's been protected from development by its sheer inaccessiblity. It is home to miles and miles of trails that weave through more ecological zones than are found in most entire countries.

The ascent through the dense and humid forest was steep and littered with bubbling streams and gushing waterfalls – it reminded me of the Himalayas. Overgrown ferns and tangles of lichen and moss spread onto our path. Crooked, contorted branches jutted out in our way. Above us, oak trees more than thirty metres high towered over the canopy. It was a tough climb, with sections that were a steep scramble up muddy paths. Mari pointed out a poison arrow frog and huge wasps, and green-and-orange bugs that no one could name. The canopy was thick and no breeze permeated the lower layers.

'I have never heard my heart so loud,' I heard Alberto gasp behind me. At an altitude of two and a half thousand metres, there's a hell of a lot less oxygen to breathe, and this was Alberto's first mountain. Howler monkeys seemed to mock us and our gasping breaths from their high lairs. All the while, toucans with their distinctive kaleidoscopic beaks hopped through the trees; wild chickens scuttled ahead of us, and a dopey-looking sloth seemed to grin like a madman at us from the branches. The whole jungle was laughing at our slow, painful climb. A giant red tarantula was enough to remind me of the presence of hidden beasts lurking on the forest floor. 'I bet it's crawling with nasty snakes, too,' said Alberto, keeping firmly away from the en-croaching undergrowth.

The trail forged on. As we climbed higher and passed above three thousand metres, this forest gave way to a bare, windy plateau – a biome known as the Páramo.

'Two people died on the mountain this year,' said Mari.

'Snakes?' I asked.

'No, one had a heart attack and the other died from exposure,' she said.

'I'm not surprised, its fucking freezing up here,' shuddered the Mexican.

'And a few years ago, a scientist came up here on his own to study the wild plants,' she carried on, ignoring Alberto's complaints.

'What happened to him?' I asked.

'We'll never know,' she said. 'He just disappeared. All they found was his camera and a hat. Probably killed by a jaguar and finished off by the wild pigs.'

Finally, after ten hours of some of the hardest walking of the expediton, we reached a little dell, sheltered from the wind. In it, across the valley, was a long building. It was the base-camp lodge where we would spend the night. I looked at my watch, it was four p.m. and behind us the sun was setting below the soup of clouds.

Who knew what tomorrow would bring? Somewhere, just a few miles ahead, hidden by the crags, was the summit of Chirripó. But for now, utterly exhausted, we staggered into the lodge and collapsed into the dormitory.

17

Paradise Found

The alarm buzzed and I shuffled awake in my sleeping bag. It was cold and I just wanted to ignore it. It was 2.55 a.m. Alberto's went off a second later and I knew it was futile. We'd come this far and there was no way we could give up now. A groan came out of Alberto's bed.

'Can I stay here?' he grumbled. 'This isn't a civilised time to wake up.'

'Come on, let's get up.' I said it more to motivate myself than him, as I slipped out of bed and into the cold dark air of the dormitory. A draught whipped through the room from an open window down the corridor and I was quick to get my clothes on. Alberto did the same. For the first time on the journey we needed woolly hats and warm jackets.

Mari was already waiting in the entranceway to the lodge, sipping on hot tea.

'Morning,' she whispered, as if speaking at full volume this early was a taboo.

'Good morning,' we whispered in reply.

We left the lodge and walked out into the pitch of night. There was no moon and yet the sky was ablaze with a billion stars and barely a cloud to disguise them. The Milky Way rose like a vast smudge across the sky, broken only by the jagged silhouette of the black mountains that surrounded us. It reminded me of the cold, clear perfection of the Himalayas.

'We're lucky,' said Alberto. 'It's clear.'

'It'll take two or three hours to get to the summit,' said Mari, 'Just in time for sunrise, as long as there are no problems.'

With Mari staying at the rear, I led with our guides, Ken and Dave, probing the path by torchlight. It was slow going in the darkness. Even with our own torches, each step was perilous as the frosty ground was slippery to walk on, and as we handrailed a cascading river we had to be careful not to slide into the freezing waters.

The path wound through the rough heath, up and down over the glacial moraine and snaking between huge boulders and lonely bushes as it led us up towards a steep ridgeline. The air was thin and cold and with each breath we exhaled a plume of warm steam. Above, a shooting star sliced the heavens in two. It gave me a rare sense of wonder, and it felt for a moment as if we were the only creatures in the world, stepping on this plateau in a land that time forgot. The climb got steeper as we progressed and Alberto started to lag behind.

'Are you OK?' I shouted back into the darkness. For a minute it was quiet, so I stood still, waiting. I looked down and on the trail were the frozen paw prints of a large animal – a wolf or a jaguar, perhaps? We weren't alone after all.

His heavy breathing grew nearer as Alberto's ghostly figure appeared out of the shadows. 'This is the hardest thing I've ever done,' he said, grimacing. I shined my torch in his face and his eyes closed. He was obviously struggling with the ascent.

'Come on, not far to go. Another hour, and look . . .' I pointed towards the distant ridge. In the darkness it was impossible to tell exactly how far away it was, but it couldn't be more than two miles away. 'There it is. Mount Chirripó.'

He tutted and shook his head. 'It's so far away and I can barely breathe. And I'm hungry. Maybe you go ahead and I'll wait for you here,' he said.

'Well, you're probably not the only one who's hungry. Trust me, you don't want to be hanging around here.' I pointed down to the paw prints of the wolf.

'Alright, alright, let's go.' And with that he steamed off ahead.

As we got closer to the peak, the trail became a series of steep, rocky ledges and steps cut out of the mountain, but with each forward step there came a little more light. It was blue to begin with, as the earth tilted slowly towards the sun, but it was heralded by the occasional flash of lightning that cracked across the distant jungles of the south.

'We'll need to be quick,' said Mari. 'The clouds will be coming, I think. We need to get to the top before sunrise.'

So we struggled on, each breath more unforgiving than the last, until we made it to the final rocky climb. By now there was no need for our torches as a glow emerged on the horizon. We were almost there. Another hundred metres away was the invisible summit, and there was just a final scramble over the boulders and crags to get there.

'Come on, mate, I'm proud of you.'

I patted Alberto on the shoulder. I really was. I couldn't believe he'd made it this far, and I wasn't going to let him not make it. With a remarkable grit and determination, he gritted his teeth and grappled his way behind me until the cairn of the summit came into view, and with it a large Costa Rican flag, flapping in the morning wind.

'Let's do this together,' I said. 'Give me your hand.'

He reached out and I hauled him up the last few steps and there we were, standing on the roof of Central America. The sun was glinting above the horizon; it was a miracle, after weeks of non-stop rain, we'd come to the highest point of the journey in the middle of the rainy season, and we'd been rewarded by a clear morning. Standing there on top of the windswept mountain, I think we were both lost for words.

'It's beautiful,' said Alberto, gazing out across the misty valleys. 'It's got to be one of the most spectacular views I've ever seen.'

'Have you ever been this high before?' I asked Alberto.

'Just in an airplane,' he smiled.

As Mari and Ken scrambled up behind us and settled onto a rock, we stood in wonderment while the sky grew redder and the sun rose above the eastern horizon. It lit up the landscape, revealing dozens of previously hidden mountain lakes glistening in the morning sun. Far away to the north, I could see a plume of smoke erupting from a distant volcano and then, as the shadows lifted further, I found the view I had come this far to see.

To the east shone the Caribbean Sea, merging into the sunrise, and with a sweep of a hundred and eighty degrees, I looked behind me and there was the golden panorama of the Pacific; two oceans from one vantage point, separated by one narrow spit of land, and here we were, balanced on its spine.

The rays of sun brought warmth and it felt as though an ordeal was over. We'd conquered Costa Rica's highest mountain and survived this far in the journey, and looking south towards the rolling hills of Panama, it felt like we'd reached a crucial milestone.

'It's all downhill from here,' I smiled at Alberto.

He laughed.

'I'll believe that when I see it,' he said.

Of course, it wasn't likely to be all downhill. But a lot of it would be, and what's more, both of us felt like we had achieved something remarkable in getting this far, and that whatever lay ahead couldn't stop us feeling victorious.

'Six hundred miles to go,' I said, watching as a vulture swept high above.

'Easy,' said Alberto. '*Vamos.*'

'Let's go.'

We descended past the shimmering lakes back down through the Páramo and into the cloud forest below. We had a spring in our step and all our worries seemed to have disappeared. We were going to do this, and dammit, we were going to enjoy it, too.

As we descended, it felt as if the morning sun brought the forest alive. Howler monkeys squealed with excitement as we passed beneath them and a host of flashing toucans danced a merry jig in the branches nearby. It's hard to explain the feeling of delight having climbed a mountain. It is more than victory or achievement, it goes beyond the ego and personal triumph. The real conquest lies in the sheer joy at having seen that view, one that few have witnessed; not because of pride or boastfulness but because, for a brief moment in time, you feel connected to the earth and all that's in it.

We came upon a flat plateau on the way down. We'd taken a different route to the south and so we ventured into an environment unlike anything I'd seen before. We entered a misty highland valley, where the ferns and plants looked oversized and surreal. The grass was long, like the elephant grasses of the

African plains, but this plain was surrounded by tall ancient trees filled with spider monkeys, and I felt like we'd been transported into prehistory. As the dew twinkled in the morning haze and we waded through the still grass, there was something magical in the air, and Alberto felt it, too.

'You know, it's not often I'm blown away by things,' he said. 'But this journey has changed me. For the better, I mean. I've forgotten about all my problems and worries, and you know what, I don't even hold a grudge against my ex-wife anymore. Nothing really matters does it? I mean, who gets to see the things we have seen, or walk in places like this? I feel like we're in Jurassic Park and I wouldn't be surprised if a Tyrannosaurus Rex walked out of that forest. It's all super wonderful,' he said, with his splendid Mexican accent.

'I know what you mean,' I replied. 'I feel very lucky.'

It took four hours to reach the village of San Jerónimo, where we could spend the night in a little lodge and recover.

The next day we walked on to a town called Buenos Aires, where we rejoined the Pan-American Highway, following it along the course of the Rio General, with its beautiful waterfalls and lush, green rainforests.

'Look,' whispered Alberto, pointing up at a tree on the side of the highway.

I looked up, expecting a howler monkey, but instead I was delighted to see up close a sloth, only ten metres away, hugging a branch.

It was much smaller than I expected, like a dog. But its down-turned eyes and permanent smile meant that you couldn't help falling a little bit in love with this shaggy little beast.

Alberto whistled and the animal very slowly came to life, raising its elongated head in the direction of the road, where it surveyed us

with dim, black eyes. Realising there was no threat, the sloth immediately turned the other way and went back to sleep.

The river was brown and powerful after weeks of heavy rain,
but it felt good to follow its course downhill and over the bridges
that spanned its mighty flow.

Everywhere the rainforest exploded in a profusion of colours
and sounds. Crickets bounded through the undergrowth and
strange mushrooms blossomed from the hedgerows, like some
ethereal vision. The beauty of nature revealed itself in Costa
Rica in a way that I could only have imagined. Everywhere we
went, we'd discover wonderful things. Bright-red frogs sheltered
from the sun under delicate roofs of greenery; these were the
poison arrow frogs of legend, the ones that the native Indians
used for their blowpipe darts. I picked one up carefully, remembering that it is only deadly if its poison gets into your bloodstream. It sat quite contentedly on my hand for a while, before
leaping off into a pool of crystal water.

This was the Costa Rica I had read about in magazines, it
came late but it was there in all its glory, even in the rainy season.

We were weary with tired, aching legs, but happy. We picked
our way south towards Guácimo through endless coffee plantations. This was the cash crop of Costa Rica, and the basis of a
cottage industry now so big that entire cultures have grown
around it across the globe. Everywhere were the tall hedgerows
surrounding vast plantations of the little berries in various stages
of growth. Here in the south of the country it was indigenous
Indians that picked it, although now wasn't the season, so there
were none around.

'They come from Panama, mostly,' said Silvio, beckoning us to
drop our bags. Mari had arranged for us to meet one of her
hippy friends, an Italian expatriate who had put down roots in

the highlands. He was good-looking, but wore a tatty, knitted cardigan and had long, matted hair and weathered skin.

'They're good workers and I pay them well,' he carried on, as I took stock of our host for the night.

We'd arrived late at the little eco-lodge that Silvio ran with his wife, a native Indian woman half his age. The house was ramshackle and full of character. 'I built it myself,' said the fifty-year-old, with his piercing green eyes. He was rightfully proud of his little empire in the hills.

'Make yourself comfortable, you can sleep in the *Palapa* next door.'

He showed us into a large, rounded thatched hut with a fireplace in the middle. Outside there was a natural volcanic hot spring. I dipped my hand in the pool of delicious warm water.

'Feel free to take a bath,' he smiled.

After the rigours of the last few days, it was a welcome rest. As night fell and the fireflies came out to dance, and the crickets filled the air with their enchanting song, we were finally able to relax and enjoy a good hot meal, whilst Silvio told us all about his coffee.

'You know, we only use around twenty per cent of the coffee in the West. We throw away the husk and the skin and that's the good stuff.' He handed me a pile of unroasted, sundried beans.

'Here, I use everything, One hundred per cent. And I don't roast it as that kills off the goodness. I just dry it out and grind it up. We call it green coffee. It's like green tea. Very healthy!'

His enthusiasm for the bean was infectious, as he described the health benefits of his magic coffee. 'We make coffee milkshakes, and coffee-flavoured dried banana,' he proceeded to dig out bags full of various types of his coffee-infused products, 'and coffee drops – and even coffee pills.'

He passed me a medicine bottle full of pills of coffee powder.

'I can't say I've ever heard of coffee pills before,' I said, astonished.

'The revolution is coming, my friend. And this is where it starts. These pills will help people to lose weight, have better metabolisms, and give you more energy than any of those energy drinks that people consume, and it's all natural and good for you.'

I was about to try one when he grabbed it from my hand.

'Not now!' he laughed. 'If you have that, you'll be awake all night and you need to sleep. Try it tomorrow.'

He was right. It was time to sleep.

The next day we pushed on through immaculate wooden villages, which looked like they'd been plucked straight out of the Alps. With dainty little Lutheran churches and picket-fences, it was hard to imagine that we were still in Central America. These were the legacy of the German and Swiss immigrants, who came in the early twentieth century to establish the coffee and chocolate industries in a country that was almost uninhabited until the Europeans arrived. At the turn of the twentieth century, there were fewer than three hundred thousand people living in this virgin jungle nation, and most of them were foreigners. The indigenous Indians, for whatever reason, had populated Panama to the south but had barely settled in Costa Rica, where only a handful had maintained a nomadic lifestyle. Most of the country was pristine wilderness, and it was only when Europeans saw the potential for coffee that anyone really bothered with the place.

So for a while we wandered through the hills to the south in a kind of fairytale land, spending nights in eco-lodges, bird watching and drinking some of the finest coffee around. It was a wonderful time and a place we were reluctant to leave. But not far to the south was the Panama border; our penultimate country beckoned.

We left the town of San Vito and walked along an unpaved road towards the border. There wasn't a single car on the road as it stretched out over the hills, and when I checked my map on the phone, it seemed that we might have already crossed into Panama without even knowing it. But after ten kilometres and a couple of hours' walking, it appeared that the map was wrong. It felt strange that there would be a border here, in this remote bit of farmland, but there was an immigration post after all, and when we arrived we were the only ones wanting to cross. There was no fence or even a line, merely a motley collection of concrete buildings, where we had to get stamped out of Costa Rica by a bored-looking man who was far more interested in watching the football on his TV. There were no questions asked, only a brief smile and goodbye.

The Panamanian side was even more disorganised. There was a village hardware shop, where a man selling machetes, hammers and pet parrots also doubled-up as the chap who stamped our passports.

'I think Panama is going to be fun,' said Alberto, as the stamp came down on his passport and the man welcomed us to his country.

We said goodbye to Mari, who had kindly walked with us this far, and she jumped in a car to go back home. I'd entered Costa Rica full of worry and doubt, but leaving it now, we were ready for whatever the Americas could throw at us. The Darién Gap seemed like a mere formality and for now we were simply looking forward to enjoying the mysteries of the jungle beyond.

18

Panama

Mist rolled in over the hills and it was getting late. 'We need to change some money before everything closes,' I suggested to Alberto, as we wandered down the hill into the village of Sereno.

Everything felt different here in Panama.

'Look, the people are all wearing traditional clothes,' said Alberto. 'It's like we've gone back in time.'

It was, too. Well, for the women at least. Where the men were all in scruffy shirts and wellington boots, the women were almost all wearing colourful, flowing dresses in lime-green, orange and purple, with gold tassels in their hair and sparkling jewellery.

'Excuse me.' Alberto stopped a lady to ask where we could change money. She giggled coyly and walked away without answering.

'What's wrong?' I asked.

'I don't know,' he replied. 'Maybe they don't speak Spanish.'

'She speaks Spanish,' came the voice of a man who'd been watching us. 'They're just shy, the women. We don't get many foreigners coming this way. Where are you from?'

We told the man, who looked like a farmer. He was leaning against a wooden shack, picking his nails with a machete. Behind him was a cage full of parrots shuffling around.

'Well, you won't need to change money then. If you've got dollars, that's what we use. We haven't used balboa in decades.'

He laughed. 'This is basically America, you gringos are welcome.'

'But we're not American, I've told you.'

'Ah,' he waved his hand, 'all the same, *mi amigo*. You're welcome. If you need anything, food, or supplies, go find the Chinese, they will sort you out. Don't expect much help from the Panamanians.'

We found a Chinese supermarket around the corner, and it did indeed seem like it was the only place in the village that was open. Actually, no, there were plenty of places open, but finding anywhere that sold what we wanted, or anywhere that appeared to have anyone working, was another matter.

'They're very lazy,' said the elderly Chinese woman who worked on the till. 'That's why we come and set up shop,' she muttered.

We walked to the town of Volcán, revelling in the excitement of being in a new and unfamiliar country. The landscape was every bit as sweeping and grand as that of Costa Rica, but perhaps even more wild. With less agriculture and coffee plantations, the whole upland pine area had a raw, untouched feel, and we arrived in the town of Volcán feeling invigorated. The journey east took us high into the cloud forests of the volcanic uplands of the Fortuna Forest Reserve. We discovered beautiful lagoons, untouched forests, and caves full of bats and creatures that I could scarcely imagine existed.

'Now I understand why you like exploring so much,' said Alberto one day, as we emerged out of a valley and crossed the Cangilones gorge. 'It's the way that no two days are the same. Like a few days ago, I literally thought my heart was going to stop beating when we were climbing up that mountain Chirripó, and yet other days we were walking through jungles that nobody has been in since the cavemen first came this way. And yesterday in that cave with those spiders, shit, they looked like something from outer space.'

We'd found ourselves in a jungle, confronted by a long cavern on the outskirts of a village, when the chief invited us to go and have a look around inside.

'I've lived here all my life,' said Justalino, a round man about my own age, 'and I've still never found the end.'

He'd led the way as we picked a path into the darkness, along a subterranean river that led deep into the mountain. Within fifty metres or so, it was pitch black apart from the narrow shafts of light from our torches. We'd walked in for an hour in almost total silence. As the water got deeper, sometimes we'd had to swim and wade along the river until we reached an underground beach. There, Justalino had pointed to the roof and we'd been treated to one of the most spectacular, and terrifying, sights of our lives. Not more than two metres above our heads was a colony of hundreds of thousands of vampire bats, swinging from their feet.

'Holy shit,' said Alberto, his eyes widening as we both cowered. We'd woken them up and a few started fluttering about. 'Aren't they dangerous?' he said, stunned.

'No,' said Justalino. 'They don't bite often, its usually just cattle, and never in here, they go outside to do that. Watch out for those, though.'

Justalino took great pleasure in pointing out a huge black spider only inches from Alberto's head, dangling on the rocky cave wall. It was as big as a tarantula, but more sinister looking, with long spindly legs and most horrific of all, two enormous pincers at its front instead of legs. It looked more like a scorpion, but without a tail.

He laughed nervously and backed away.

There was suddenly a splash between my legs and I shone my light down to see a school of perfectly blue fish with no eyes swimming around my feet; the result of some freakish cave evolution, which meant that everything that lived in here was completely blind.

We left the cave the same way we came, trusting Justalino's judgement that the cave was indeed endless and led to the centre of the earth. It was one of many incredible encounters that we'd found along the way, and one of the reasons that I maintain a desire to keep exploring, even when it seems the whole world has been explored.

'And now,' Alberto carried on, as we reached the famous gorge, 'here we are faced with yet another death-defying jump into the unknown. But I'm not even scared any more. If you'd told me four months ago that I would have to climb mountains, and hack through jungles, and eat termites and see those fucking spiders, and jump off cliffs into rivers full of crocodiles, I'd have said you must be crazy.'

He grinned and patted me on the back.

'But now, it's totally normal, and we've seen things that most people will never get to see.'

He flung himself into the gorge, jumping three metres into the flowing waters. I followed soon after, bags and boots and all, and let the current take me down to a beach on the other side, where we could get out of the river and carry on walking. It didn't matter that we were wet. Nothing like that mattered any more. If we were cold, so be it, we'd warm up by walking. If we were wet, so be it, we'd dry off in the sun. If we were hungry, that didn't matter either, because sooner or later we'd find food.

I suppose it was all about having faith, letting go of your worries and trusting that things will all work out the way they are supposed to. We were both in good health. In fact, we were both as fit as we'd been in a long time, and there hadn't been any accidents or injuries, and so what more could we ask for? It was time to be grateful for being on the road and take whatever came our way, so that's what we did.

Heading south-east, we left the mountains behind and descended into the rolling countryside of central Panama, where we skirted the Pacific coast for the first time since seeing it from the top of Cerro Chirripó in Costa Rica. Here we joined the Pan-American Highway once again and even though it was one and the same road, it felt good to be on it. Perhaps it was the knowledge that in only a couple of hundred miles we'd reach the comfort of Panama City, and then we'd be on the home straight; or maybe it was simply the fact that we'd broken the back of the expedition and thought, rightly or wrongly, that the hardest part was behind us.

It was the thirtieth of October and we'd spent the morning walking along the highway, which was virtually deserted on account of the fact that it was a Sunday morning. I enjoyed it when it was like this and we had the road to ourselves; it meant that we didn't have to worry about getting flattened by a truck, or dodging drunken drivers. It was a pleasant walk, especially since we were no more than a few miles away from the Pacific Ocean and occasionally we'd be treated to a view of the vast expanse of water in between the hills and palm trees.

We'd become used to starting the day without breakfast now. Often it simply wasn't available, because the Panamanians didn't get up till late, and when they did, it took them at least two hours to knock up a meal; and sometimes we just wanted to start walking early so that we could avoid the heat of the day and get some miles done before lunch. Today was one of those days. But it was almost noon now and we were both very hungry.

'There's nothing on this road at all,' said Alberto.

He was right, there hadn't been a single service station, shop or stall the whole route. The only other human being in sight was a boy standing under the shade of an acacia tree selling crabs.

'Have you got any cooked?' I asked him, salivating at the thought.

'No, just these, they're all alive. Buy one from me.'

I looked at the string of crabs, all tied together writhing their pincers and stalky eyes. I felt sorry for them. 'No thanks.'

'Where can we find some food?' Alberto asked.

'You can try El Nancito, up there,' the boy nodded towards a side road that led up the hill off the main highway.

We thanked the boy and gave him a tip, before following his advice and walking off up to the village of El Nancito. It was a detour of a mile or so, but since we were so hungry, we decided it was worth it.

When we arrived, there was a little shop selling bananas and nuts, so we had to make do with that. It wasn't exactly the most filling meal, but I'd learned to appreciate the power of serendipity. Whilst we only managed to find a meagre meal, what we discovered at El Nancito reminded me yet again about why I loved ground-level exploration.

There, in the middle of the quiet little village, we discovered a field full of giant boulders covered in prehistoric carvings. These were the little-known petroglyphs of Panama. Tucked away behind a rusty wire fence lay one of the wonders of Central America.

'How do we get in?' I said to Alberto.

'Let's climb it,' he suggested.

It didn't sit too well with me, climbing over a fence to get into an archaeological site, but it seemed like there were plenty of holes that we could scuttle through. We asked the man in the shop what he thought.

'Nobody's been here in ages. They sometimes open it if there's any tourists, but there haven't been any all season. Anyway, it's a Sunday so the caretaker isn't around. Just go through one of the holes, that's what we all used to do as kids.'

We left a donation for the caretaker with the shopkeeper, in the vain hope that it would get to its rightful owner, and climbed through the fence.

The boulders seemed out of place, I guess they must have been spewed out of a volcano somewhere in the recesses of the past, but here they were, dozens of them in all shapes and sizes, some balanced precariously on each other like gigantic marbles. One or two had split down the middle and now had trees growing out of the centre. What united them all, though, was the fascinating etchings that had been engraved on their surfaces.

The shapes looked aboriginal in design, mostly abstract shapes of wiggly lines and dots; but some were clear representations of the physical world. There was a cross and an arrow and a sun, and what looked to be a human with his manhood very much on display. These were the markings of the ancient Ngobe tribe. Probably. The thing is, there is no accurate way of ever dating these inscriptions, or translating what they say. There was never an empire or real civilisation in Panama, only the sporadic evidence of hunter-gatherers who liked to draw pictures on rocks.

'How old are they?' asked Alberto.

'Impossible to say. But from what I've read, they're at least two and a half thousand years old. But some people think they might be double that age.'

'There's still a lot we don't know, isn't there?'

'There certainly is.'

It occurred to me that we will never know the full story of pre-Colombian civilisation in the Americas. At least in places like Egypt, the sand kept archaeological ruins fairly intact. But here in the jungle, the rain and the trees meant that nature would always succeed in wiping away all but the most hardy traces of man's existence. Trees, moss, roots and vines have disappeared entire cities in this unforgiving environment, and a world without metal is almost impossible to rediscover. But one thing is for sure, there's plenty more out there somewhere.

We carried on east, following the curvature of Panama past the city of Santiago and the towns of Pocrí and Penonomé. It took almost a week to reach the slopes of El Valle de Antón, but it was a beautiful walk. We'd found the paradise of the postcards at last. Here, on the shores of the Pacific, wandering through the farmlands and rolling hills of Coclé and the central highlands, was a kind of rare magnificence. It didn't matter that the Panamanians were some of the most idle and disinterested folk imaginable, their backyards made up for it. Teak trees lined the country lanes and exquisite stallions roamed the fields. Even the snakes were wondrous. One day, as we were traipsing along the road to Penonomé, a two-metre boa constrictor was slithering across the road. It was clearly wounded, somebody had tried to bash it in for fear of it eating the pet dog, so we picked it up and carried it to a wild bit of forest where we could let it go in peace.

Huge blue butterflies danced around the wildflowers, and bananas grew wild from the hedgerows. As we ambled by, the accompanying soundtrack was one of crashing waterfalls, singing cicadas, and the ringing of cows' bells. It was a scene of man's early happiness, unchanged in centuries. It was Independence Day here, too. Panama got to have an entire month's worth of celebrations since it had its independence from Spain, but also Colombia, which had once ruled the country.

That meant that everywhere we went, we would find girls in long, flowing gypsy dresses, a legacy of the Spanish tradition. There were ladies with fans and castanets and gold jewellery drawn across bare shoulders. There was dancing in the streets and cross-dressers galore, and the boys playing trumpets were all kitted out in their best straw hats and white linen shirts. Despite it being the rainy season, we'd come at a time when the whole country was having a party.

Alberto had long forgotten about his blisters and we were covering a rapid pace. Even the occasional rain did nothing to dampen our spirits, as we began the ascent to El Valle de Antón. This was a place I'd been excited to visit for a long time. We got higher and higher up towards the crest of the mountain – this was the largest inhabited volcano crater in the world.

According to legend, Indians came to live here thousands of years ago, attracted by the magical properties of the warm waters, the abundance of wood, and I imagine, the rather splendid views from the top across the country. Nowadays it's the playground of the Panama millionaires, a country retreat for the wealthy businessmen and their families from Panama City forty miles away. The walk to the top was hard work, but worth it. Looking back from the top of the rim, we could see the glistening Pacific and the jungle-clad shoreline in all its turquoise glory, and then ahead was a perfect ring of pristine rainforest circling this ancient valley. We looked down in wonder.

'There's a town in there?' said Alberto in surprise.

'I know, you can hardly tell,' I said. It looked like a flat expanse of green; only the occasional flash of blue or red from a rooftop, and a few patches of garden and road, gave away the presence of a settlement inside the crater.

We ran down the road for a mile into the heart of the volcano, into the canopy of the forest below. It was like entering the Lost World in the twenty-first century. Beautiful mansions were hidden behind walls of mahogany, and little lanes joined the manicured gardens and bungalows. Everywhere there were brand-new cars and buggies being driven by city folk having fun and celebrating their freedom. Boys cantered along on horses amid the meadows and babbling brooks. The red flowers of the acacia and towering teak trees almost obscured the sky from view, as we walked through this mini-paradise to find a bed for the night.

'I can't believe we've almost made it,' said Alberto. 'We're nearly there and I'm so happy.'

'Me, too, and you know what, thanks for coming along. This journey wouldn't have been the same without you,' I said.

I was genuinely getting a bit emotional about the fact that there were only a few weeks left to push, and I knew I'd have to say goodbye to my old mate. If I'd learnt anything on these journeys, it was that friendships matter. People matter. You can be in hell, but as long as you're with someone you trust and you enjoy their company, then it's bearable, and sometimes even fun. Likewise, you can be in the most beautiful place on earth, but if you don't have anyone to share it with, then it loses its magic. Luckily, I was here in this extraordinary place with a good companion.

We were tantalisingly close to Panama City now; a mere forty miles on the far side of the crater to the east. We left El Valle de Antón content that we'd found somewhere so incredibly special that it would be a place that would stay in our hearts for a long time. The road wound back down the volcano towards Las Lajas where we reconnected with the highway. It took three more days to reach Panama City as we walked towards La Chorrera. The closer we got to the city, the more built-up the road became. After a spell of beautiful clear skies, we thought that perhaps the rainy season had all but passed us by, and we were feeling quite smug about the fact. But then one afternoon, as we started to leave the outskirts of a town, it began to rain so hard that I thought we might get washed away.

'I've never seen rain like it,' said Alberto, 'and that's coming from someone who's been in hurricanes most of his life.'

The motorway vanished in the pounding rain and visibility was suddenly cut down to barely a few metres.

'It's too dangerous to walk along this road in this rain,' I shouted through the noise of the thunder. 'We'll get hit by a lorry. Let's find some shelter.'

I looked around. We were on the edge of an industrial park and the only place with any lights on nearby was the glowing golden arches of a McDonalds restaurant up ahead. It was the first one we'd seen, I think, on the entire journey.

'That'll have to do.'

We ran through the ankle-deep puddles across the road and darted through the revolving door into the dry safety of the fast-food joint. We were drenched through and the cold blast of the air-conditioning sent a shiver down my spine.

'Let's wait and dry off a bit. It shouldn't last too long.'

The restaurant was full of rich Panamanian kids filling up on burgers after a weekend of fun in El Valle de Antón.

'Hallo, guys, where are you from?' The voice was English with a European accent. Dutch, perhaps? I looked around to see two men, travellers, every bit as soaking wet as Alberto and I were.

'Looks like you got caught out, too,' said Alberto to the first man. The pair looked like they were in their late twenties or early thirties. The one who had greeted us was slim and looked like he'd been travelling a while. The other, dark and bearded, wore cycling shorts.

I told him that I was British and Alberto was Mexican.

'Ah, great, we were in Mexico a few months ago,' said Tom, the slimmer one.

I asked them what they were doing.

'I'm hitchhiking to South America and Peter here is cycling. His bike is outside. We're from Belgium.'

'Are you travelling together?' I asked, wondering how that worked.

'No, it's weird we're both from the same place and started at the same time and now we keep bumping into each other along the way, every day or few days we find ourselves in the same place. How strange we all meet in McDonalds like this, eh?'

It was strange indeed.

'You're walking to Colombia?' asked Tom, clearly surprised that we were heading in the same direction.

I couldn't help but enquire about their plans to reach South America. These were the first travellers we'd met on our route that were planning on trying to get to Colombia, and as far as I was aware, nobody had succeeded in crossing by land in years, if not decades.

'Well, we are also trying to cross the Darién Gap,' he said, sounding confident in his plans.

'How are you going to do it?' I asked.

He went quiet for a second and eyed me up and down. 'We don't have a plan. We just thought we'd get to Yaviza and pay the Indians to tell us the way across.'

He was either very clever and keeping his cards close to his chest, or else he was very naïve, if not downright stupid.

'What about you?' he said to me. Alberto kept quiet and gave me a glance.

I didn't want to tell this stranger our route for fear of him getting there first. Not because it was a competition, but because if these two amateurs went and pissed off the army or the Indians, they could screw it up for us. The Darién Gap hadn't been crossed, legally at least, since the 1970s and the last thing I needed was a couple of ill-prepared backpackers messing up my plans. Well, whatever plans I had.

Originally, we'd had a notion of going straight through the middle of the jungle and either crossing the Atrato river to get to Turbo, or else heading south-west towards the Pacific coast at Jurado. But to be honest, it was all up in the air. We'd been granted nominal approval by the Panamanian border force – SENAFRONT – to get through their side of the forest, and a tip-off from the Colombians, who said that we should get through and ask questions later. But really, it all came down to the tribal chief on the day and what mood he was in. The Embera and Kuna Indians were notoriously fickle and suspicious of foreigners, and since we were doing things by the book, my worry was that these Belgians could ruin our chances on a whim.

'Look, mate. We're not sure which route we're taking yet,' I told him the truth. 'But the reality is this. If you go into the Darién, you're going to need SENAFRONT approval and a local guide to get you through. Who are you speaking to?'

Tom looked at Peter and back at me. 'Nobody yet, maybe you can give us your contacts.'

'I can't do that,' I told them.

I began to feel sorry for them. They hadn't got a clue about how serious this border was, and how dangerous the jungle could be for them. I felt like I should at least give them some advice, since I'd been planning this journey for months. There was something else, too. Here I was, almost at the end of a large-scale expedition, having had the privilege of a back-up team in the UK, television support and a pretty decent budget, and yet these lads had done the same thing with no money on a wing and a prayer. I was vaguely jealous of their freedom and sense of confidence, however unfounded.

'What equipment do you have?' I asked, wanting to see how prepared they were.

Peter showed me a tiny backpack. 'This is all I need.'

'What about tents or hammocks? Boots?'

'I don't have anything like that. Maybe I'll pick something up in Panama City,' Tom replied.

'Yes, you might want to do that,' I said, bewildered at what they thought they were letting themselves in for.

'Have you ever been in the jungle?' I asked.

They both shook their heads and smiled. 'We'll be fine.'

And with that, they shook our hands and headed off just as the rain died down.

'Good luck!' I shouted after them.

God knows, they were going to need it. I didn't know if they would ever be seen alive again.

19

Crossing the Panama Canal

On the eighth of November, we turned off the Pan-American Highway at La Chorrera and walked south, with the intention of getting as close to Panama City as we could by the end of the day. All that remained between us and the town was a short fifteen-mile walk and I thought it would be rather more pleasant to follow the Pacific coast rather than walk along the motorway.

'Not one of your shortcuts again?' Alberto rolled his eyes, as we looked down off the embankment of the motorway in the direction of a country lane. 'You always get us lost.'

'That's simply not true. We always have more fun on my shortcuts,' I said.

The leaves were beginning to fall on the deciduous trees that lined the track and there was a distinctly autumnal feel in the air, despite its tropical warmth.

'Come on, then, let's go. If we want to get home for Christmas, we can't hang about.'

When you're on an expedition like this, there are some days when nothing happens. Literally you wake up, walk all day, find a bed and sleep. In fact, I'd probably say that's the case fifty per cent of the entire journey. Often it can be so dull that you don't even find anyone to talk to, and you spend the day lost in your own thoughts. So for the sake of the reader, I've tried to cut out or skip over as much of the humdrum daily grind as possible.

Then again, some days everything would happen at once. Today was a day like that.

For a start, it was election day in the United States. The chatter on the streets was all about Donald Trump and Hillary Clinton and who would be the next president. Alberto joked that all his fence climbing would come in handy, now that a wall to keep the Mexicans out was on the cards.

We made our way to a small fishing village called Puerto Caimito, which stood on the west bank of a wide river estuary that spilled its brown flow out into the sea.

'We can't swim across that,' said Alberto, looking out across the bay. It was almost a mile wide, and even though we were both good swimmers, we had our bags to think about.

'Let's ask one of these fishermen to give us a ride across,' I suggested, watching as the seagulls swooped down in bids to steal the day's catch from the slimy decks of the boats.

A wiry man in a football shirt, with delicate painted fingernails, offered to take us across the river for thirty dollars. It was a rip-off, but there was no other choice at that moment, so we agreed. Alberto loaded his bags on first and gave me a hand clambering onto the little motorboat from the shallows. The journey, which should have taken five minutes, ended up taking almost an hour, as we ran out of petrol halfway across the bay and the prospect of floating out into the shark-infested waters of the Pacific Ocean became a very real possibility. Luckily the wiry fisherman with his painted nails persisted with his efforts to restart the engine solely on fumes, which seemed to do the trick and get us at last floating in the right direction.

On the other side of the river was another small fishing port with a sandy beach and the wrecks of three old boats, now rotting half-submerged in the sand.

'Follow the road along the coast and it will take you to the city,' said the captain nervously, as we jumped out into the knee-deep water. He paddled away rather more slowly than he would have wanted.

Alberto and I walked up the beach and onto a raised road that went off up a hill to the east. On the far side of the road were some buildings with flags hoisted above them. Just as we were walking away, a man emerged from the building and started running after us.

'Stop there!' he shouted.

We stopped and turned around. The security guard was armed with a pistol, but he looked more intrigued than malign.

'Where are you from?' he said frowning. 'Are you Cubans?'

'No, I'm Mexican,' said Alberto. I told him I was British.

'What are you doing jumping off a boat onto that beach? You know this is a private port, don't you?'

We didn't and apologised.

'Are you trying to get to the United States?' he said, confused.

'No, we're going south.'

'Oh, I thought you must be illegal immigrants.'

Alberto laughed. 'No, we're going the other way.'

The guard told us that we'd still have to go through immigration and they'd need to check our passports. So off we went down the road, where a huddle of equally confused immigration officials quizzed us as to our intentions.

They let us go after Alberto worked his usual magic, and soon enough we were back on the track. The guard had suggested we take a shortcut along the beach from Vacamonte to La Playita, which would save us a mile or two. So that's what we did, we scrambled round the rocky headland and found ourselves walking across a wide beach as the tide was out. Cockle- and clam-pickers squatted in splendid isolation as silhouettes against the distant shoreline, searching for a meagre living among the rock pools and sand.

We picked our way, trying to stay dry by hopping from rock to rock. Inland there was a dense mangrove thicket and from experience I knew that it would be flooded and hard to get through. Ahead there was high ground a mile away, where the headland separated us from the next village, but first we had to carry on along the beach. After another few hundred metres, we were confronted by a wide but shallow-looking stream that ran through sand.

'We can walk across that,' said Alberto. 'It's not deep.'

I led the way. We'd made good progress since leaving the port despite our brief detention by the immigration people, and both of us were looking forward to getting to the city, maybe even by that evening, so we picked up the pace. Now we were walking on flat sand where there were no rocks and it was easy going, so I wasn't anticipating what happened next.

Just as we reached the little stream that flowed out of the mangrove and went out to sea, I took a step forward and suddenly found myself plunged into a bog of mud.

'Shit!' I screamed, as I flailed waist-deep in the quagmire.

Alberto, only a few steps behind me but still on dry land, laughed out loud.

'*Chinga!* Is that quicksand?' he said.

I'd crossed swamps and rivers aplenty before, and found myself stuck in the mud on several occasions on most continents, but in all my travels around the world, I'd never fallen foul of proper quicksand before.

'Yes, it bloody is!' I shouted. 'Give me a hand.'

I reached out, but Alberto didn't want to make the same mistake that I did and couldn't quite get to me. I was sinking fast. It was a terrible feeling of utter helplessness. After only a few seconds, I was up to my chest. I couldn't move my legs at all; the sand was so viscous, it was like being stuck in superglue.

Alberto had stopped laughing now and was looking around for a stick, or something to pull me out with.

'Use your bag,' I told him. 'Hurry.'

Alberto took off his rucksack and got down on his knees at the edge of the gloop and held it out with both arms. I was just able to grab a hold of one of the straps as the sand came up to my shoulders. 'Now pull!'

He pulled and I tried to kick as best I could. He did well and after a few minutes he'd managed to get me loose enough so that I could haul myself out and onto dry land.

'That was close,' he said. 'Imagine if I wasn't here and you were alone, you'd be screwed.'

He was right. It was a good reminder why I didn't try and do these journeys on my own.

For a while I lay on the dry sand covered completely in mud, filthy but otherwise happy to be alive and not currently gurgling my last breaths under a tonne of soggy grit.

Sometimes you simply have to take the long way around.

'I told you your shortcuts were a bad idea,' Alberto winked and jogged off before I could clout him around the ear.

After cleaning myself off in the stale water of the mangrove swamp, we made it onto the headland and were treated to a view of indescribable beauty. The hills were covered in long pampas grass in dazzling white tussocks that danced in the after-noon wind. It was like a vision of heaven from the movies and neither of us could manage words, possibly because we were so knackered from traipsing through the swamp, but also we were genuinely moved by the sight of such unbridled natural splendour. From the top of the hill, we could see for miles ahead to the east as the coast stretched out. Inland the Pan-American Highway carved through the forest, and ahead a string of lovely coastal villages heralded that we were close to the city.

I looked at my watch. It was already four o'clock and if my calculations were right, Panama was still too far away to make it tonight, so we would need to find some accommodation soon.

We descended the hill and walked through the village of La Playita. We found a group of men sitting on the veranda of their bungalow, a little wooden house. All the men were black Afro-Caribbeans, like the Garifuna we'd met in Belize and Guatemala, and they wore white singlets with gold chains. They eyed us suspiciously as they were counting large piles of dollars and smoking spliffs. All around the garden there appeared to be dozens of cages. I squinted to see what was inside. They were filled with cockerels.

'They're for fighting,' said Alberto as we walked past, smiling at the men and greeting them politely.

'Cock fighting?' I said, surprised that it was done here.

'Yes, we have it in the little villages in Mexico, too, although it's illegal. Looks like here they do it in the open. Those cocks are worth thousands.'

'I think we banned it in England about two hundred years ago,' I told him.

'Yes, but it is popular across all of Latin America, people become millionaires from it.'

I thought it best that we didn't stay in the village, there were no guest houses anyway. 'Let's do another mile the other side and camp on a deserted stretch of beach,' I suggested.

As the sun got lower in the evening sky and the ocean started to glow a deep red, we found a trail that led through the woods to what looked like an empty bay.

The deeper we got, though, the thicker the undergrowth became, and before we knew it, we were hacking our way through dense forest until to our surprise, we stumbled upon an abandoned building. In fact, it was a whole complex of buildings, all overgrown and lost to the jungle.

'It looks like a hotel,' said Alberto. 'Look at the rooms and the toilet blocks.'

It was as if the apocalypse had already arrived here. Whatever had happened, the place had never been finished. Half-built rooms were now filled with vines, trees grew out of the roof, and animal droppings were scattered across the dirty tiles. A lone shoe sat with mushrooms and moss growing out of it. It was a sneaker of a very 1980s style, perhaps indicating the date when the place was abandoned. Maybe it was destroyed by the Americans when they invaded in 1989, or it was one of the dictator Noriega's investments, lost after he was ousted. Either way, we had no choice but to make use of it for the night as the sun set.

'We'll put up our hammocks on those trees,' I said, pointing to a thicket next to the ruined bar by the beach. So we did. As the dusk turned to complete darkness, we set up camp on the cliff, listening to the sound of the waves crashing on the rocks below. I imagined what a wonderful place this would have been if it had been finished. The only inhabitants now, though, were the lizards and tarantulas.

'Goodnight, *muñeco*,' said Alberto, zipping up. As we got into our nets, I gave the scene a final sweep with my headtorch. All around were the sparkling eyes of hundreds of spiders, big, hairy ones, reflecting in the glint.

'Goodnight, mate,' I said, thinking it was best to keep that to myself.

The next morning, we woke at dawn to the lapping rhythm of the Pacific on the beach below. Out to sea a steady stream of ships were silhouetted against the crimson horizon. It was beautiful. I looked at my phone and it was six a.m. If we were lucky, we could decamp and head back to the road, then cross the canal before lunchtime and eat a good meal in the city, so we wasted no time in packing up. Just as I was planning the movements, I got a news-flash pop-up. Donald Trump had won the US election.

'No way,' said Alberto. 'OK, now I'm not going home,' he joked. 'Mexico will be too full. I think I'll stay in Panama.'

An hour and a half later, we reached the crossing point over the Panama Canal. Ahead lay the grand metal beams of the *Puente de las Americas*, a vast bridge spanning the famous canal and also the gateway to Panama City, which lay like a beacon of incongruous modernity on the far side of the bay.

'It's huge. I never imagined it to be so big,' said Alberto, as we stepped onto the 'Bridge of the Americas', dodging cars and trucks that rumbled over the sixty-metre-high conduit.

It is exactly a mile long and we were the only pedestrians; no one else was daft enough to risk the perilous walkway that ran along the edge of the speeding traffic. The only other people not contained in their cars were the workmen; engineers and labourers, dangling from ropes high above with welding gear and face masks; working on the incessant repairs that are needed to keep this feat of engineering alive.

But the real masterpiece wasn't the bridge, of course, it was what it spanned. Looking down into the distant waters, we were reminded that we were in the presence of something very special.

The Panama Canal must be considered one of the modern wonders of the world. It was started back in 1881 and at a cost of almost twenty-eight thousand lives was eventually finished in 1914. Every day an average of forty container ships pass through, generating billions of dollars in revenue for the country. It used to be owned by the United States, who extended an exclusion zone along the canal to keep the locals out and the money flowing back to America, but after a long and painful process, the canal was finally handed back to the Panamanian government twenty-seven years ago.

To the right, on the far side of the road, extended the Pacific and a long line of ships, waiting to enter the canal on their voyage to the Caribbean. I could just make out the headland where we'd camped by the ruined hotel the night before. To the left, down below, were the dockyards and refuelling stations and customs ports that serviced the fourteen thousand ships a year that transited the canal. There were vast yards filled with shipping containers, stacked ten-high in all colours from every country in the world. There were ships moored from China, the Philippines and Norway; surrounding them were the yellow cranes that picked them up and dropped them down. From up here, they reminded me of those machines at amusement parks that grapple teddy bears and drop them down a chute if you win.

Beyond the industrial littoral zone, the canal stretched out to the north; it became narrower and ultimately disappeared as it rounded the bends in the valley, where jungle-clad hills were a reminder that this man-made miracle was still beholden to the forces of nature.

'Look down there,' said Alberto, with a spring in his step. He pointed to the east, where the suburbs of the city sprang from the coastline. 'It doesn't look real.'

In the distance, I saw the glittering skyscrapers and flyovers of a very modern, confident metropolis, quite unlike anything we'd seen thus far on the expedition.

It took another hour to leave the bridge and follow the highway. It was still the Pan-American – the same road we'd been following for weeks, but here it struck like a knife straight through the centre of the town. Fringed with palm trees and flanked on the one side by the corniche of the Pacific and on the other by a great wave of plush hotels, fancy restaurants, and boutique shops selling designer watches and Ferraris, it was hard to imagine that only a few hours before we were pulling each other out of quicksand and hacking through tarantula-infested jungles. It was as if we'd suddenly been teleported into Miami.

Before long the road had taken us into the middle of the city and we were surrounded by billboards, busy streets full of busy people, and flash cars whizzing past. 'I feel quite claustrophobic now,' said Alberto. I could sympathise. 'Well, we may as well make the most of it,' I said. 'After this we're back into the jungle and there's the Darién Gap, let's enjoy ourselves for a few days.'

And so we did. We checked into the most expensive hotel we could afford; a sixty-storey glass monstrosity overlooking the promenade, with a pool deck and a Jacuzzi spa and a rooftop bar that sold overpriced margaritas and rum cocktails with little umbrellas in them. There was a sushi bar and a breakfast buffet and a shopping mall. It felt indulgent and initially quite uncomfortable, after seeing all that poverty and injustice along the way. But does punishing oneself achieve anything? Sometimes, perhaps, but we'd reached a milestone in the journey and from here on in we were on the homeward leg. It felt like we were allowed a little luxury after the rigours of the road, so for three days we rested up and ate good food and restocked our supplies of medicines, batteries and other bits that had disappeared or fallen apart along the way.

We'd been walking for almost four months now and I'd almost forgotten what time of year it was. The tropics have that effect, but when you suddenly get sucked into a city, there's no avoiding those little indicators that remind you of another reality and another life, away from the road. People walking hand in hand with their partners; friends having fun in pubs and bars; families enjoying time together in the parks and shopping malls. The stores all had their Christmas decorations up and though it was incongruous to see inflatable Santa Clauses and twinkling Christmas trees next to the palm-fringed swimming pools, there was no denying that we were both thinking of home.

Before we carried on, there was one thing left to do. By pulling some strings and making flagrant use of contacts, I managed to blag us a ride on a helicopter. Ostensibly this was to get us a good view of the city from above and obtain some nice aerial footage for the documentary, but there was another reason, too. I wanted to see what lay ahead.

As we got into the little AS350 helicopter and buckled up, the pilot giving us the thumbs-up as the rotary blades started and we wobbled into the air, I kept my eyes on the horizon to the south-east. The chopper rose higher and higher, making its way over the canal where the ships looked like little toys, and then in a grand circle over the ocean back towards the old colonial town with its ancient fortress and iron cannons, then high above the skyscrapers and there, beyond the shanties and favelas, I saw the highway disappear into the distance as the jungle extended for as far as the eye could see into Darién province.

Somewhere out there was the end of the road, the Darién Gap, and, beyond that, the gateway to South America.

20

The End of the Road

We left Panama City and the Pacific behind, following the Pan-American Highway east and inland. We were feeling rejuvenated and fit after a rest and we were starting to cover distance quickly. Thoughts of home and Christmas spurred us on, as did the prospect of succeeding in our mission and making it to Colombia. At first the road carved its way through the agricultural plains and gritty villages of Pacora and Chepo, before winding through the valley of Lake Bayano, where the fringes of the jungle began to get thicker and more wild. The further east we got, averaging twenty-five miles a day, the quieter the road became.

'There's nothing beyond Yaviza,' I said to Alberto, but it was more to remind myself of where we were going. 'Nowhere for the trucks to go.'

The road gradually deteriorated until the prevalence of potholes and the deep mud meant that only the sturdiest 4x4s could cope with the terrain, and often we would not see cars for hours on end. By the time we got to Avicar one day, after relentless rain and silent walking, the reality dawned on us that we weren't out of trouble yet.

Occasionally we'd stumble through military checkpoints, where soldiers in olive-green uniforms and camouflage webbing would stop and take our details. We'd already been warned that when we arrived in Santa Fé or Yaviza, we'd have to report to the SENAFRONT headquarters, but for now we told the soldiers that we were walking as far as Yaviza. Mentioning the Darién Gap at this stage would probably end up with us getting detained at every roadblock.

The jungle closed in on either side of the road. I wondered what might have happened to the Belgian backpackers, Tom and Peter. They were a week ahead of us and by my reckoning they must be well into the Darién Gap by now. I wondered if by some miracle they'd already made it to Colombia, or if maybe something terrible had happened. I had visions of stumbling over their corpses somewhere in the jungle. Perhaps they'd got lost or been bitten by a snake, or swept away in a flash flood, speared to death by the Indians, or shot by the rebels.

'We can't dwell on that,' said Alberto. 'They're grown men, and it is big boys' rules out here. You tried to tell them that it was a foolish thing to do, but they didn't listen.'

We slept in little guesthouses when there were villages, but with each passing day they grew further and further apart. For hours at a time our only company were the howler monkeys that growled like dogs from the canopy surrounding us, and the watchful vultures that soared high above, waiting patiently for a car to come and squash a lizard, or run over a feral dog. Ten miles south-east of Avicar, we crossed the unmarked border into Darién province.

We'd finally made it to our last hurdle. The town of Santa Fé rose off the highway to the right-hand side. It was only a large village really, full of ramshackle bungalows and a few shops clustered around a main community park. As we walked along the main street, I noticed an old soldier waving frantically in our direction.

We stopped and smiled.

'What's up?' said Alberto. The soldier, a tiny man in his late fifties, mouthed something incomprehensible. I thought he might be drunk, so I merely shrugged my shoulders. He put his hand against the side of his head and mumbled something and pointed to a nearby building.

'I think he's deaf and dumb,' said Alberto.

'Show us where you want us to go,' I said in Spanish, feeling embarrassed.

We followed the old man to an army barracks, where the insignia of SENAFRONT was plastered across a concrete wall. Behind a barbed-wire fence was a reception room filled with soldiers armed to the teeth. Sat on the bench were a group of young men in dirty civilian clothes. They looked nervous and were sat in total silence. I assumed they must have been new recruits or local criminals. Either way, they didn't look like they wanted to be in there.

'Where are you going?' asked a burly sergeant to me and Alberto.

I told him we were going to Yaviza.

'You must the ones wanting to cross the Darién Gap?'

Damn, I thought. Those bloody Belgians had spread the word.

'We've heard about you,' he said knowingly. 'Everyone has.'

It was futile to lie.

'Yes, we're trying to get to Colombia,' said Alberto.

'I know. You've been summoned to the headquarters in Meteti tomorrow. Make sure you're there for six p.m., Colonel Carrion wants to meet you.'

Meteti was twenty miles away to the south, and where we were supposed to be arriving tomorrow anyway, so logistically it wasn't a problem. It seemed we had been on their radar for a while and I suspected that SENAFRONT might have their own ideas about our journey.

'Of course,' I said.

While we waited for the sergeant to photocopy our passports and documents, I sat down next to a boy on the wooden bench.

'*De donde eres?*' I asked. 'Where are you from?'

He didn't look me in the eye. He looked scared.

'He doesn't speak Spanish,' said the sergeant.

'Where is he from then?' I asked.

'Nepal,' he said. 'He's the only one with a passport. The others,' he motioned to a group of other lads in their twenties, who were stood by the wall, 'don't even have identification, but I think they're Indians or Bangladeshis.'

'Illegal immigrants,' said Alberto. 'They come the same way the Congolese did, through Brazil and Ecuador.'

Poor lads, I thought, they'd made it this far only to be arrested. I tried to be friendly and said a few words of Nepali to the lad, and even showed him some photos on my phone of the Himalayas, but he was too terrified to respond and sat staring at the floor.

'What happens to them?' I asked.

'We send them to a camp in Panama City, where they get processed.'

'And then what?'

The sergeant winked. 'They are usually just let go, and sent to the Costa Rican border. We don't want them here and we don't want to pay to deport them, so we let them carry on towards the USA.'

The next day we walked to Meteti, another meagre little town, but at least there was a small hotel and a Chinese super-market where we could stock up with final supplies. We'd been told to go to the military headquarters, which lay on the edge of the town, so that's what we did.

It was already dark when we were met at the gate by two officers. One was a shifty-looking man in civilian clothing who didn't seem to want to look anyone in the eye and was constantly checking his phone. The other, a well-built, smart man in uniform, was Colonel Carrion. He was smiling and polite.

'Gentlemen, follow me.'

Alberto and I walked behind the two men past the rows of barbed-wire fences and around the side of the main barracks, where young soldiers were washing their boots in the outside ablutions. They jumped to attention when we walked past.

'I am Comisionado Carrion and this is Major Fernandez, head of intelligence for the special forces,' said the colonel as we walked. The major said nothing.

'This is the headquarters for SENAFRONT special forces group in the Darién province. We are very interested in your journey.'

Alberto and I looked at each other.

'Come, this way.' He led us into a room. It seemed to be an operations centre. The walls were covered in maps and aerial photographs. In the middle was a table and on it was a large model of the barracks with stick-in pins indicating the locations of ammunition supplies, weapons and vehicles, as well as defensive points and escape routes.

'We were informed of your expedition by the Brigadier in Panama City. It seems you are well known for your walking,' said the colonel with a smile.

Before I could reply, he carried on.

'My sources also tell me you are an army officer, no? A Paratrooper.'

I nodded.

'Well then, in the spirit of brotherhood we shall do all we can to help.' He flashed a grin and pointed to his paratrooper's wings sewn onto his camouflage shirt.

I had half been expecting him to tell us that we weren't going to be allowed to venture into the Darién Gap, but it seemed he was just curious.

'Normally we don't let anyone go across into Colombia by land. It's too dangerous and we don't want people getting killed on our territory. But it seems you have done your homework and made it this far, so we will do what we can to assist your mission.'

I felt a wave of relief fill my body. Alberto smiled.

He pointed to the map. It was the most detailed map of the region I had seen and far better than anything we'd been able to look at before now, even with months of planning.

'Which route do you want to take?' he asked.

'Well, we'd like to get to Colombia, either straight down the middle to the Atrato River and beyond, or else following the Rio Balsas to the west and try to get to Jurado on the coast.'

The colonel laughed out loud.

'Look here,' he pointed to the Rio Balsas. 'All this area is full of ELN rebels on the Colombian side. Our troops are fighting them every week. Also, this is the most remote part of the Darién, it'll take you weeks. The Colombians don't have any military there, so it's totally lawless.'

I nodded. I knew that already.

'And here,' he carried on and pointed to the central route which led to the Atrato. 'It's one big swamp. You'd have to go by boat, there's no way of walking through that. In any case, we can't let you go that way at the moment, as it's the main drug-smuggling route and since the FARC ceasefire the whole area has been taken over by the cartels and criminal gangs. They don't take prisoners.'

Alberto nodded.

'At least with FARC you can do business. They have stopped killing foreigners since they've tried to become legitimate, but the gangs don't want anyone walking through their turf. They've got nothing to gain and everything to lose. As far as they are concerned, they want the Darién Gap to stay as off-limits as possible.'

It looked like our options were running out.

'Well, I can see only two options. You can just take a boat around the coast like everybody else ...' then he smiled, 'but I think you don't want to do that, no?'

'No,' I said.

'In that case the only way to go is east, up the Rio Membrillo to Canaan and over the mountains to Puerto Escocés and Carreto. From there you can follow the coast to La Miel and cross into Colombia at Sapzurro.'

I studied the map. It felt like a cheat. We wouldn't be crossing the main portion of the Gap, or even following in the footsteps of John Blashford-Snell.

The colonel sensed my disappointment and chuckled.

'What's wrong? Not hard enough for you?'

'Well, it's not the route I was planning, that's all.'

'Don't worry, you'll get plenty of excitement. It's still the Darién Gap, but it's the shortest way through. Nobody has been allowed to do this legally as far as anyone can remember. It's off-limits to most people, but you still might find illegals – it's the way that immigrants try and sneak in, the ones that can't afford to get a boat. So you'll need to be careful.'

'Also, isn't Puerto Escocés the place you were telling me about, where the Scottish made their settlement all those years ago?' said Alberto.

He was right, of course. I'd almost forgotten about the Scottish Darién scheme, but now we'd been presented with the perfect opportunity to see the place that created the United Kingdom first-hand.

It was serendipity, and if there's one thing I'd learnt on expeditions, it was to embrace change and go with the flow.

'OK, we'll go that way,' I said.

'I hope you know what you're letting yourself in for,' said the colonel.

'What will be our main challenges, do you think?' said Alberto.

The colonel shook his head. 'Just stay away if you see any gangs of people. The smugglers – the Coyotes – can sometimes be armed. I think you already know the other main dangers. Wild boars, spiders, snakes, there's plenty of those. Flash flooding can happen quickly, so don't camp on river beaches. Make sure you carry enough food and water, of course. Get some Indian porters from Canaan to help you carry stuff. They will know the way, but you should remember this . . .'

He paused for effect and glanced at the intelligence major.

'Never trust the Indians.'

Major Fernandez nodded solemnly.

'I'll let the outpost at Canaan know you're coming so that they don't arrest you,' said Carrion. 'We already captured two gringos the other day trying to cross into Colombia illegally.'

It couldn't be, could it? I thought of the two backpackers, Tom and Peter.

'They weren't Belgians, were they?' I asked. 'What happened to them?'

'Yes, something like that. Europeans. One of them was trying to take a bicycle through the jungle,' he chuckled. 'But my men captured them, because they didn't ask for permission or have an exit stamp.'

'And?'

The colonel shrugged his shoulders. 'So they put them in prison for a few days and now we're deporting them, of course.'

Poor buggers, I thought, after getting so close. But at least they weren't dead.

Colonel Carrion stared at me and then at Alberto. 'Whichever way you go, there will be dangers and risks. I will let you continue, but we are not responsible for you or your safety. Do you understand? Crossing the Darién,' he said slowly and deliberately, 'is a suicide wish.'

He patted me on the shoulder. It was time to leave.

The next day we walked south, bound for Yaviza and the end of the road. With the colonel's words ringing in my ears, we trudged on in silence as the road became narrower and more decrepit. There were almost no cars at all now and on both sides a wall of thick, dark jungle rose up like an impenetrable green barrage of vegetation. For two days the stillness was unnerving. In the heat of the day even the crickets seemed to quieten down, and the only movement was the occasional rustle of the grass, as a lizard would scuttle away into the undergrowth.

We reached the outskirts of Yaviza at noon on the seventeenth of November. I remembered that John Blashford-Snell had described the place to me back at the RGS as little more than a clearing in the jungle. That was 1971. It appeared times had changed a little. The road was still paved in parts and a lot of land had been deforested to make way for fields and banana plantations. A few of the outlying huts were still of the traditional kind, with thatched roofs and wooden stilts, but in the centre of the town modernity had arrived. Most of the buildings were low-level, breeze-block bungalows, with bars on the windows. Almost every house had a satellite dish, and radios and TVs blared music. There were a few grimy snooker bars, cantinas, and hotels that looked more like brothels. Everyone, it seemed, was drunk. Some things, at least, hadn't changed.

'Look at him,' said Alberto, pointing to a man being pushed along in a wheelbarrow. '*Boracho!*' he said, totally drunk. Almost all the inhabitants were black. Most of them were Colombians from the coast, who'd come to Panama in search of dollars and work and forgotten to go home.

'We've got a nice life here,' said Alfredo, a wrinkly old man with enormous lips and wiry grey hair. 'I came forty years ago chasing after a woman and decided to stay. It's better here than in Colombia. I hear it's safe over there now, but back then too many drugs. Too dangerous, man.'

'How did you get here?' I asked, wondering which route he'd taken across the Darién.

'Ha, ha,' he laughed out loud. 'I came by boat. I ain't stupid. I've lived here since the 1970s and never even been in the jungle. No sir, I stay at home and drink, that's all I need.'

We left the old man to his beer and carried on towards the river. The road just stopped. Literally it hit a wall, on the far side of which was a little hill covered in gravestones. It was the town cemetery and an ominous sign.

Speaking of which. There, where the tarmac finished, was an

actual sign, just below the cemetery wall. It read: *Bienvenidos Yaviza. 12,580km to Alaska.*

I looked back the way we came. I couldn't quite believe it. We'd been following the course of the Pan-American Highway since Nicaragua and barely walked a fraction of this, the longest road in the world. But I felt we'd done enough.

'This is where it ends,' said Alberto.

'Or where it starts,' I said, 'depending on your point of view.'

We walked along a muddy path to the left of the cemetery, which led to the main street where the river port was. A couple of hundred metres away was a hanging bridge spanning the Yaviza river, and local Indians were walking across from the little village on the far side carrying stacks of fruit on their heads. Down some steps was a little jetty where dugout canoes were being loaded with boxes and bales. Oranges, bananas and bags of rice were coming and going. The Indians did the work and the blacks shouted at them. Otherwise people sat around and smoked and drank. Nobody was in any hurry to do anything here.

Further along the river bank we came across the ruins of the old Spanish fort, which Blashers had told me to go and inspect. 'Go and see if it's there, old boy, let me know what state it's in,' I remembered him saying.

There wasn't much left at all. The sign had faded into obscurity and the perimeter fence was all but torn down. The old bricks were cracked and weathered and plants were sprouting from between the holes. The river had encroached on the spoil underneath and pulled down most of what would have been there. Now there were just two walls, crumbling and sad, marking the last visible remains of the old civilisation. Nature had won out here and the locals didn't even know what it was, and they cared even less.

I looked out over the brown waters as they swirled into frothy eddies. The sky was dark and brooding and the water was high. It was already raining somewhere upstream and the jungle on the far banks looked dark and menacing. This was the start of the Darién Gap, the nemesis of overland exploration, and our final battle.

21

The Last Jungle

We travelled back north to Puerto Limon, a little village strad-
dling the Rio Membrillo at the point where the river flowed
out of the wild mountains and into the lowland plantations. It
was where we'd agreed to meet the boatmen who would take us
upriver to Canaan, where we'd find our porters and begin walking through the Darién.

'Be careful with that,' said Segundo, an enormous man with
hands like spades. He looked like a bouncer with his crew-cut
hair and wide shoulders. A long machete as big as a sword swung
off a leather belt. The Indian boatmen did as they were told.

'That is fragile stuff. The gringo has cameras and things that
will break, do you understand?' He adopted the tone of a
concerned father, rather than one of anger. 'They are like my
children,' said the giant, grabbing one by his arm gently and
patting him on his head. Segundo was to be our chief liaison
man. He was of mestizo stock – mixed-race African, indigenous
and Spanish – but spoke some of the Indian languages and knew
the jungle like the back of his hand. Once, for fun, he had run
across Panama from coast to coast. He'd been recommended to
guide us, at least as far as the Indian settlement at Canaan, by
Rick Morales, the only man in the know in the whole of Panama
when it came to expeditions, so that was endorsement enough
for us.

As Segundo supervised the loading of the boats, I made a mental note of our equipment and supplies. Enough rations for seven days for fifteen people. Who knows how many Indians we'd need to take? Blashers took sixty, so I hope we can get away with that. Water filtration system and emergency purification tablets. Snake gaiters? Yes, I supposed, just in case. Satellite phone, check; hammocks, yes; lots of mosquito repellent; first-aid kit and a stretcher, essential. It was all there in the waterproof grip bags laid out in the narrow tree trunk that passed itself off as a dugout canoe. The indigenous Indians grinned that they'd got it all in without anything falling off into the water.

'Are you ready?' asked Segundo.

I looked at Alberto and he nodded. 'Let's do this.'

I went first, balancing to get into the wobbly little boat and sitting on top of my rucksack. The Indians waved goodbye to their womenfolk, who'd walked down to the waterside out of curiosity. Then our captain for the three-hour boat ride punted us away from the shore using an eight-foot pole, until we were out of the shallows and floating in the middle of the brown muddy river.

Once we were deep enough, he lowered the small motor into the flow and kicked it into action with a splutter. We were off. The floating tree trunk carrying us and our rations for the forthcoming quest sped along at a rapid pace, gliding upriver like a water skate. The captain navigated the bends with grace and skill, sometimes swerving around fallen trees and floating deadfall. Dugout canoes aren't the most comfortable form of transport, especially for us fat-arsed Westerners, and it takes some getting used to, sitting still and not causing the thing to capsize. Having said that, the knowledge that the river was teeming with crocodiles and electric eels was enough to keep us from fidgeting too much.

As we travelled upriver at the relatively breakneck speed of twenty miles an hour, we could finally relax and take in the scenery. What we had forgotten or left behind now we'd have to do without. For the next week or so we would have to be completely self-sufficient, with no backup, little by way of communications, no roads or resupply, and no one to blame but ourselves.

All around, the jungle closed in. Everything seemed enormous. The trees were the biggest I had ever seen; huge ceiba and mahogany and teak loomed on both sides. We passed through prehistoric swamps, where we saw the crocodiles basking on the matted knots of vegetation. Howler monkeys swung like Tarzan through the branches and dangled from vines as they tried to get a closer look at these intruders into their domain. A six-foot-long python was wrapped around a log as we buzzed past; the slippery length unfurled itself to reveal a small but menacing set of eyes that watched us with intent. All around there were beasts of the jungle: sloths, giant iguanas, toucans, vultures and swooping herons. With every mile we covered, the land got wilder and wilder.

After an hour or so, the river seemed to get broader, which was unusual since we were going upstream, but it also got shallower. On either side was a great swamp and the trees seemed to emerge directly out of the water. Here, though, it was clearer with less sediment, so you could almost see the bottom. Shoals of fish darted around the boat and sometimes we would bottom out on the gravel and sandbanks so that we'd have to get out and push the canoe. Segundo led the charge with his massive frame, twice the size of the Indians, and he seemed to relish the challenge of hauling the boat up the rapids.

The river snaked its way uphill and soon the terrain on either side grew steep and to the north-east, vast green mountains loomed under the clouds.

'We're not too far from Canaan now,' said Segundo, 'another hour, so we should get there before dusk.'

At that moment, I saw a flash of red on the east bank of the river about a hundred metres away. Something was moving behind a log and it wasn't natural.

'What was that? Did you see it?' I said, squinting to see what it was.

'I think it was a person,' said Alberto.

There it was again. This time I saw the distinct form of a human, no, there were two, crouching behind a log, clearly trying to hide.

'Immigrants,' said Segundo quietly.

I looked again. The man in the red was watching us through the fallen branches.

'Cubans,' whispered the boat captain.

After a few seconds we had rounded a bend and they were out of view.

'How do you know?' I asked.

'They are the only ones who don't use coyotes. They travel in pairs and don't follow the main trails.'

We pushed on. It was late afternoon and it gets dark early in the jungle, so we didn't have time to hang around.

By four o'clock we reached a wide meander in the river, where several dugout canoes were moored up on a sandbank. Dogs barked at us from the banks and some naked children eyed us warily from the beach where they'd been playing. This was Canaan, the last village this side of the mountains.

Segundo jumped out of the dugout and tied the boat to an overhanging tree and helped me and Alberto get off and onto the bank, where a load of villagers had emerged out of the bush to come and see the new arrivals.

'Come,' said Segundo, 'the boatmen will unload the bags, let's go and let the soldiers know we are here.'

We followed our lofty guide through the crowd of villagers along a trail that led to a large clearing, where the village spread out before us. There were about a hundred houses, all of them wooden on stilts spread at equal distances apart. I presumed that the raised platforms were in case the river ever flooded, as well as to keep the people safe from snakes and other beasts. Most of the roofs were thatched from palm leaves and grass, but a few were made of metal tin.

As the sun fell below the trees across the camp, the shadows of the huts stretched across the clearing where kids played football and women sat on the ladders chatting. These were the Embera tribe that I'd heard about from Blashford-Snell. 'Rings through their noses ... up for a laugh ... tits jiggling all over the place ...'

I looked around. There was barely a breast in sight, apart from a few women suckling their brood and a couple of octogenarians combing their long black hair in the sunset. Most of the tribe were in fact fully clothed; the result of proselytising Christian missionaries, no doubt, who'd been meddling with the Indians for the last forty years.

'A shame,' said Alberto, 'I haven't seen a naked woman in months.'

Semi-feral dogs ran around yapping, searching for scraps of food underneath the houses, only to be chased off by decrepit old men with no teeth. All the men wore tatty old football shirts and rubber boots; hand-me-downs from charities in the US and Europe. They'd done the trick and 'civilised' the natives. No more poor naked savages here, I thought. Just poor clothed ones instead. A tame people, who'd lost their culture and traditions. There wasn't a spear in sight. There was, however, a large number of satellite dishes, so that even here the locals could tune in to MTV and watch other tribes on Discovery channel. A bizarre thought.

We weaved our way between the stilted houses.

'At least they're friendly,' said Alberto.

Everyone waved and said hello in Spanish or Embera. On the far side of the village, just before the trees started again, were some green tents and a hut with camouflage netting surrounded by sandbags. Four soldiers stood inside in uniform and one was patrolling the perimeter with a machine gun. The boss came outside, a stocky sergeant called Gutierrez. He didn't smile.

'These are the foreigners who are crossing to Colombia,' said Segundo. 'You should have been notified by Colonel Carrion.'

The sergeant grunted. 'Show me your papers.'

We handed over our passports for inspection and a letter from SENAFRONT that stated we had permission to leave Panama through the jungle.

'You can stay with them tonight,' he said, cocking a head towards a group of men who were watching proceedings.

'Who are they?' I asked.

'It's their chief and his leaders,' said Segundo.

We walked over. A short, skinny man in his late forties or fifties, wearing a red T-shirt, offered a hand.

'Ernesto Konde,' he said. 'I'm the chief.'

He didn't look like a chief. He was wiry and shifty-looking and didn't seem to have much leadership presence. He looked like a shoplifter.

'You can stay in my spare house,' he said, motioning for us to follow him.

It was like the others, six feet off the ground and held together by rusty nails. It was only half built and Ernesto had to move a load of timber so that we could climb up the stepladders onto the platform. Still, it was better than nothing, so we thanked him and strung our hammocks as darkness fell.

'When you're done, come over for food.' He pointed to the next hut along, ten metres away.

'What do you think is on the menu?' said Alberto.

'More fried bananas, I would imagine,' I replied.

We were both pleasantly surprised to discover then, when we went over for dinner, that a plate of freshly roasted venison was waiting for us, as well as plenty of fried bananas.

Ernesto grinned. 'Jungle deer,' he said, giving us a thumbs-up. 'Very tasty.'

I had visions of Ernesto and his men out in their loincloths and body paint, stalking through the jungle with bows and arrows and blowpipes. I told him so.

He laughed. 'No, my grandfather used to do that stuff. And we sometimes watch the Brazilian tribes on National Geographic. But we don't do that anymore.'

'So how do you hunt?' asked Alberto, as he chewed on the succulent meat.

'Guns, if we have enough ammunition,' he said. 'But usually we send our dogs after the animals and kill them with machetes.'

It sounded brutal, but then again, so was all life in the Darién.

After we'd finished eating, Ernesto's wife came and sat down next to me. She was old and withered, but had a twinkle in her eye that betrayed a lifetime of laughter.

'Do you want to buy something?' she said in a conspiratorial tone.

'What?' I asked, expecting to be peddled some tribal beads or needlework, like we'd seen in the markets of Panama City.

Instead she pulled out of her apron a cloth, which she unwrapped and then pulled out a white thing, the size of a thumb. It was a tooth.

'It's from a jaguar,' she said.

I grimaced. Poor thing, I thought. They've probably killed it to sell the teeth.

'No, thanks,' I said, explaining that I didn't want to encourage poaching. She thought about it and shrugged her shoulders, wrapping it back up in the cloth.

'OK, I have something else,' she said with a sigh. 'I've had it a very long time, but I want to sell it.'

From another pocket came another cloth, this time bigger. Before she unwrapped it, she looked me in the eye and stared.

'These are very rare,' she said in a whisper.

'Let me see.'

She placed the object into my hands and I felt the heavy coldness of something old and triangular in shape. In the half light of the room, I couldn't tell what it was. Two of the sides were razor sharp and serrated. It felt like some sort of Stone Age spearhead made of flint. That must be what it was, evidence of a prehistoric society in Panama, perhaps?

'No, it's not a spear,' said Maria. 'It's a *Uña de Rayo*.'

'She says it's a nail of lightning, like a fingernail. I think she means it's a thunderbolt,' said Alberto.

I laughed out loud. She frowned and grasped it out of my hand. 'It is, it is, that's what it is. My grandmother found one. They are only found in the Darién, nowhere else. We some-time find them underneath trees that have been burned by the sky.'

I supressed my chuckles and felt bad that I had laughed. Maria genuinely thought that it was the tip of some sort of supernatural thunderbolt, presumably petrified upon impact with the earth.

If it wasn't a spearhead (it was too big and irregular for that) and it wasn't a thunderbolt, there was only one thing left that it could be. It was a shark's tooth. But this wasn't any old shark's tooth, it was that of a prehistoric megaladon; a thirty-metre monster ten times bigger than your average Great White, that swam in the oceans over three million years ago. One thing was certain, that this ancient fossil was formed at a time when Central America was nothing but a ridge of underwater volcanoes, but then again, who was I to argue with this wise lady and her dreams of thunderbolts?

Even if I had a notion to correct her, what is a more likely story: a flash of lightning striking a tree and leaving a piece of stone in the shape of an arrow, or a giant sea-monster leaving its teeth in the middle of a jungle? The old dear had never even seen the sea! So I told Maria that I would love to buy her thunderbolt, even if it was a hundred dollars. I didn't barter.

The next morning I woke to the sound of bullfrogs croaking in the reeds and the patter of children's feet, as they shuffled around the village collecting water from the well.

'Come on, Lev, you're the last one up, it's time to go,' said Alberto.

I peeled myself out of the hammock and got dressed. Outside on the ground below the hut, Ernesto the chief was waiting and behind him was a crowd of men.

'These will be the porters,' he said. 'We will take you over the mountains to Carreto into Kuna Yala.'

'So you're coming too?' I asked the chief. This was a surprise.

'Of course,' he said. 'It'll be an adventure.'

'Do we really need all these men?' I asked Segundo. 'There's a lot of them.'

'The chief plus eight, and me.'

'You as well?'

'I need to supervise the Indians. You remember what the colonel said?'

'That they can't be trusted?'

'Exactly. We can't let them rob you and leave you in the jungle.'

'They seem nice enough,' I said.

'Yes, but the Kuna are troublesome, and we'll meet them on the other side.'

In any case, I thought, having an extra pair of hands would be useful, especially ones as big as his. So it would be a rather large band of merry men after all.

We ate a breakfast of steamed rice and plantain over in the chief's hut, while the porters made carrying systems from old bits of rope and bicycle inner tubes, which they wrapped round the bags and carried either like rucksacks, or on their heads. Segundo went around tightening straps and tying away loose ends. He'd make a great platoon sergeant, I thought.

'Go and have a blessing from the women,' said Ernesto. 'They're waiting for you.'

Apparently it was Embera tradition to get a tattoo dyed onto your skin before setting off on a journey, so Alberto and I sat topless as the old women drew a pattern on our arms with some sort of plant extract, which left a black stain on our skin.

'It lasts for a week,' they said.

'I hope so,' said Alberto, as the lady slipped with her stick and made a messy smudge across his bicep.

And with that, we set off out of the village and into the jungle. To begin with, there was a muddy little single track. Ernesto and his chief porter Leo led the way, followed by me and Alberto, then all the Indians with Segundo at the back. We followed the course of the Membrillo river, which after a while became unnavigable, but we were able to hear its gushing current and the noise of the streams and waterfalls that flowed into it, even as the path wound up and over ridges and hills.

Soon enough, the trail petered out. This was clearly the limit of most Embera explorations. They didn't need to go far to hunt. Already that morning we'd seen two 'tigrillos', which are black cats similar to leopards, as well as a small deer, a wild pig and plenty of huge iguanas and monkeys, all of which got eaten around here.

'Look at that,' said Ernesto, pointing to something in the branches of a tree not far away.

It was a hawk eagle with a dead rat in its talons.

'They're a magical animal,' he continued. 'The jungle is full of magic. Some is good and some is bad.'

We followed our superstitious chief, hacking a new trail through the undergrowth. It began to pour with rain and it wasn't long before we were soaking wet with sweat, and up to our knees in mud as we splashed and waded our way through the swamps and streams. It was hot and humid and even though we'd travelled through plenty of forests on this journey already, nothing could have prepared us for the sheer brutality of the terrain that we encountered in the Darién.

At least the porters were cheery. For the Embera, it was a well-paid holiday away from their wives. The older and bolder amongst them had been this way before, five or ten years ago; they couldn't remember when exactly. Only Leo knew the route, at fifty-seven years he was the oldest of the group. Even the chief hadn't been this way in over twenty years and couldn't remember the path. For several of the youngsters it was their first major outing, and if they made it, it would be the first time they had ever seen the ocean. A few of the lads wore old trainers and flip-flops. Only one had boots. The rest were quite content to walk in rubber wellies.

'We're used to it,' grinned the chief. 'But if you want to donate any of your boots at the end, we won't say no.' He winked.

The first day in the Darién we walked for five hours and covered only six miles and by the time we found a suitable place to camp, on the bank of the river, Alberto and I were utterly exhausted. Even the Embera and Segundo looked tired. We cleared a patch with our machetes and strung our hammocks and cooked some rations up to eat. By six o'clock it was pitch black and there was nothing left to do. Each of us slid into our hammocks as the noise of the forest roared in the darkness. Only then did it finally sink in how far away from civilisation we really were. This was true wilderness, and if anything went wrong here, there would be no one coming to find us.

22

The Darién Gap

I was lying in my hammock strung between two palm trees. All around I could hear through the darkness the faint whispers of Scottish highland accents. They were talking about tomorrow and the fact that they'd get started on the fort in the morning, if only they could find fresh water. Even though it was dark, I could see the outline of the *Caledonia* with her rigging up, moored in the bay. It was 1698 and I was the captain of the ship. I was happy to be here in the New World, away from the cold and on a true mission of exploration in this unexplored region called the Darién. I was going to make Scotland rich. My hammock was white, made of old sails, but it was comfortable. Better than being on the floor of that infernal boat.

Hang on. Why was my hammock white? My hammock is normally green, and how had I reached the coast already? I didn't understand what was going on. Suddenly, there was an explosion. I sat up with a jerk and then almost fell out of the hammock as I rolled over. I couldn't get out. What was happening? Was it the Spanish? Were they attacking us already? Or was it the Indians? We hadn't seen any yet. What was going on?

'Deadfall!' shouted Alberto.

I opened my eyes. A tree had come crashing down ten metres away. I was sweating and terrified. Thank God for that, I thought to myself. I thought I was about to be speared by a Choco tribesman.

'What are you talking about?' came Alberto's voice from the blackness. 'Didn't you hear me? It was a tree.'

'Nothing, I was just dreaming, that's all.'

I looked at my watch. It was five a.m., and the sun would be coming up in an hour. I tried to go back to sleep, but after the nightmare it was impossible and I found myself shuffling deeper into my cotton liner in the early morning chill.

At first light, I got up and went down to the river. Leo and Ernesto were already up and huddled round the fire. They'd been fishing in the night with their machetes.

'How do you catch them?' I asked.

Ernesto replied, 'You hold a torch in one hand and wait for the fish to come to the surface. They are stupid and think its daytime. And then ...' He raised his knife. 'Whoosh. You just hit them and they die.' He grinned and handed me a crispy black fish that he'd grilled on the smoky fire. It tasted good and was a nice break from dehydrated rations. Alberto came wandering over in his underpants and flip-flops, yawning.

'Sleep well?' I asked.

'No, I did not,' he said. 'That tree fell right next to my hammock. I thought I was going to die. And all you could talk about was Indians and spears, or some shit. I thought you'd gone mad.'

He shivered and knelt by the fire.

'Honestly, Lev, if I survive this jungle and get to Colombia, you know what I'm gonna do?'

'No, tell me.'

'I'm gonna go home to Mérida and meet the mayor and tell him I want a statue in the main plaza. Me ... the only Mexican to walk to Colombia.' He patted his chest.

'In fact, no, fuck the statue. The birds will shit on that. I want them to name a leisure centre after me. That way, the kids will know my name.'

We set off, following the course of the river. We'd given up worrying about getting wet feet now and spent the whole day wading upstream; slipping and sliding over rocks and boulders, sometimes having to swim across the deep parts. Kingfishers swooped for their prey as we ploughed through the virgin waterway, unnavigable since time began. Either side of the river, the jungle arched up in vertical cliffs that were impossible to climb. If there was a flash flood now, we'd be swept away in an instant, but for the time being the rain had abated.

Leo led the way again, with me, Alberto and Ernesto trying to keep up. Segundo and the porters kept a steady pace behind, lugging baskets on their heads. Compared to us, they seemed to glide over the rocks with relative ease. The deeper into the jungle we got, the hotter and steamier it became. By eleven a.m., the temperature had soared to over thirty-five Celsius, just as we reached a bend where a gorge made it impossible to keep wading up the river.

'It's too deep ahead,' said Leo. 'We'll have to go over the ridge.'

He pointed up to what looked like an almost sheer climb of vertical jungle. There was no choice but to leave the river behind.

Grasping onto a vine, we pulled ourselves up onto a rock, where Leo started hacking away at the foliage to create a new trail. It took some time before a sufficient gap could be made so that all the team could follow on. From there, we encountered one of the most brutal, skin-tearing, lung-busting jungle climbs I have ever endured. For hours we scrambled up through the bushes and trees, battling with thorns, razor-sharp grass and spiders' webs, and getting covered in ants, termites and millipedes. Sometimes we'd have to scale waterfalls, clinging onto the rocks for dear life, and at others we'd descend into chasms of swamp and quicksand. Evil-looking insects crawled up our legs and even the very flowers appeared malevolent and bent on our destruction. This was the Darién Gap of my dreams, and now, it seemed, my nightmares.

After an eternity we crested the ridge, although the only way of knowing this was that there were occasional glints of sunlight at head level on two sides. That was the clue we had reached the top. But I wasn't about to congratulate myself just yet. There were plenty more ridges and mountains to climb ahead. By my reckoning, we'd managed to cover only fifteen miles in the last two days. At this rate, we'd run out of food before we could get to Carreto and the coast.

'We need to push on,' said Ernesto, as we began the descent to another river. The little chief took the lead ahead of Leo and began a steady jog down the steep decline, flailing his machete at the dangling vines. There was a sapling in the way, which he swiped and sliced almost at the base, leaving a lethal-looking spike poking out of the ground. I turned around to warn Alberto of the danger below, and then suddenly I slipped.

I felt my left foot give way to the squelching mud and before I knew it, I was horizontal mid-air and then ... Bang! I landed straight on my back. At first I couldn't feel any pain, I was just winded, and thought it would be best to get right back up, which I did.

And then it hit me like a lorry. A shudder of searing pain flowed through my entire body, starting with the base of my spine. I looked down to see the spike below me. I'd clearly fallen directly on top of it. My first reaction was one of relief. If I'd landed an inch further up, the spike would have rammed itself straight up my arse. As it happened, it had jarred against my coccyx instead. I flopped to the ground.

'Are you OK?' came a voice. I felt so faint, I didn't know who it was.

The pain was now so acute that I wanted to vomit. Alberto offered to carry me, but I knew that I had to sit still for a while and wait for it to pass. It had been a lucky escape. It could have been a lot worse, but even so, I knew that it was going to slow me down even more. After fifteen minutes, I got up and slowly made my way down the hill, this time with more caution and each step with deliberate restraint.

'I have something that will help.' I looked around and saw Leo. He had a dirty plastic bottle in his hand.

'What is it?'

'Medicine,' he said, handing me the bottle and unscrewing the cap.

I smelled the stuff and almost puked up.

'What on earth is that?'

He raised his eyebrows, 'It's kerosene, of course.'

'What do you do with it?' I asked.

'It gets rid of the pain. We rub it around the area that hurts and then drink some, just to make sure.'

I politely declined.

For four more hours I walked on, my spine still hurting with each step. Alberto, despite falling over every ten metres, managed to somehow avoid any serious injury, but he was slowing down by the day and found himself covered in insect bites. At one point his hand had swollen so much from a spider bite that it looked like a balloon and he couldn't get his watch on his wrist. When we stopped for food by the rivers, we'd check our feet and the scene was grisly. Almost everybody looked like they'd been sitting in the bath for a week – which is basically what we had done. Trench-foot was beginning to set in with some of the team, as the soles of people's feet wrinkled and cracked into bloody pulps.

All the gear was wrecked. The cameras were completely destroyed by water damage. Our boots were sodden, our clothes torn and our skin ripped to shreds. But we had no choice other than to carry on. We climbed another two or three ridges and crossed more rivers than I can ever remember. No wonder this place had taken so many lives, I thought, glad at least that we'd got the Embera. I couldn't imagine attempting something like this without a guide. The colonel was right, it would be suicide. Even Segundo was struggling. The man-mountain had been silent for forty-eight hours now. He was plodding along like some sort of giant sloth. I suppose that even the locals were only human and this kind of terrain wasn't picky about on whom it chose to inflict suffering.

Having said that, what I will say about the Embera is that they never lost their sense of humour. Even at the toughest times, they would chuckle and joke about the weather, the terrain and the magic of the jungle. They'd point out the dangers and laugh. They showed me the magical 'penis' vine: a local plant that apparently makes one's appendage grow to exactly the size you want it, depending on how much of the potion is used. Blokes everywhere, it seems, find the same things amusing.

As we reached the watershed of the mountains, Ernesto pointed out a particularly big ceiba tree. It stood proud on top of the peak, and I remembered Keats's poem: 'Silent, upon a peak in Darien.' Keats clearly hadn't met the Embera, who didn't stop chattering the whole time.

'This is the limit of our Embera ancestral lands.'

He pointed down towards the endless sea of jungle, which disappeared into the clouds.

'Everything down there is Kuna Yala.'

'Do you ever meet with them?' I asked, as Leo stopped beside us.

'No, not for many years. We speak different languages and have very different cultures. The legends say that many years ago, hundreds of years before the white man came, we were the same tribe and lived in Colombia, and then we moved north into the Darién. One day there was a big war and the tribe split – into the Embera and the Kuna. We won, and sent the Kuna away, out of the jungle and towards the great ocean, where they now live by the Caribbean.'

'Sounds like the Kuna got the best deal,' Alberto joked.

'No, we don't like the sea,' said Ernesto. 'You can't even drink it.'

'But you've been there before?' I asked.

'Yes, but not for decades. Leo here has been many times. He went to school in Carreto, because there were none in our area when we were children.'

Leo smiled and gave me a thumbs-up. 'I like to go and see the women. They have beautiful ladies in the Kuna lands.'

We followed a ridgeline down to the river. Finally, we could walk downstream as the waters flowed north-east to the Caribbean some fifteen miles distant. As long as we kept the pace, then tomorrow we should reach Carreto, but for now we needed to make camp in the jungle.

Leo led us to a stony beach by the river. I was surprised to see that there was an old shelter made of wooden poles and palm leaves hidden away on the banks.

'Who built that?' I asked the chief.

He shrugged. 'Maybe narcos, or the people smugglers, this is the way they bring the immigrants.'

We were so exhausted, though, that none of us cared much about the drug traffickers or the smugglers any more. We needed a rest, so set about cutting a clearing around the shelter and stringing up the hammocks.

Suddenly there was a commotion next to the shelter. One of the porters, Rodrigo, was jumping about like a madman. 'What's up?' I shouted, running over.

'Snake! Snake!' he said.

'Did it bite you?' I asked.

By now he had his trousers round his ankles and was pinching the skin at the back of his thigh. The other porters and Leo ran over to help.

I looked down at the ground to see the snake. It was a tiny viper; a baby no longer than a foot and a half.

'Poisonous! Poisonous!' the men chanted.

'He smashed its head, look,' said Leo.

'What kind of snake is it?' asked Alberto.

'A fer-de-lance,' they chimed.

It was one of the most infamous and deadly snakes in the Americas. The same that had almost killed Aron in Belize.

I looked at Rodrigo's leg. It seemed the snake had darted out of a hole in a tree and tried to bite him on the leg, but instead had caught its fangs with their lethal poison on the material of his trouser leg, thank God. It was a lucky escape. The babies, I'm told, are the worst, because they unload all their venom when they bite. And when they do, you've got less than twenty-four hours to get the hell out of there and find a hospital with anti-venom. Out here, in the middle of the jungle, he would almost certainly be dead.

The snake was writhing around on the jungle floor, half-alive. But the men took no chances and proceeded to finish bashing it over the head with a stick until it stopped moving. After that Rodrigo danced over the snake in an Embera ritual, jumping three times over the dead creature.

'Why do you do that?' I asked.

'So we won't get bitten by another one,' he explained. 'It's like a magic spell and keeps them calm. Maybe the mother snake is around here somewhere.'

All of the Embera did the same dance, and I did, too, just in case.

The next morning, we followed the river down through the rainforest, where Leo found a narrow track. It was the first trail we'd seen in days. 'This leads to Carreto,' he said, proud that he'd remembered the way.

'God knows how he did that,' said Alberto. 'With no map, no trail and no GPS. All by memory. These Indians are incredible.'

As the path got more discernible, we were able to cover ground more quickly and before long we found ourselves among plantations of banana and cacao; the first semblance of human habitation since leaving Canaan.

'We have to be careful,' said Ernesto. 'The Kuna can be dangerous.'

I remembered the words of John Blashford-Snell, who'd warned me that they were troublesome and hostile and their only love was of money.

Ernesto spoke with Leo in their Embera tongue and they seemed to have a heated debate.

'What are they talking about?' I asked Segundo, who knew the language.

'They are arguing. Ernesto wants Leo to pretend that he is the chief, because he went to school here, but Leo says they won't believe him.'

'Why?'

'Because Leo can speak Kuna since he learnt it as a child. But Leo isn't sure he can pull it off.'

Leo stamped his feet and walked on ahead. It seems the chief, the real one, had got his way, and Leo was now the unwilling pretender.

Luckily the old porter performed admirably. After an hour of meandering between the banana trees, we met our first group of Kuna. They were three men in their twenties, all wearing dirty T-shirts and ripped trousers. One of them carried a hunting rifle. They stopped for a second on the track and then came closer.

Leo went ahead and with his biggest smile, he greeted the opposing tribesmen with a handshake and a hug.

'See, they think he's the chief,' Ernesto laughed.

I saw the Kuna men point down the track and we all followed Leo's lead, saying hello to the Kuna men as they passed us. They didn't smile or reply, only giving us a perfunctory nod.

A mile down the track, I saw the outskirts of the village hidden amongst the trees. We passed a clearing where the remains of a military-style bunker had been made out of sandbags. Nobody was manning it, but it was hardly the most welcoming sight. The younger porters looked nervous as we entered the village, closing together as a group, and keeping a close eye on the reactions of their elders. Leo did his job well and shook hands with everyone we met, as the whole team bumbled into the middle of Carreto.

Soon we seemed to be in the centre, surrounded by wooden shacks with thatched roofs. It was as if we'd been transported back into the Middle Ages. Unlike the Embera with their satellite dishes and tin roofs, there was almost nothing to suggest the twenty-first century was coming here any time soon. Villagers started to crowd around us. First there were dozens, and then hundreds of children in varying states of nakedness; and then the women, all in traditional dress: colourful red and yellow sarongs, and wearing a kind of headscarf that covered their long black hair. Their chests were adorned with reams of handmade jewellery; gold and beads and shells. Only the men wore Western clothes and a kind of straw hat, which gave them a dignified formality despite their obvious poverty.

'Who are you?' asked one of the old men, who was leaning on a stick.

'I am Leo, of the Canaan Embera. I came to school here fifty years ago.'

The old man's eyes lit up.

'It can't be?'

Leo grinned, 'It is, Silas.'

The old man came forward and grasped Leo, his old friend, hugging him tightly. 'Then you are welcome. Come and meet the chiefs.' He nodded in our direction, 'Who are the whites?'

Leo motioned for us to step forward. 'They like to walk. We brought them this far, but they want to carry on.'

Silas, which meant 'elder' in Kuna, looked us up and down with a calculated glare. He pointed at me. 'Where are you going?'

I told him.

'Colombia.'

He nodded.

'We will decide on that.'

23

New Scotland

We followed Silas through the narrow alleyways to the beach, where the Caribbean Sea unfolded before us. After the confines of the jungle, it felt surreal to be in such an open space with nothing but turquoise waters for as far as the eye could see. The young Embera who had never been here before stood as the waves lapped against their wellies. Rodrigo just shrugged. 'It's nice, but I prefer the jungle,' he said.

'This is where we leave you,' said Ernesto, shaking our hands.

'Now you're in the hands of the Kuna,' said Leo. 'They will look after you, as long as you tip them well.'

It was advice as well as a hint. We paid our Embera guides and the porters, and tipped them well, too. They'd done us proud, and although we hadn't quite crossed the Darién Gap yet, we'd got further than we ever imagined possible and it was down in no small part to their help.

We waved goodbye to the hardy men. Now that they'd shed their loads, and us, they said they'd be able to make the homeward journey in only three days. But for now, they wanted to share a moment of friendship with the Kuna – something that hadn't happened in years. Rodrigo and the youngsters played football with their Kuna counterparts, while Leo and Ernesto went off to get drunk.

The Kuna elder stayed with us. 'Colombia is still three or four days' walk from here. But before we can let you carry on, you will need to speak with the chief.'

'No problem,' I said, more than used to the formality of introductions to chieftains and tribal elders by now. 'Where is he?'

Silas looked out to sea.

'Caledonia.'

The word sounded strangely familiar. Of course. Now I remembered. We were just a few miles distant from the exact same spot where the Scottish made landfall all those years ago. I checked my map. There was nothing to suggest that there was any settlement there now – not even a name. I asked Silas.

'Puerto Escosés,' he said. 'Yes, it's the next bay along.'

Puerto Escosés. That was Spanish for 'Scottish port'. It made sense.

The old man pointed to a headland along the beach.

'But why do you want to go there? There's nothing there.'

I was going to launch into a history lesson, but thought better of it. Alberto gave the short answer instead.

'He wants to see the place where his people came to live.'

That would do, I thought.

Then Silas nodded. 'Well, you still have to go to Caledonia first. It's an island. We can arrange a boat for some money.'

It seemed there was no choice. We needed to get to the Colombian border, but the Kuna were notoriously bureaucratic, and if we needed to meet the chief then that's what we'd have to do, even if it meant a little boat detour. And in any case, we couldn't come this close and not see New Edinburgh.

So we paid up and got on a little motorised canoe that bounced over the waves of the Caribbean. We sped around the headland and out to sea towards a little island about a mile offshore. The sky was clear and the water warm as it splashed against the keel and into our faces. Suddenly a shoal of dolphins crested the surface and ploughed alongside us in a graceful welcome. I looked back at the shoreline. The wild jungle extended for miles along the coast and the mountains of the Darién loomed like vast spectres. I couldn't quite believe we'd walked over them.

Ahead, Caledonia came into view. It felt strange to think that it was still called Caledonia after all these years. Shacks rose from the island and little huts on stilts poked out of the sea. Not a single square inch was left untamed, it seemed. Rickety jetties protruded from the coral and rocks that had been piled up in an effort to reclaim some land from the water. Smoke spiralled from the village houses and skinny dogs barked as we approached.

'We're here,' said the boatman. 'I'll wait while you meet the chiefs.'

We disembarked and immediately we were surrounded, as we had been in Carreto, by the curious villagers. Similarly all the ladies were resplendent in their traditional dress. Some wore a familiar pattern in their skirts, which bore a startling resemblance to tartan. I remember hearing a legend that these people were trading with the Scottish, and though the dates don't quite work out, you never know.

We were led by some youngsters to the island long house: a hut bigger than all the others, with an enormous thatched roof, which was filled with long benches like church pews, and yet there were hammocks dangling from the rafters, too. It served as a church, a community gathering place and a wedding venue, as well, it seems, as the place where the old men liked to hang out.

All the Silases were horizontal, lounging in the hammocks. They didn't bat an eyelid as Alberto and I were escorted in and told to sit down. For the umpteenth time, I recounted our journey and told the elders that we wanted to walk through their lands for the final leg of the expedition, to reach the Colombian border. It would take us along the coast and through a last bit of the Darién's jungle to a place called La Miel. From there, it was one final hill to get to the border post.

They listened quietly.

I was expecting the worst, given all that I'd heard about this tribe. Maybe they would refuse permission and send us back across the Darién Gap. Just as bad, they might tell us to get on the boat and we'd have to go by sea to Colombia and we'd fail in the mission. Or even worse, they would confiscate all our equipment and money and leave us stranded on a beach somewhere.

But none of that happened. We merely paid a small 'registration fee' and they said we were free to go. We could visit Puerto Escocés on the way if we wanted. 'But there's nothing there to see,' said the chief. 'You can have one hour there, no more. And take Andres with you. He knows the place.'

Andres Ortega was the village drunk. He stumbled into the hut holding a can of beer and introduced himself.

'I am the best guide in the whole of Kuna Yala,' he announced, dead serious. 'There is nowhere I don't know on this coast. Tomorrow I will take you to see the Scottish port.'

So we spent the night on the floor of a hut, waiting for our new guide to sober up. Our boatman had lost his patience and gone back to Carreto, so we ended up having to pay for another boat. It reminded me of Egypt, where the entire tourism industry is based around the concept of keeping you there for as long as possible until your money runs out.

The next morning Andres arrived, albeit an hour later than we'd planned, and together we walked back down to the jetty where the new boat was waiting. But as we walked past the village school – the only breeze-block building on the whole island – I heard some strange music emanating from inside. I recognised it as familiar, but couldn't immediately put my finger on it. It was so out of place that I'd almost forgotten my own national anthem.

'God Save the Queen' was pumped out of the school radio, and all the kids were singing along in unison. The language was different though, the words were Kuna, not English or Spanish, so neither of us could understand. Quite what the British national anthem was doing being played out in a tribal village in one of the most remote parts of the world, I don't think I'll ever know. But I have to say it did make me chuckle and I felt a little warm glow inside. I was almost home.

Andres got onto the boat. I could smell booze on his breath. He was clearly still half-cut, but we didn't have any other options so we thought we'd give him a chance. At least he wasn't driving it. As we set off, though, it turned out he was actually quite a good tour guide and the inebriation didn't stop him recounting some history.

'When did you last go to Puerto Escosés?' I asked.

'I've been three or four times,' he replied. 'I went there first in 1993 with another Englishman.'

'Oh really?' I was surprised. 'What was his name?'

Andres squinted his eyes, deep in thought.

'Hmmm, he was in the Army. What was his name . . .?' He scratched his head, and then it came to him. 'Basfordsmell.'

Basfordsmell? No, surely it wasn't. But of course, who else would it be?

'You mean Colonel John Blashford-Snell?'

'Yes, that's it. Blashford-Snell. We did an archaeological dig and we found lots of things. Pots and smoking pipes and some old coins. But he was very strict – he wouldn't let us take anything away. He said it was important that it stayed in Panama.'

The boat trailed parallel with the wild shoreline.

'Look at that beach,' said Andres. 'It's where Balboa was executed.' Balboa was the first Spaniard to cross the Darién in a bid to reach the Pacific. He managed to trek right across the coast and return alive, only to be beheaded by a jealous Spanish rival who wanted all the glory of the exploration for himself. This remote stretch of coast had certainly seen its fair share of world-changing events, although to look at it now, it was hard to believe humans had even contemplated living here.

'You know when people talk about the Darién Gap nowadays, it's because it is the only break in the Pan-American Highway, right?'

'I knew that, yes.'

'Well, that's not what it originally meant. Before, the Darién was seen as the easy bit of Central America to cross, because it's so narrow.'

'Trust me, it wasn't easy,' said Alberto, scowling.

'Yes, but back in the old days, think how remote and impossible it would have been to travel through the jungle in Costa Rica and Nicaragua. That's why nobody lived there. They were the real problems. Now they are tame and this is the only wilderness left.'

He was certainly right about that much.

As we got closer to the rocky headland, Puerto Escosés, or Nuevo Scotia, came into view. There it was, New Scotland. Now, nothing left but an empty bay a mile across and a jungle-clad hill, where the fort of St Andrews stood for a couple of years from 1698 until it was abandoned.

'Where do you want to land?' said Andres.

I looked at the bay. I couldn't understand why the Scots had chosen to make this the site of their new colony. I'm no sailor, but it felt pretty obvious that Carreto, with its wide, sandy beach and natural harbour, would have been a far better choice. Here there were rocks and shallows and lethal sandbanks everywhere. There were no real beaches to land on and the coast was all mangrove swamps. What on earth were they thinking? I could only put it down to the fact that, if they'd been sailing from the north where the bays were all worse, this must have seemed like the best option. If only they had carried on another five miles, perhaps the world might have been a very different place.

'Over there.' I pointed to a narrow stretch of sand just ten metres across. It was the only place I could imagine that anyone would have been able to moor up. Behind was the one bit of flat land that the pioneers would have been able to build a settlement on, and it was in the shadow of the hill on which I reckoned the fort must have been placed.

The captain steered us into the shallows, where we jumped into the clear water up to our knees and waded ashore.

'Yes, yes, this is where we came with Mr Bashfordsmell,' said Andres.

'Blashford-Snell.'

'Over there we found many things.'

We walked up the beach, which was littered with driftwood and weeds and bits of rubbish that must have washed ashore having drifted from the Kuna Islands. The place was hot and the air stale. There was no breeze this side of the bay. We walked into the scrub and found ourselves picking our way through mangrove roots, palms and banana trees. These must have been planted by the Scots, I thought. Coconuts were strewn in the undergrowth, which was thick with thorn bushes. It was hard to imagine that anyone had ever lived here. Nature ruled supreme now and there was no trace left of any settlement.

In my mind, I was going to unearth a Claymore sword, or find some buried gold, or at least discover the remains of the graves of the poor Highlanders. But there was nothing here. Nothing at all. Whatever treasures might have been left behind, they were all gone now.

'A ship came eight years ago. Foreigners who paid the Silases five hundred dollars so they could loot with their magic sticks.'

'Magic sticks?' said Alberto, who was clearly unimpressed by the grisly patch of swamp that I'd led him to.

'I think he probably means metal detectors,' I said.

'Yes, they came and took everything away. They even found a big cannon.'

'Let's climb the hill,' I suggested, thinking that if nothing else we might find something of the old fort.

So we hauled ourselves up the slope, grabbing at the vines and the branches, sweating in the staid atmosphere of the tropical jungle for forty-five minutes, until at last we reached the top.

We stood amid the gnarled branches of a ceiba tree, its roots snaking through the uneven hilltop. There was no sign whatsoever of the fort, not even some stones or bits of wood. In the gaps of the foliage we could look out across the Caribbean and back down towards the bay. This was St. Andrews and I tried to imagine the captain of the *Caledonia* as he stood in the same spot, surveying his new empire. I suppose for him, and the hundreds of Scottish colonists, there must have been some inkling of hope that their new life was going to be better than the one they had left behind. Driven by a desire to escape the poverty of seventeenth-century Scotland, and spurred on by tales of glory, wealth and the dream of a tropical paradise, maybe this little mosquito-ridden peninsula was in some way betterment.

Stubbornness and dogged determination had got them this far, but it was also their downfall. As the settlers tried to tame this inhospitable wilderness, they exhausted all their energy and within a matter of months, almost all had perished. I wondered where they lay now. Somewhere down there were the remains of almost two thousand men, women and children, who had left the hills of Scotland to find a new and better life in the New World, only to discover nothing but disease, hunger and ultimately death.

It occurred to me then that the situation had not been all that different for the modern migrants and refugees fleeing poverty and violence in the Middle East, Africa and Latin America, in their bid to find the American dream. The grass, it seems, is not always greener.

24

Colombia

We left New Scotland behind and walked east towards the Colombian border, keeping the lapping waves of the Caribbean within earshot. There was a little trail that followed the coastline, weaving its way through the palm trees and sandy beaches and occasionally over rocky headlands. The remoteness and isolation of this shore gave me the feeling that we were somehow nearing the edge of the world. It was raw, beautiful and menacing, all at once.

We passed by the village of Puerto Obaldía, a little outpost of Afro-Caribbeans – Garifuna – who'd inhabited this place for longer even than the Kuna. One of the local men, Maximillian, offered to guide us the ten miles remaining to the border post.

'It's still hot out there, man, you don't want to do it alone,' he said.

'What do you mean, hot?' I asked.

'It's got bandits and coyotes and irregulars. It's the way the immigrants come,' he said, shaking his head.

With only a few miles left to push, I didn't want to take any chances. We agreed to have him along and so off we went. Maximillian led the way, firstly through the banana groves and then up a steep jungle climb. There was a trail, but it was muddy and covered in litter. Our guide pointed out the discarded plastic bottles, rags and clothes.

There were jackets and shirts strewn around the bushes. Some had been tied to trees deliberately.

'So they don't get lost,' Max said. I thought back to the two thousand Congolese that were still stuck in the refugee camp in Costa Rica. They must have passed by this way on their route.

Then there was underwear; bras and knickers just abandoned at the side of the trail. Max explained, 'They come at night when the army ain't patrolling and bad shit happens. Some get robbed and their stuff gets stolen. People even die here.'

It was a shocking thought and I remembered the confessions of Tony in Nicaragua. We followed the trail of garments as it led us over a series of ridges and valleys. This was the final push through the Darién Gap. We were almost there. Despite knowing that we might bump into a gang of people smugglers at any moment, we were now fixated on getting to the border as fast as we could, so we ploughed on through the steamy heat of the forest.

The path descended a hill and emerged onto a beach that backed up against a meadow of sparse palm trees, beautiful pools and wildflowers. It was like a little Garden of Eden. We went to cross a small stream that was flowing out of the woodland, when suddenly I noticed a group of men ahead. From afar they looked dark-skinned, but not like the Garifuna that lived along the coast. One of them approached me. He looked nervous and fidgety.

'Excuse me, sir, do you speak English?' he said, taking me aback with his perfect command of my language. He clearly wasn't a local.

'Yes, I am English,' I told him.

'Oh, wonderful,' he said. 'My name is Javed. Just come for five minutes. Not far, we have a camp very close.'

I followed the man, intrigued, as he led us fifty metres through the palm trees to where three others were standing by a makeshift shelter. They were all remarkably smart, in clean polo shirts and pressed trousers. One of them, the oldest, had a long beard and wore a brown shirt. He looked like a mullah.

'My name is Amaar,' said another of the men. 'We are from Pakistan.'

I looked around to see if there was any danger. There were four of them and they seemed harmless. They were clearly more worried about being here than we were.

'Can you help us sir?' Amaar said.

He explained that the group had crossed from Colombia into Panama illegally after undertaking the same journey that the Congolese we'd met had taken. Their route was through Brazil, Ecuador, Peru, Colombia, and now they'd found themselves here on the edge of the Darién Gap.

'We are waiting for our agent,' he said, as if talking about Thomas Cook.

'You mean your coyote?' said Alberto.

He looked over his shoulder, as if someone might be listening.

'Yes. He's meant to be taking us on a ship around the mountain, because that's the easiest way.'

I told him that he needn't fear us. That we were going on the opposite journey, trying to get to Colombia.

'Can you tell us how far it is to the next village?' he said. 'If you've come that way.'

I told him that Puerto Obaldía was around the bay, only an hour's walk.

'We've been stranded here for four days and we're running

out of food. Are there any soldiers or police there? Do you think they'll arrest us?'

I told him that there was a small SENAFRONT outpost, but they needn't worry. The Panamanians would probably be quite helpful and from what we'd heard, they would just send them north and help them get to Costa Rica.

Amaar seemed relieved.

'You must've had a very hard journey,' I told him. 'Are you going to the United States?'

'Yes,' he said. 'Well actually, that's what we'd planned. But now that this Donald Trump will be the next president, I think we'll keep going to Canada.' He laughed. 'So you guys are from London?' he said.

I told him that I was.

'Which part of London?'

'I'm from Hampton Court,' I said, not quite able to compute the fact that we were discussing London suburbs in the Darién Gap.

'I know it well. I've been there. I used to live there for seven years,' he said, quite casually. 'I used to work on London Underground trains.'

I couldn't quite believe what I was hearing. But then again, I'd discovered that the world is a very small place indeed at times, and that nothing should come as a surprise. I asked him why he wanted to get to North America.

'Once you live in London, you cannot live in Pakistan again. We come from Kohat in the tribal areas of the North West Frontier. There is nothing there. No jobs, no security, nothing. We just want a better future, if not for us then at least for our families. I loved London. I got deported after seven years for not having any papers, but I still have an aunt in Croydon. I love the fact people run around with a coffee in one hand and a croissant in the other, rushing around. It's amazing. The Central line, the Bakerloo line, I miss them.'

I felt very humbled. I knew that what these men were doing was illegal, but I had to respect their resolve to undertake such a mammoth expedition against the odds in a bid to find a better life. If I was them, I'd probably be doing the same. I wished them luck with it and we said goodbye. Whilst we were at the end of our journey, they were only at the start of theirs.

We carried on along the beach towards another village called La Miel, a couple of hours along the bay, and there we were met by a soldier from SENAFRONT.

'We've been expecting you,' said the corporal. 'Headquarters said that you should be arriving any day now. Welcome. The border isn't far from here. I'll show you the way.'

We followed the soldier up a hill, where some steep steps led to a bunker surrounded by sandbags. Two more Panamanian soldiers were sat there manning the border post. If that's what you could call it. Next to the bunker was a stone monument. On one side it said Panama, with the country's coat of arms. And on the far side it had the Colombian one. Above it two flag poles demarked the invisible border, with each nationality's flag fluttering in the afternoon breeze. We'd made it. We'd crossed the Darién Gap. One step forward, and we were in Colombia.

Alberto raced up the steps behind me and smiled. 'We've done it.'

I don't think he could quite believe it himself. We both stood there on top of the hill under azure skies and looked down the valley towards the bay of Sapzurro, where a little village was nestled between the palm trees, and the waters of the Caribbean stretched out beyond. That one view was worth all the pain and hardship.

'There's only one thing left to do,' I said, 'and that's get in the sea.'

Alberto smiled at me, he didn't need a second hint. 'Absolutely. I've been waiting for this for four months.'

We ran down the steps on the other side, down the hill into the Colombian settlement. The afternoon sun slanted through the palms to reveal a vision of paradise. Everything seemed colourful and vibrant and full of energy and hope. Everybody we passed just laughed and waved at us in a warm welcome. At the beach front was a jetty, with some boats moored up against it. The expedition was done. The journey at an end.

We didn't need an invitation. Dumping our bags, we ran as fast as we could along the wooden pier and together we dived off the edge into the emerald sea. This was the gateway to South America. My Mexican fashion photographer slapped my cheek, as we struggled to tread water fully clothed, our boots weighing us down.

'So, are we going to carry on walking to the bottom of South America?' he joked.

'Not right now,' I said. Maybe that's an adventure for another time.

After over four months of walking, I said so long to Alberto, knowing that it wasn't goodbye. He flew home to Mérida and on to Tulum, where he had a load of Brazilian models waiting for him to look after them. I returned to Panama City and from there flew home via Madrid. In London, it was grey and misty. The only optimism was that it was almost Christmas and the lights and decorations at least brought some cheer to the gloom. I took a taxi to Hampton Court, where my house was finished. The building and decoration was complete, so that now I could finally call it home.

It was cold outside and even as I dumped my bags on the kitchen floor, I could see my breath steaming inside. I lit the fire with some logs that had dried out nicely over the summer and watched as the smoke danced up the chimney. Even though it was only four in the afternoon, it was already dark and the lights of the palace twinkled in the festive night sky. The street lights flickered on and I drew the curtains.

One little walk before bed, I thought to myself.

So I put on my warmest jacket and wrapped a scarf around my neck, locked the door and wandered down to the palace gardens. Nothing had changed, except in the courtyard an ice rink had been set up for the winter festivities. It was filled with families and children skating and enjoying the fun. A vendor in a flat cap stood over a stall selling chestnuts and mulled wine, and the smell made me hungry.

It was busy and there were more tourists than locals by a long stretch and I smiled as I listened to the chatter from around the world. Amongst the German, French, Urdu, Polish and Russian, there were the familiar, beautiful tones of New World Spanish: Mexican, Costa Rican or Panamanian, perhaps? A woman, short with broad shoulders, a gold necklace and black hair tied back in a ponytail, led her two young children by the hand towards the chestnuts. One of them wore a T-shirt that said 'I love London'.

From the river, I looked up at the south front of the new wing, built by Christopher Wren, with its baroque windows, circular fountains and manicured hedges, looking, as he intended, like the Palace of Versailles. The world, it seems, had just got a little smaller.

Acknowledgements

No expedition is, of course, a one-man show. I think it's clear to the reader that this journey would have been far less interesting, enjoyable and perhaps even impossible, without the enthusiasm and tenacity of my guide Alberto Cáceres. It is to him that I owe this journey.

There are many more people that I must thank for their advice, help and assistance before, during and after the expedition itself. The planning for such a mammoth task took months of bureaucracy, emails and logistical wrangling.

A big thank you goes out yet again to the team at October films: Adam Bullmore, Jos Cushing, Jane Manning, Martin Long, Rebecca Duke, Marta Garcia and Letitia Meruvia for their months of hard work, research and advice.

Thanks to Jamie Berry for his directorship and inspired vision as a filmmaker, and of course to Neil Bonner, who introduced me to this world in the first place and Tom Cross who brought in a real dedication to the art.

The expedition was supported logistically by Secret Compass. Tom Bodkin and the team did a great job navigating the logistical and security issues related to the region.

In his capacity as expedition leader Dave Luke brought this journey together, kept us out of trouble, and dealt with local police, soldiers and bureaucrats with skilful aplomb. He's a

Acknowledgements

fantastic yoga teacher too and kept the team in supple flexibility throughout.

Simon Buxton came out as the expedition photographer and provided some truly excellent images as a result.

I must also thank John Hay and the team at Channel 4, who yet again had faith in me to undertake and document the journey and of course Melanie Darlaston and Chris Sutherland at Group M for their financial backing.

I owe the book to Rupert Lancaster at my publisher, Hodder & Stoughton, and all the team involved especially Kerry Hood, Cameron Myers and Caitriona Horne.

Of course I couldn't have done any of this without my wonderful agent Jo Cantello who yet again has kept me on the straight and narrow.

I also wish to thank those incredible companies who have sponsored and assisted me with financial and material support over the past year: Craghoppers, IWC, Clinique, Belstaff, Leica, Altberg boots, Sub-4 Orthotics, Global Rescue, Oliver Sweeney.

And in no particular order to all of the following for their words of wisdom, floor space, companionship on the trail, logistical assistance or just a cup of coffee:

Ceci Alonzo who introduced me to Mexico in the first place; Don Victor Alonzo and Doña Leonor Echeverria, Mari and Aaron Diaz, the doctors of Merida hospital, Maritza Carbajal, Aron Tzib, CO BATSUB, Xavier Molina, Max Baldetti, Renato Lacáyo, Daniel Pacheco, Ashwin Bhardwaj, Pete Wood, Mari Jimenez, José (Chan) Fabián Ramírez Tinoco, Levinton Marin, Urial Lanzas, Roberto Duran, Chris Mahoney, Holly Aguilar, Bansi Shah, Mark Galley, Rick Morales, Segundo Sugaste, Lt. Col. Carrión and all the Officers at SENAFRONT, Ernesto Konde and the Embera of Canaan, Siobhan Sinnerton, Dominic

Acknowledgements

Harrison, Mark Ogle, Charlotte Tottenham, Will Charlton, Tom McShane, Clare Howes, Mark Ogle, Nigel McIntyre, Lt. Col. John Blashford-Snell OBE, Brigadier Alastair Aitken, 77th Brigade, all the team at UNICEF UK, Sophie Bolsover for all her support, and of course my long-suffering parents.

Finally, my gratitude to the people of Mexico, Belize, Guatemala, Honduras, Nicaragua, Costa Rica, Panama and Colombia for their generosity and kindness.

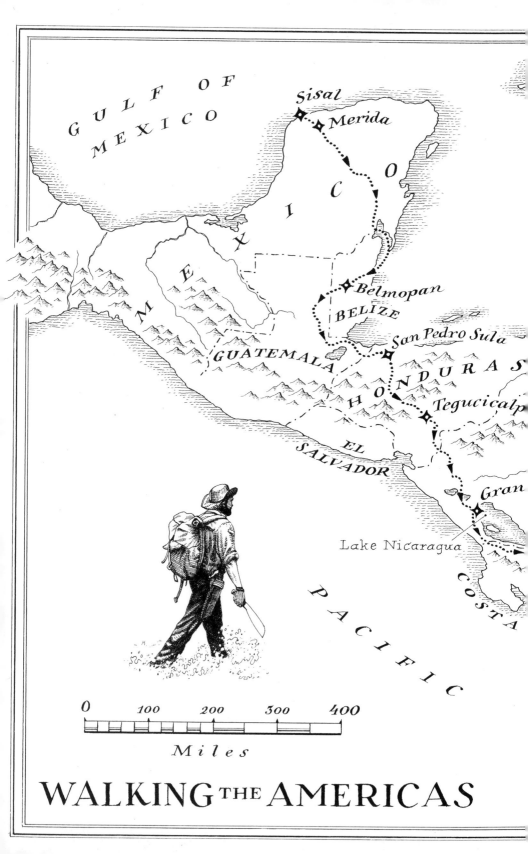

WALKING THE AMERICAS